The CBT Career Guide

Becoming and Developing as a Cognitive Behavioural Therapist

Helen Moya

The CBT Career Guide
Becoming and Developing as a Cognitive Behavioural Therapist

© Pavilion Publishing & Media

The author has asserted her rights in accordance with the Copyright, Designs and Patents Act (1988) to be identified as the author of this work.

Published by:

Pavilion Publishing and Media Ltd
Blue Sky Offices, 25 Cecil Pashley Way
Shoreham by Sea, West Sussex
BN43 5FF

Tel: 01273 434 943
Email: info@pavpub.com
Web: www.pavpub.com

Published 2024

All rights reserved. No part of this publication may be reproduced, stored in a retrieval system, or transmitted in any form or by any means, electronic, mechanical, photocopying, recording or otherwise, without prior permission in writing of the publisher and the copyright owners.

A catalogue record for this book is available from the British Library.

ISBN: 978-1-803883-79-3

Pavilion Publishing and Media is a leading publisher of books, training materials and digital content in mental health, social care and allied fields. Pavilion and its imprints offer must-have knowledge and innovative learning solutions underpinned by sound research and professional values.

Author: Helen Moya
Cover design: Emma Dawe, Pavilion Publishing and Media Ltd
Page layout and typesetting: Phil Morash, Pavilion Publishing and Media Ltd
Printing: Independent Publishers Group (IPG)

Contents

Acknowledgements vii
Foreword ix
About the Resources page xi
Preface 1

    Chapter 1 Introducing the ARD model of CBT career development 3
    Chapter 2 Building a CBT therapist 13
    Chapter 3 What does a CBT career look like? 23
    Chapter 4 Diversity in CBT 37
    Chapter 5 CBT career roadmap: Pathways to becoming a CBT therapist 55
    Chapter 6 Gaining relevant clinical experience 71
    Chapter 7 The Knowledge, Skills and Attitudes (KSA) route: building your portfolio 85
    Chapter 8 Preparing for CBT training 103
    Chapter 9 Getting the most from training 117
    Chapter 10 Managing rejection and failure 133
    Chapter 11 Accreditation 141
    Chapter 12 Maintaining skills and knowledge 149
    Chapter 13 Maximizing clinical supervision 163
    Chapter 14 Managing stress and preventing burnout 175
    Chapter 15 Your CBT career vision 187
    Chapter 16 CBT career options 193
    Chapter 17 Working independently as a CBT entrepreneur 209
    Chapter 18 Promoting CBT careers 223

Appendices 235
References 245

I dedicate this book to my family, who accept and support me through the good times and the challenges of life.

Acknowledgements

This book has been a long time in the making.

Ever since being the Course Director of the CBT training programme at the University of Nottingham, I have been thinking of ways to facilitate the career progression process. My work on the course brought me into contact with two incredible trainers and esteemed CBT therapists, Anne Garland and Philip Kinsella. Along with Professor Patrick Callaghan, who was the Head of School at the time, they have inspired me on my own career path.

I give thanks to all the people who have shared their stories in this book. It has been a privilege to learn from you, and to pass your wisdom to those who are following in our footsteps.

Finally, on a personal note, I am grateful for all the patients, clients, trainees, and supervisees I have ever worked with. You all have played a role in shaping me into the CBT therapist and entrepreneur I am today.

Foreword

It is a pleasure to be asked to introduce this innovative book by Helen Moya.

Although Helen and I have never met in person, we exchanged emails when she started developing her CBT career development model as a potential paper for *The Cognitive Behaviour Therapist* journal (for which I am Editor-in-Chief). That paper became a much larger proposition – a full book!

As someone who has spent much of his career thinking about how best to help CBT therapists develop basic competence and then continue to develop procedural skills and knowledge over the course of their career, it was obvious that I was going to be intrigued. Also, as someone who has worked as a clinical lead within an NHS Talking Therapies service (previously known as Improving Access to Psychological Therapies) since the programme was launched, and who spends a lot of time considering how to support staff in embarking on and developing within CBT careers, I was excited to read her ideas on these key areas.

Helen is extremely well equipped to write this book given her experiences as a CBT therapist, supervisor, trainer, author and CBT course director over her career. Equally importantly, Helen is committed to increasing equity within CBT, whether this is equity of access to therapy, supporting CBT staff to make appropriate adaptations to ensure equitable outcomes or as this book demonstrates, a commitment to making the CBT profession (at all levels) representative of the population. The data we currently have from some CBT services suggests that, for example, the proportion of CBT therapists from minoritised ethnicities reduces as the pay bandings increase, which clearly suggests a major issue that needs to be addressed. Chapter 4 is one of a small number of discussions of identities, intersectionality, and diversity in CBT currently available in the literature. Helen's experience, values, and willingness to acknowledge the impact of our identities on our professional selves over our careers has helped her to identify the issues that are presented at each stage, and furthermore allows her to show real empathy for these challenges, providing guidance around how these can be addressed.

Often, when interviewing people for trainee CBT posts, I have come across individuals with real potential in terms of values and interpersonal skills, but who are not quite ready to train – usually due to a lack of ability to access CBT-informed supervision from an accredited CBT therapist or a lack of knowledge about what introductory courses to access (avoiding some of the low quality course that are appearing online offering to train someone to be a CBT therapist in a few days!). There is always a risk that such people may give up on their CBT dream and pursue other careers, and I have always wished that there was a book I could recommend – one that would answer all the key questions and provide a practical guide on how to embark on CBT training and get the most out of it. Ideally such a book would explain what careers in CBT could look like across the various patient groups, reframe and answer frequently asked questions, and give detailed advice on every stage of CBT career development. This is that book! I will be recommending it to this group of people as soon as it is published.

But this book doesn't just contain useful material for people in the stage of preparing for CBT training. It is much more ambitious, and is structured around Helen's newly developed ARD (Attract, Retain, Develop) model of CBT career development. As already mentioned, the initial chapters are based on how to attract people to careers in CBT and how those of us in the profession facilitate this process. There is no equivalent book out there that covers this background, and I can see this being extremely useful for people doing their A-levels right through to qualified professionals considering CBT training to develop as a clinician.

The middle section of the book addresses how to support staff in **retaining** their skills and knowledge. This is also aimed at services in terms of **retaining** staff given the challenges with the role. These chapters are focused in the main on those first few years post-CBT training where staff are seeking accreditation, consolidating, and developing their skills as they see more patients and start to really develop more advanced procedural skills, meta-competence, and their own style as a therapist. Chapter 13 provides guidance on how to maximise learning in supervision with these tasks in mind and Chapter 14 focuses on the key task of maintaining wellbeing and preventing burnout in what is a challenging role.

The final group of chapters focuses on how to continue **developing** as a CBT practitioner across the whole of your career whether this involves clinical expertise, leadership, research or delivering training (or some combination). Many excellent CBT practitioners can struggle to progress in their careers or may not even be aware of the potential options. This section of the book will be particularly useful to qualified and experienced CBT therapists, but it is also helpful for service leads and managers to consider how they can support their experienced CBT therapists in developing further.

Whilst some readers will want to read the whole book in order, some may choose to dip in and out depending on their stage of career or who they are advising and recommending it to. I would recommend that all readers start with Chapter 1 to get an overview of the ARD model, and then either read the whole book in order (it is very readable) or dip in and out based on your needs and interest.

However you choose to approach it, I have no doubt that this book will provoke thoughts and ideas in novice therapists, established therapists, supervisors, service leads and trainers. Enjoy scribbling in the margins!

Dr Richard Thwaites
Consultant Clinical Psychologist and Cognitive Behavioural Psychotherapist
Editor-in-Chief, *The Cognitive Behaviour Therapist*

About the Resources page

To supplement the contents of this book there is an accompanying website where you can download worksheets and brief guides that summarize some of the content presented in individual chapters. This will be referred to throughout the book as the **Resources page**, and it can be found at:

www.pavpub.com/the-cbt-career-guide-resources

Preface

With a career spanning more than thirty-five years in the caring professions, I am extremely fortunate to have seen some major changes in the development of CBT.

Training as a learning disability nurse in the 1980's was an exciting time, with behaviour therapy heralded as a radical approach to aid learning for people deemed unteachable. I was introduced to psychology, and it has been my passion and the central force guiding my career ever since. I have developed and applied my knowledge and skills across clinical populations, settings, and academia. In 1997 I became one of the first learning disability nurses in the UK to complete a PhD. This examined identities in care relationships using a narrative approach. Identity is a thread I have woven into every role I have occupied.

I was a lecturer in mental health and social care at the University of Nottingham for over a decade, teaching learning disability and mental health nurses. I was privy to the change in philosophy of care in mental health nursing from a predominantly medical model to the recovery model. This elevated the lived experience of the person as the means to understanding mental distress. This aligned with my values relating to an identity-focused approach and represented another interesting progression in UK mental health care.

When the Improving Access to Psychological Therapies (IAPT) initiative was introduced (now referred to as NHS Talking Therapies), I requested to be part of the first cohort at Nottingham, taking a voluntary placement in a local IAPT service alongside my lecturing post. I became Course Director of the Level 2 accredited CBT programme, which is an IAPT curriculum. I held this role for six years alongside an honorary contract with a local mental health trust in the Department of Psychological Medicine, providing CBT to people with persistent physical symptoms and long-term physical health conditions.

In 2018, I immersed myself back into full-time clinical work and made the radical move to a band 7 CBT therapist post in an NHS Talking Therapies service. I value having clinical credibility as an educationalist, and I wanted to re-connect with CBT on the frontline. I worked in this service for four years, integrating my academic background and encouraging the development of a part-time clinical trainer role.

I set up my own private practice, Moya CBT, in 2020 on a part-time basis. Rather than just providing private CBT treatment, I used it to create a career development service for CBT therapists at all stages of their journey. I set up some Facebook communities including the CBT Careers group which now has over two thousand members from diverse backgrounds and career stages. I also set up a KSA (Knowledge Skills and Attitudes) portfolio group for peer support. In 2022 I completed additional training in CBT for children and adolescents. I have lived experience of ADHD, and I have developed clinical expertise in this area and can work across the life span. I have produced a range of CBT self-help materials relating to ADHD, and I offer training to CBT practitioners and organisations.

Preface

I see myself as a CBT entrepreneur – providing information on CBT and career opportunities, delivering training events and clinical supervision to a wide range of relevant organisations and practitioners, and continually developing my own skills and interests. My passion for CBT and career development has culminated in this book.

Chapter 1
Introducing the ARD model of CBT career development

On average it takes eight years of study and clinical practice to become a cognitive behavioural therapist. There are different pathways, so it is important to understand this before embarking on your journey. This book is aimed at anyone considering a career as a cognitive behavioural therapist, or seeking advice for career options beyond training in cognitive behavioural therapy (CBT). You may already be a mental health professional and would like to specialize in CBT, or still at school with an interest in psychology, or maybe you have had CBT yourself and have been inspired to change your career.

Considering the wide application and ongoing development of CBT in the UK, no models exist to guide a CBT career journey. I created a conceptual model to provide a framework for CBT career development. This is the ARD model (Moya, 2022), which covers the processes of **Attraction** (A) to becoming a CBT therapist; **Retention** (R) of skills and knowledge to maintain the role; and options for further career **Development** (D).

Figure 1.1 – The ARD model of CBT career development

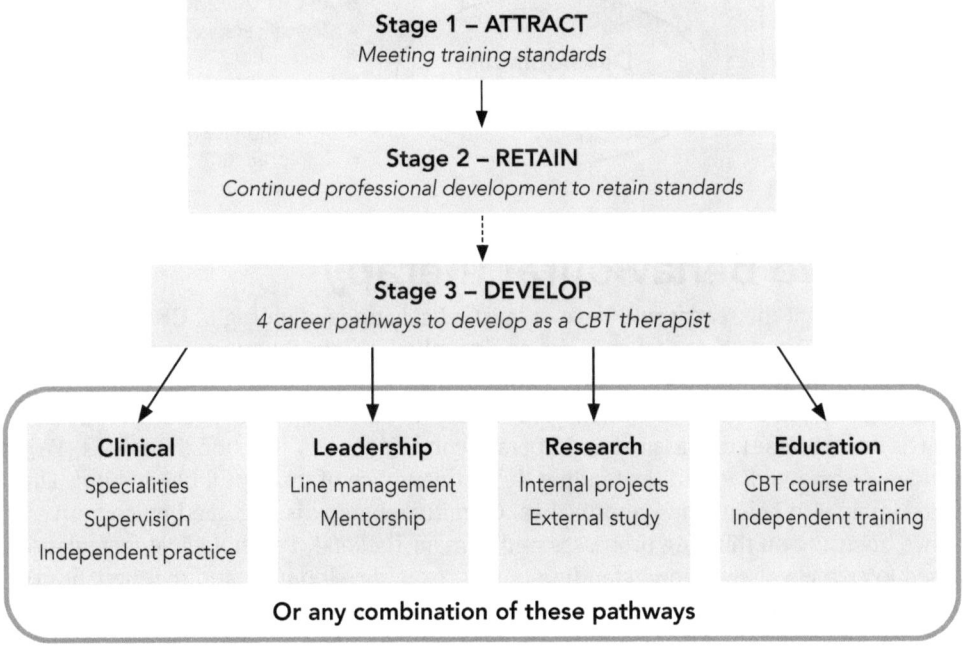

The ARD model will be broken down in more detail throughout the book, and provides a structure to discuss each part of the journey. Considering the broad scope of the model, the book will appeal to many people. Most of the content is aimed at a UK audience, which includes people from other countries who want to practice as a CBT therapist within the UK. The scope of this guide includes all parts of the career journey from contemplation through to very experienced CBT therapists looking at ways to develop their career in a new direction. The book will also appeal to educators and employers. Figure 1.2 depicts the scope of the audience this book is aimed at.

Figure 1.2 – Audience for *The CBT Career Guide*

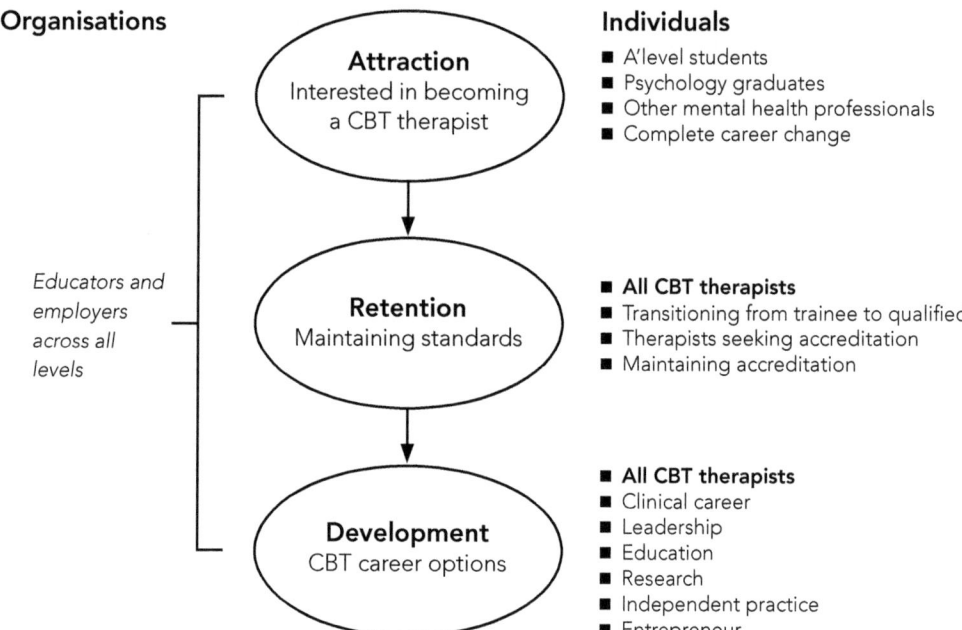

Cognitive behavioural therapy

It is assumed that the reader will have at least a basic understanding of CBT. The book will refer to CBT in its broadest capacity as an umbrella term covering a variety of approaches informed by different psychological theories. This includes learning theory, which seeks to understand the function of behaviours and how they become reinforced through the processes of classical and operant conditioning. A functional analysis (FA) provides a framework for understanding the maintenance of unhelpful behaviours. This is fundamental to behavioural approaches. Cognitive therapy is informed by cognitive science, focusing on thinking processes and content (beliefs). Psychological formulation is used to create a shared understanding of the onset, development and maintenance of beliefs. Most CBT approaches fall somewhere between these extremes. The emphasis placed on behavioural and/or cognitive aspects will vary, and a range of approaches have developed over time. It could be argued that some of these approaches may overlap or belong to a different point on the diagram shown in Figure 1.3, but this is intended as a simple overview only.

Figure 1.3 – CBT approaches

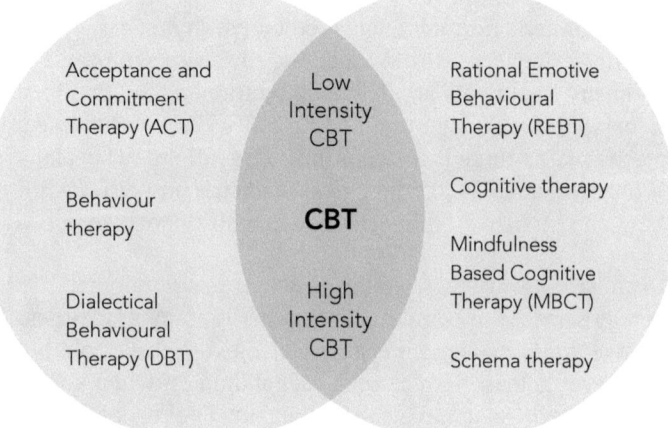

There are features of CBT that are agreed upon across approaches: it is **goal driven**, **collaborative**, **structured**, **evidence based**, and needs to be practiced between sessions using **homework** tasks. It is the role of the CBT therapist to work collaboratively with their client to make sense of what is maintaining their emotional difficulties, then use CBT theory and clinical skills to make meaningful changes to reduce their emotional distress. This is a very simple description of the role, and as we work through this book, we will see how complex the process is to become a competent CBT therapist.

If this brief description is not detailed enough for you, there are many excellent introductory textbooks on CBT (Beck *et al*, 2019; Kennerley *et al*, 2016; Simmons & Griffiths, 2017).

CBT in the UK

CBT is one of the most popular psychological therapies currently practiced in the UK. Although it has been used for several decades in mental healthcare, it was only available to very few people until more recently. The introduction of the Improving Access to Psychological Therapies (IAPT) initiative in 2008 saw the proliferation of CBT as an alternative to medication alone for the treatment of depression and anxiety. This is now referred to as NHS Talking Therapy services and the terms may be used interchangeably throughout the book. This model is based on a stepped-care approach that assigns the appropriate 'dose' of CBT for the level of severity of the presenting problem. The stepped-care approach was recommended by the National Institute for Clinical Excellence (NICE) for adults with common mental health problems (NICE, 2011) and comprises three steps:

- Step 1 – identification and assessment of mental health problems. Monitoring.
- Step 2 – low-intensity psychological treatment for subthreshold symptoms (mild to moderate).
- Step 3 – high-intensity psychological treatment for moderate to severe symptoms.

This goes from threshold and mild symptoms of depression or anxiety, suitable for step 2 or low-intensity interventions normally delivered by psychological wellbeing practitioners (PWP) in IAPT services. Step 3 relates to moderate to severe symptoms of depression, for which high-intensity treatments are delivered by trained CBT therapists accredited by the British Association for Behavioural and Cognitive Psychotherapies (BABCP). For more complex presentations there is a step 4 for interventions in specialist secondary and tertiary care services, such as psychological medicine and other adult mental health services where CBT can be delivered in accordance with the evidence.

CBT continues to cause controversy in terms of how it has dominated the UK's psychological therapy services in comparison to other therapy modalities. The historical and political context for this movement is acknowledged in this book, but not covered in any detail. It is a moveable feast and, as such, depending on when you read this book, the CBT landscape in the UK may have changed again. The reader is therefore advised to explore this wider context of CBT to gain a personal position.

CBT for children and young people

Most training courses are focused on using CBT to treat adults. This is due to the established evidence base which largely stems from research with the adult population. Treatment protocols for the different anxiety disorders and depression were originally adult focused. However, CBT for children and young people (CYP) has developed more recently since the onset of the IAPT enterprise in 2008 (as mentioned, now called NHS Talking Therapies). This led the way to specific training for therapists wanting to use CBT with younger clients, and an increase in research to develop and adapt protocols and treatment approaches more suitable for children's developmental stages. NICE guidance for working with children and young people focuses on depression as there is more robust research evidence in relation to outcomes using CBT (NICE, 2019). Pass & Reynolds (2020) produced a step-by-step guide for using behavioural activation for depressed adolescents. Anxiety tends to be viewed more generically with treatment taking a transdiagnostic approach, especially with younger children (Stallard, 2020). Protocols have been developed such as a 'coping cat' for younger children, and a version for adolescents (Kendall & Hedtke, 2006b). This manualized therapist resource can be used with children and families (Kendall & Khanna, 2008) and a randomized controlled trial by McNally *et al* (2013) found some therapeutic gains for children with co-morbid anxiety and autism depending on developmental functioning. More recent CBT approaches to help children with anxiety include Cresswell *et al* (2019) parent-led CBT and Triste's (2023) cognitive behavioural map.

Like with adult CBT, you can work at low- or high-intensity levels depending on the needs of the child. The IAPT child and young person (CYP) training programme was introduced in 2011 to increase access to psychological therapies for children and adolescents experiencing common mental health problems. This was to ease pressure on the step 4 services, mainly Child and Adolescent Mental Health Services (CAMHS). There has been increasing pressure on children's mental health services in recent years, leading to legislation and policies to improve access and care pathways. Most of this stemmed from the *Future in Mind* report produced by a collaborative mental health task force aiming to create a vision for mental health services for children and young people (NHS England, 2015). This gave rise to **the** government green paper in 2017 called *Transforming Children's and Young People's Mental Health Provision*, which picked up on the key recommendations from the mental health task force. One of these was to offer low-intensity psychological therapies to children and young people in schools. The stepped-care model for children with depression (NICE, 2019) was developed in response to the *Future in Mind* green paper and the response by the Care Quality Commission called *Are we listening?* published in 2018. It covers five steps:

1. Detection and recognition of depression and risk profiling in primary care and community settings.
2. Recognition of depression in children and young people referred to children and young people's mental health services (including CAMHS).
3. Managing recognized depression in primary care and community settings
   – mild depression.
4. Managing recognized depression in steps 2 or 3 CAMHS
   – moderate to severe depression.
5. Managing recognized depression in steps 3 or 4 CAMHS
   – unresponsive, recurrent and psychotic depression, including depression needing inpatient care.

Another major difference between working with children as opposed to adults is the use of a systemic approach. This means acknowledging the systems around the child such as family, school and any other agencies or organizations involved in the child's current care. Working systemically involves collaborating with these other stakeholders to fully understand the presenting problems in context. Dummett (2010) provides a comprehensive model for developing a systemic CBT formulation. It is well worth a read even if you are not working with children.

Recent legislation has given rise to more varied opportunities to use CBT with children and young people in different settings, including schools, as part of a mental health support team (MHST). The low-intensity version of a PWP is a Children's Wellbeing Practitioner (CWP), and the newer role of Educational Mental Health Practitioner (EMHP) extends the options for a CBT career working with children and young people. Training for these roles includes a greater emphasis on developmental issues that may impact therapy such as the stage of the person's cognitive development or poor attachments with their primary carers. More information on these roles is provided in subsequent chapters and on the Resources page.

Accreditation in the UK

The British Association of Behavioural and Cognitive Psychotherapies (BABCP) is the principal professional body that sets standards of professional practice for CBT therapists in the UK. One means of achieving this is through the process of accreditation. It is akin to registration required by other healthcare professions such as nursing or medicine. In other countries, a CBT therapist may have to be licensed or registered with a professional body that governs health and social care practice in that country. As with all these processes, accreditation sets the standard for good, safe and ethical practice to protect the public and the practitioner, ensuring that they are working within their competency level. The BABCP provides accreditation to individuals and to courses that meet the minimum training standards (MTS) deemed suitable for practice as a competent practitioner. For many years, partly due to the funding of IAPT being largely driven by Health Education England (HEE), the focus of accreditation had been on practitioners completing training in England. However, the BABCP have addressed this issue by broadening the MTS to include equivalent systems in Scotland, Wales and Northern Ireland.

Until recently, CBT has not been recognized by the Professional Standards Authority (PSA) for health and social care as a protected profession. This essentially means that anyone can call themselves a CBT therapist without any legal redress. This has made the profession vulnerable to people who may not have the adequate skills, knowledge or attitude to provide safe and effective CBT therapy to vulnerable people. With unregulated online courses marketed as 'CBT training', it is also confusing for well-meaning practitioners who want to specialize in CBT.

Accreditation requires a substantial clinical background in mental health and qualifications that demonstrate a sound knowledge of psychology before completing additional training in CBT. There are many variations on how to meet these requirements, and they will all be considered in this book. A summary of the minimum training standards and core curriculum is presented in the appendices.

Identity approach

Becoming and developing as a CBT therapist is more than a job or a set of skills. It is a professional identity, and you will be at different stages of this identification process. Whether you have a core profession or not, CBT is the approach you have chosen, and this commitment will guide your career journey. This book focuses on identity throughout, to help you recognize your personal qualities, aspirations and resources that will help you progress. There are regular 'reflections boxes' to encourage you to pause and relate the content to your personal perspective, which may or may not be challenged throughout the book.

In recognition of the importance of identity, this book presents storied accounts of CBT therapists at various stages of their career and from different backgrounds. I am very grateful to everyone who has shared their story. They serve to promote identification with others who have chosen a CBT career. Each contributor was given the choice to use their real name or a pseudonym.

Reflection

Reflective practice has been part of health and social care professional practice for many years (Johns, 1994). It requires a space to stand back and learn from experience. There are many models to guide reflection which tend to view learning as a continual cycle (Gibbs, 1988). A popular one used in CBT is Kolb's (1983) learning cycle, as this provides an appropriate explanatory framework that supports the scientist-practitioner model of CBT. More recently, CBT from the inside-out model (Bennett-Levy *et al*, 2014; Thwaites *et al*, 2014) provides a dynamic approach to experiential learning through the application of the CBT tools for self-practice and self-reflection.

Figure 1.4 – Kolb's learning cycle

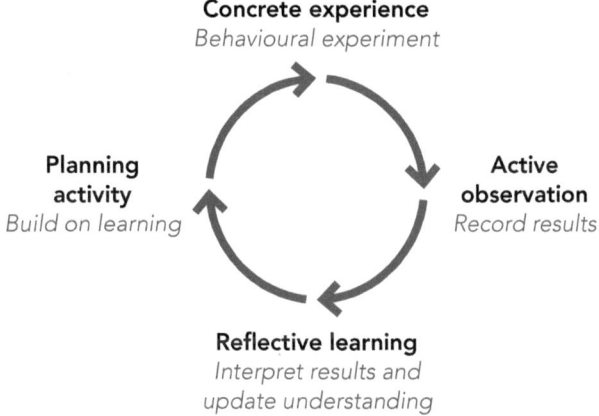

The helicopter model is a simple framework that encourages critical reflection at three levels: individual (micro level), local environment or community (meso level), and the bigger picture (macro level), which considers political, cultural and systemic issues impacting any situation. The therapy process model encourages reflection on the interaction between therapist, client and therapy. A copy of each of these models is presented in the appendices and in the Resources page for easy reference.

We will refer to all these reflective frameworks throughout the book. The reader is encouraged to approach their learning from a reflective position. As mentioned, there are 'reflections boxes' in each chapter to provide space to develop a personal position on the contents of the book.

Reframing some frequently asked questions

When seeking information about your career progression, it is important that you are asking the most helpful questions. It is a human instinct to want to seek the quickest route to a goal, but in this profession there are no shortcuts and there are many potential pathways to meet your goals. Table 1.1 provides some common questions which can be reframed to help your investigations.

Table 1.1 – Reframing commonly asked questions

Common question	Reframed	Comments
What is the quickest route to becoming a CBT therapist?	With my current qualifications and experience, which CBT pathway would be the best fit?	The pathway must fit your qualifications and experience so the time it takes will vary. The emphasis on speed can detract from the journey.
Can CBT training help me get onto the clinical or counselling doctorate programmes?	Which career pathway am I seeking? Do I want to be a clinical or counselling psychologist or am I completely committed to a CBT model?	Experience as a CBT therapist is relevant for doctoral programmes, but there is already a lot of CBT content in the clinical psychology and counselling psychology curricula, so being a CBT therapist before applying is not necessary. There is also the issue of funding. Both these programmes are currently funded by Health Education England (HEE) so you must choose the pathway you want to allow others who are motivated for a CBT career to have a greater chance to access CBT training places. Sometimes motivation for a career can change, which is different to approaching CBT training with the goal of using it as a stepping-stone only.
Will a master's in psychology get me on a CBT training course?	Do I currently meet the requirements for CBT training, and if not, what are the gaps I need to fill?	There is a trend for psychology graduates to jump straight into a master's course believing this will increase their chances of accessing mental health professions. However, for CBT training, a core profession is a pre-requisite, or a psychology-related degree plus relevant clinical experience. Your Bachelor's degree is enough, so use the time to seek clinical work or clinical training such as low-intensity CBT (PWP, CWP or EMHP) as this will provide better opportunities than two academic qualifications in psychology. If, however, you have sufficient clinical experience to meet the KSA route but no formal degree in psychology, then a master's might fill a gap in your knowledge. It really depends on your circumstances.

Structure of the book

Throughout the book, there are a series of diagrams and frameworks to help navigate your needs. Each chapter contains reflection points to help you assimilate the content to your journey. The whole book is intended to be a roadmap leading to information at each stage. It does not need to be read in order as it is appreciated that there is a broad audience.

The book is divided into three main sections based on the stages of the ARD model. Before this, we will consider what it takes to be a CBT therapist in Chapter 2: Building a CBT therapist. This is followed in Chapter 3 by an illustration of what a CBT career can look like through stories of people at different stages of their CBT career journey and from different backgrounds. This sets the scene for considering your own journey. Chapter 4 provides an exploration of diversity in CBT from the therapist's perspective to reinforce a message of inclusion for all who want to become cognitive behavioural therapists. This chapter is not only aimed at potential or current therapists, but all of us from different backgrounds and stages of our careers, including managers and leaders as issues relating to equality and diversity are everyone's business. Actively addressing discrimination and unconscious bias within the psychological therapy workforce is a necessary part of developing a transcultural approach to CBT.

Section one focuses on the stages leading up to and including CBT training. This is for people who are interested in a CBT career but do not know how to proceed. It provides information that applies to a broad range of people, from college students who have not yet chosen a university course to people who are seeking a complete career change. Chapter 5 presents a map of the different pathways to becoming a CBT therapist and the specific requirements of each. Chapter 6 focuses on gaining relevant clinical experience to increase your opportunities for accessing training in CBT down the line.

The KSA route is the focus of Chapter 7, which provides a detailed overview of the requirements of the KSA portfolio and advice on how to get started. This links to preparing for training in Chapter 8, including the application process and preparing for interviews. Chapter 9 makes suggestions for getting the most out of training. The final chapter in this section, Chapter 10, addresses the difficult issue of managing failure and rejection to help you move through the challenges and continue with your CBT journey.

Section two is the retention part of the ARD model and applies to therapists who have completed basic training in CBT. It is a time of building competence and confidence. Chapter 11 outlines the requirements for accreditation as a practitioner with the BABCP, as not everyone will have accessed a level 2 accredited course that allows a direct route to practitioner accreditation. This applies to people working in the UK who may have done their basic training in another country and want their experience and qualifications to be recognized through accreditation with the BABCP.

Chapter 12 addresses how to maintain your skills and knowledge and build confidence. Often an intense time follows training, as you try to consolidate learning and work autonomously. This chapter encourages you to focus on this difficult period as an essential part of your personal growth as a CBT therapist.

Supervision is a fundamental part of CBT practice, so Chapter 13 is dedicated to developing your supervision skills to maximize learning and development. The final chapter in this section, Chapter 14, acknowledges the demands of the CBT therapist role and encourages reflection on your wellbeing and how to manage stress and prevent burnout.

Section 3 moves to the development part of the ARD model. It is easy to get stuck in a rut following training. The chapters in this section provide a bigger picture that is difficult to contemplate when you are caught up in the daily challenges of the here-and-now. Chapter 15 asks you to consider your personal career vision, and Chapter 16 provides a framework of possible career pathways you may not have considered. This will help to navigate and inspire you in your journey. Chapter 17 focuses on working independently and looks beyond having a private practice to consider a flexible and creative way of working as a CBT entrepreneur. Finally, Chapter 18 considers how we can promote CBT careers across different organizations and communities to raise awareness and maintain the growth of the profession.

Getting the most from the book

It is your career, and you are in control of it. Once you have information about the bigger picture, you can develop a plan that fits your personal situation and goals. Remember that it does not have to be set in stone. There are many different pathways to becoming and developing as a CBT therapist. The advice echoed throughout this book is to slow down and focus on taking one step at a time so that you enjoy each stage of the journey.

Disclaimer

It is acknowledged that the information in this book may change over time due to changes in policy and services. Most of the views and ideas expressed are those of the author.

Chapter 2
Building a CBT therapist

What is required to become a CBT therapist? This is probably the question I am asked most often, and people expect just a list of qualifications and clinical experience. Clearly, these are essential requirements, but it takes more than this to be successful in CBT. Figure 2.1 presents a framework for discussing how to build a CBT therapist. It begins with a set of **personal qualities** and values which some might say cannot be taught. This relates to the identity of the person and is the foundation on which the skills and knowledge are built. The word 'identity' is carefully chosen to avoid rigid notions of personality types or traits. There is not one 'type' of person who will make a better therapist than another; it is more about the values we hold that motivate us to want to help others.

The **essential knowledge and skills** derived through years of study and clinical practice are rooted in psychology and mental health. Given how long it takes to become fully qualified to the level of professional accreditation, it is important to see the whole journey as part of this building process and not just the end goal.

Working as a mental health professional is more like a vocation than a job as it takes a solid level of commitment which is not always rewarded financially, and which can result in significant wear and tear on the physical and mental health of the practitioner. Once qualified, we need to manage our wellbeing and maintain our drive to develop in our CBT career. This takes careful use of our **resources**, which are a mix of personal qualities that drew us to a caring role in the first place and practical support strategies to reduce the risk of burnout over the long haul. Not only will this protect you, but it will increase confidence over time as you develop.

In this chapter, we discuss the requirements for becoming a CBT therapist in terms of both internal and external factors that form the necessary building blocks in this process. It is an overview, and some of the elements covered will be addressed in more detail in further chapters.

Figure 2.1 – Building a CBT therapist

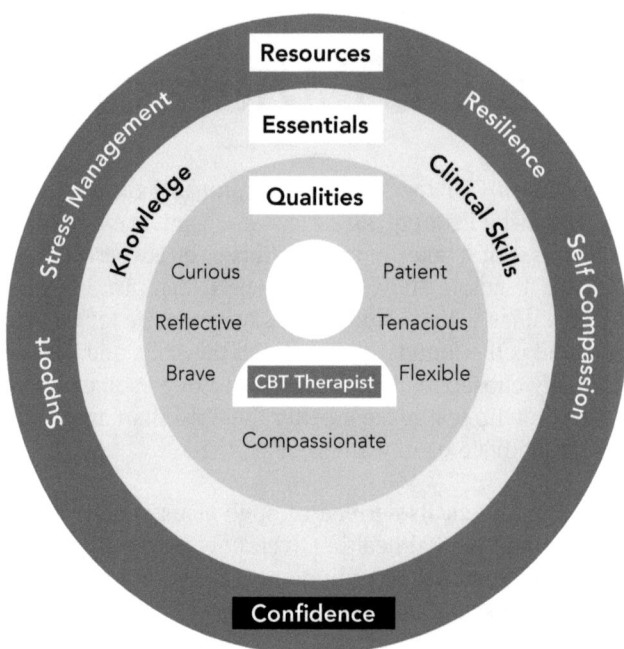

Qualities and values

This is the foundation level and comprises a mixture of personal qualities and values gained through our life experiences. So what qualities are helpful for working in a psychological therapy role? Occupational psychology seeks to develop profiles for different occupations based on personal characteristics. Other branches of psychology have also sought to understand why some people are drawn to certain career choices. This informs HR managers when creating specifications for job roles in the employment market.

While the research is interesting, we need to be mindful of the complexity of human beings and individual differences that are often massaged away in scientific studies when trying to determine specific types of people. Individual differences should be seen as strengths for the CBT role. Throughout this book, when discussing identity, we will be assuming a commonsense notion. In other words, a combination of attributes that guide how we define ourselves.

The importance of identity

When we meet someone for the first time, we often introduce ourselves by giving our name. This is a primary identity marker. Other markers include the personal details we are regularly asked to disclose on application forms and other documents. There is a legal framework regarding identity to protect it from being stolen or misused. Here are some of the common characteristics we may refer to when describing who we are. Of course, we may not disclose all of these and there are an infinite number of additional items that could go on this list. It is intended to promote reflection at this point:

- Name
- Age
- Gender identification
- Sexuality
- Where we live
- Where we were born – heritage, culture, ethnicity
- Family
- Relationships
- Education
- Values
- Interests
- Strengths
- Religious beliefs
- Occupation

Reflection point – who are you?

How would you answer this? Draw on the attributes that make you who you are. How does this help us to understand the identity of others?

How we define and present ourselves to others changes over time, and according to the situation or context we are in. As previously stated, we will not be using a specific theory of identity although the research literature is fascinating and well worth exploring. A list of references is provided to guide reading and a summary of identity theories in psychology is provided on the Resources page.

Understanding who we are is fundamental to our functioning and interactions with others. When attracted to psychological therapies it is likely that we have an intrinsic interest in people and issues relating to the mind and mental health. The reasons for this may be varied but there are some qualities we can agree are necessary for helping others to understand and address their difficulties.

Compassion

The drive to help others can be defined as compassion. There are other words used to describe this quality such as empathy, humility or altruism. To be consistent, the term 'compassion' will be used in this book to refer to this broad spectrum of qualities relating to the desire to understand the lived experience of others. There is a large body of literature on compassion, and we will be drawing on this throughout the book.

Patience

This may seem obvious, but patience is a fundamental quality necessary to be a therapist. This does not mean that therapists are more patient than others. It may not be a quality that transcends all areas of your life, but it can be honed when your focus is on helping others. This is one of the qualities that can grow over time when working as a therapist. It is also one that is tested most as the desire to help people can lead to rushing rather than going at a pace that optimizes therapeutic gains. Sitting with discomfort and waiting before acting are critical elements of patience when applied to therapy.

Curiosity

Interest in people and behaviour requires a degree of curiosity. This is the drive to want to know more about people and leads to questions that you want to explore. Curiosity is a key quality of CBT therapists as the approach is based on the scientist-practitioner model that assumes an investigative style of enquiry when seeking to understand what has brought a person to therapy.

Reflection

Being able to take a step back and think about a situation or experience to learn from it is what reflection allows us to do. This is not to be confused with rumination, which is when we get stuck in a cycle of negative thinking relating to events that have happened that does not generally lead to a new position in thinking. Rumination tends to reinforce negative beliefs that already exist, whereas reflection allows an open and more flexible way of processing experiences. Reflective practice is a fundamental part of CBT.

Flexibility

When considering this quality, we are referring to the ability to remain open-minded and switch from one pathway to another. It is a thinking style that allows us to recognize that there is more than one way to approach a task or goal and to know when our way isn't productive. The opposite of this is rigidity in thinking, which leads to a very black-and-white view of the world and is characteristic of perfectionism or radical opinions. That doesn't mean perfectionists cannot make good therapists. In fact, there is likely to be many people working in all healthcare professions who would consider themselves to be perfectionists. While this may limit some areas of functioning, it is still possible to be open-minded when it comes to helping others as this is likely to drive caring behaviour.

Flexibility is also required to be a critical thinker. Related to reflection, keeping an open mind helps us to develop a position on an issue that can change based on the acquisition of new information or consideration of another perspective.

Tenacity

Helping people requires strength and determination. Mental health is complex and multifaceted and can be conceptualized from many different perspectives, so tenacity is necessary if you are to hold your ground when expressing or defending your position. It also helps when addressing difficult situations that require grit and perseverance, such as helping someone experiencing tragedy or trauma, or working with someone who has very different beliefs and values to you. It is the drive to keep going and see things through.

Courage

Related to tenacity and resilience, it takes courage to work in the mental health field. We are working with people who are experiencing mental distress and this can be scary and challenging. Regardless of our backgrounds, being brave is something we share when it comes to being therapists. People come to us for help, which assumes we know how to overcome problems and adversity in our own lives. This is not always the case. Many therapists lack confidence but will face all sorts of complex situations and difficulties in their CBT role.

> ### Reflection point – my qualities
>
> This list of qualities is not exhaustive. Add any other qualities you think are important to work in a caring role. Spend some time reflecting on each quality and how this applies to you. Write down some examples of each one. How does it make you feel when you reflect on this?

Beliefs that shape our identity

So far, we have discussed qualities that may appear intrinsic to our identity. We now turn to the experiences and beliefs that contribute to our desire to help people. From a CBT perspective, we recognize the importance of our beliefs in forming and maintaining a sense of identity. Early experiences lead to the development of a set of beliefs about self, others, and the world. Beck *et al* (1979) called this the cognitive triad. This is the level of cognition called core beliefs, which are formed in response to our experiences through interpretation. These interpretations become lenses through which we view ourselves, others, and the world around us, leading to reinforcement over time. This makes core beliefs appear like facts. They can be positive or negative and tend to be carried throughout our lives if not recognized or updated.

Sometimes core beliefs are referred to as schemas. The definition of 'schemas' may vary according to theoretical persuasion, but they are generally recognized as mental processes that help us to make sense of the world and our place in it, which is akin to the lens analogy used above. Leahy (2001; 2002) identified schemas that relate to therapy, and these will be examined in more detail below.

Common beliefs shared by therapists

Through the process of psychological formulation, we can map out our beliefs and the experiences that influence them. Formulation is a fundamental part of CBT theory and practice as it drives the therapy process. Understanding our own belief system will help to develop the knowledge and skills necessary to help others. This process is not easy and can be emotionally challenging, as some of our beliefs may be very negative and have been informed by adverse and traumatic events in early life. Later in the book we will return to this process, but for now we are only considering a broad set of beliefs that are common among mental health practitioners.

Although early experiences are unique to each person, there are some themes common among therapists. As previously discussed, the drive to care for others is likely to manifest in some beliefs about self as being caring ('I am caring', 'I am sensitive to the needs of others'), others as needing our help ('others are vulnerable'), and inequities in the world that render the need for people to support others ('the world is unfair', 'the world is harsh'). This triad of beliefs makes the perfect basis for leaning towards a career in the healthcare profession.

Figure 2.2 – Cognitive triad of beliefs about helping

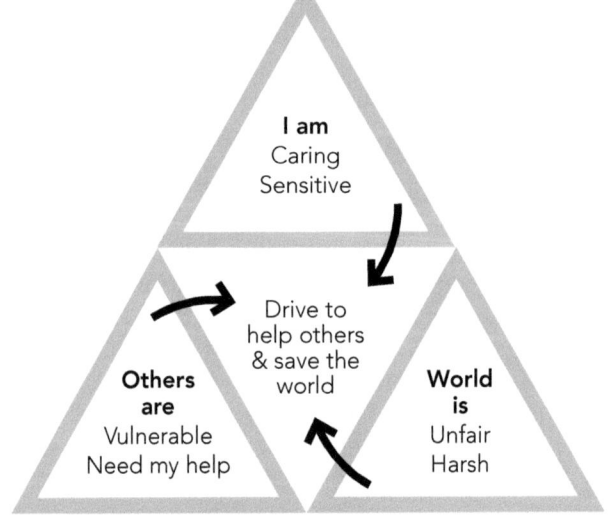

It has been suggested that a significant proportion of mental health professionals will identify with adverse childhood experiences (ACE) (Simpson *et al*, 2019; Vallianitou & Mirovic, 2020). Putting the needs of others before your own may have been a survival strategy in childhood to please and appease others, which then became a rule for living. This rule is not exclusive to people with ACEs, as any experience may lead to a catastrophic interpretation that exaggerates the level of threat associated with that specific experience. It does mean that therapists are likely to fear negative judgement by others, which is compounded by their intrinsic need to help people.

Common schemas identified in therapists include self-sacrifice, emotional deprivation, and unrelenting standards (Leahy, 2001; Haarhoff, 2006; Saddichha *et al*, 2012). Self-sacrifice and emotional deprivation lead to the approval-based rule described above, driven by the need to help others and avoid rejection. Unrelenting standards are associated with perfectionism and push the therapist to do more and more to help the person recover. All three schemas carry a high risk of burnout, so we will return to this when we come to the 'Resources' level of building a CBT therapist (see Figure 2.1).

Essential knowledge and clinical skills

This is often the list that most people want to know. Given the desirable qualities, what knowledge and clinical experience is necessary to become a CBT therapist? With the average journey taking eight years, it is important to know the best route for you to follow. This section provides a brief overview of the essential skills and clinical experience required to enter a CBT training programme or meet the minimum training standards for accreditation with the BABCP. Chapter 5 examines pathways to becoming a CBT therapist in detail and presents a CBT career-map diagram.

CBT is a psychological therapy which is based on theory from various areas including clinical, developmental, social, and cognitive psychology. For this reason, it is a basic requirement to have a psychology-related degree. This does not have to be a pure psychology degree, but it must have a significant amount of psychology theory included in the curriculum. A first degree in psychology is not adequate to meet all the requirements for CBT training but does provide a basis on which to build your clinical experience.

Chapter 5 indicates an alternative route to gaining adequate psychological theory through having a core profession related to mental health. Psychology is a fundamental strand of the theory informing mental health core professions. It also provides the necessary clinical experience to enter CBT training making it the smoothest route to becoming a CBT therapist. Without a core profession, you will need substantive clinical experience of a minimum of four years before starting CBT training. Chapter 6 explores some options for gaining suitable clinical experience.

Resources

At this level, we identify the skills and practices necessary to manage the demands of being a CBT therapist over the long haul. It begins with self-awareness of our own beliefs and values identified in the 'Qualities' level of building a CBT therapist, and how these can impact our wellbeing. Being driven by rigid beliefs and schemas leads to stress-vulnerability and a risk of burnout. Asking for help perpetuates negative beliefs but by addressing and normalizing these difficulties, the therapist will build confidence, which is the most important resource we have. We begin by considering the internal resources of resilience and self-compassion, before addressing external resources including support and stress management. This section will be expanded in a later chapter on maintaining wellbeing.

Resilience

We identified some key qualities that therapists may share. Resilience can be viewed as the sum of these qualities: reflective, patient, curious, tenacious, courageous, compassionate. Engaging with these qualities helps us to learn from difficult situations in the therapy process and apply that learning in new ways.

Padesky & Mooney (2012) developed the personal model of resilience (PMR) which is based on a strengths-based approach to CBT. Recognizing our strengths is the first step in building resilience. The model encourages us to identify examples when we have overcome difficulties in our lives which may not seem threatening, then applying this understanding to more challenging situations. For example, starting a recipe and realizing you don't have one of the ingredients. How did you overcome this? You may have thought of a replacement or experimented with changing the recipe. When faced with a challenge in therapy this learning can be applied – can I replace the intervention I was going to use or experiment with something completely different and see how it turns out?

Self-compassion

Being compassionate to others is often easier than applying it to ourselves, especially when we have rigid beliefs about helping people. In terms of therapist schema, this refers to the three common schemas that make self-compassion difficult: self-sacrifice (I must put this person's needs first); emotional deprivation (I must hide my feelings/can't be myself); and unrelenting standards (I must get this person better at all costs). Putting the needs of others before our own not only feels more natural – it is also reinforced through positive feedback that acknowledges how much we have helped someone or defines us as caring and kind.

In terms of the broader theory on compassion, we can turn to the work of Paul Gilbert who drew together an evolutionary perspective on compassion in his book *The Compassionate Mind*, published in 2010. It draws our attention to three systems – threat, drive and self-soothing – that correspond to brain functioning and guide behaviour.

Figure 2.3 – Three systems of the compassionate mind model

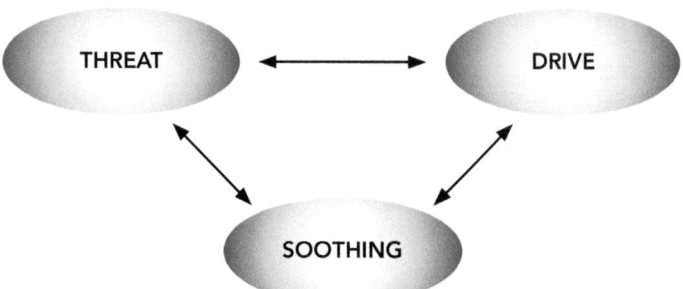

Gilbert suggests these systems have been present throughout evolution since the primitive brain developed through to the sophisticated modern brain we understand today. The threat system is the amygdala, which produces adrenaline and, when fired, puts us into fight-flight-freeze mode. This tends to activate the drive system which motivates us to solve and resolve problems by taking action. The soothing system allows us to recognize when we are in distress (threat system activated) and helps us to calm ourselves through self-care, empathy and kindness. Sometimes the threat is what we believe is happening such as someone judging us negatively. This will produce adrenaline, which makes us feel the symptoms of anxiety. Rather than soothing ourselves through this distress we often jump straight into the drive mode and try to reduce the threat through actions like pleasing others. This means we lose the ability to recognize when a threat is overestimated and learn that we don't have to firefight every situation. Sometimes soothing ourselves is the more effective way of restoring emotional balance, but over time this becomes eroded.

Therapists tend to operate between the threat and drive systems constantly, leaving little in the way of self-soothing. This can be due to a lack of awareness of this process, but it can also be due to our beliefs about self-compassion – that it is for others but not us, or it will make us selfish if we focus on ourselves. We will also likely believe that being proactive in the drive mode is the best way to respond as this is related to unrelenting standards.

Learning to engage with the soothing system requires a different response to the threat system, which is not easy. It requires recognition of our self-critical voice and learning to respond more compassionately. At this point, we are only drawing attention to this important process, but it will be elaborated in the chapter on maintaining self-care with practical ways to incorporate self-compassion into our lives.

Support

Asking for help can be challenging, especially when you are driven to help others. You may not recognize your own needs, or you might ignore them, pushing through challenging times until the difficulty passes. This leads to increased stress and is not a sustainable strategy. Knowing what you need and how to address that need is a skill that will help you maintain your resilience.

Clinical supervision is the fundamental level of support for continued professional development. It is an ongoing requirement to maintain accreditation and provides a space to reflect and learn from your clinical practice. We address how to get the most out of supervision in Chapter 13.

Networking with other therapists is another important source of support. When working remotely, we become isolated, and this adds to stress. Sharing experiences informally with people who understand helps to normalize our difficulties and concerns, and we can learn strategies from each other to cope better. If you work in a service, try to set up a regular time to have an informal meeting with other therapists. There are online forums for therapists to meet and provide mutual support. There are some links in the resources section at the end of the book.

Support extends beyond clinical practice. You are likely to have other demanding roles that add to your stress. It is important to apply the same strategies across all areas of your life. This may involve asking a partner or family member to look after your children to give you a break. Down time is essential when you have a challenging job. Make sure you have some dedicated time to engage in pleasurable activities, either alone or with others. Staying connected to people outside of work reduces time spent ruminating and worrying about work and encourages a present-moment focus. By practising mindfulness, we not only support our wellbeing, but we can model this to the people we work with.

Stress management

The CBT career journey is stressful at all stages. Gaining the specific requirements takes time and patience. You will be studying alongside doing a demanding job and probably have other commitments and responsibilities. CBT training is extremely intensive so having strategies to manage stress is essential. Even when qualified, the process of gaining competence and confidence is ongoing and continues to be challenging.

Chapter 14 focuses on managing stress and preventing burnout by exploring evidence-based approaches used in CBT. Taking a CBT from the inside-out approach (Bennett-Levy *et al*, 2014), you are encouraged to apply some of the techniques and interventions to manage stress and maintain your psychological wellbeing across the long-term journey.

Summary

This chapter has provided an overview of the building blocks to become and develop as a CBT therapist. It sets the scene for the following chapters which will address some of these issues in more detail to help you at each stage of your CBT career journey.

Chapter 3
What does a CBT career look like?

This is a useful question to ask when considering a career in cognitive behavioural therapy. The previous chapter described the qualities, knowledge, and skills necessary to build a CBT therapist, but CBT is practiced in many different settings with different client groups, so the personal experience of each therapist and their journey are unique and varied. This chapter presents a series of stories by CBT therapists to give a snapshot of what the role looks like, and the steps taken to get to this point. In most cases, the time it takes to become a CBT therapist goes far beyond the average of eight years. The most important message is that each step is valuable.

As the evidence base for CBT has developed, so have its applications across different presenting problems and age groups. CBT can be used across the life span, which allows choice for working either with adults or children and young people. This adds to the options for pathways into a CBT career as you may already be in a role working with children or young people and have developed a particular interest in mental health and want to know what options are available to you.

In addition to the career stories in this chapter, we will consider what a typical day in the life of a CBT might look like in different settings. This is just a snapshot, to give you an idea of the different clinical roles within CBT practice. Alternative career options, including independent practice and roles with a non-clinical focus, are discussed in more detail later in the book. The chapter finishes with a series of tips therapists have provided regarding what they wish they had known before embarking on their CBT career journey.

CBT across the lifespan

It is possible to work as a CBT therapist with any age group. Originally developed for adults, CBT is becoming increasingly recognized as an effective approach for treating emotional difficulties in children. There has been a rapid growth in research over the past 20 years into CBT for children and young people, which has produced treatment models that account for developmental and systemic factors (Dummett, 2010). Although CBT training for working with adults is different to the training for working with children and young people (CYP), it is possible to transition between these roles. Table 3.1 provides an overview of some of the settings, approaches, and common presenting problems you can expect when using CBT with adults and children. A Landscape version is available to download on the Resources page.

Table 3.1 – Comparing CBT for adults and children

Aspect of CBT	Adults	Children and young people (CYP)
Settings where CBT is delivered	■ NHS across all tiers: 　■ **NHS Talking Therapies (IAPT)** for mild to moderate problems 　■ **Secondary care** – mental health teams, early interventions in psychosis (EIP) 　■ **Tertiary services** like psychological medicine for medically unexplained physical health problems 　■ **Specialist services** (e.g. eating disorders, substance misuse services, oncology and perinatal mental health) ■ **Prisons** – there are mental health services within the prison service offering both medication and therapeutic approaches including CBT. ■ **Military** – there are mental health practitioners within all the armed forces and this includes the use of CBT as an evidence-based psychological therapy often associated with the treatment of PTSD. ■ **University counselling services** – CBT is one of the therapeutic approaches offered to students who are struggling with their mental health. ■ **Third-sector organizations** – including mental health charities like MIND or Anxiety UK offer CBT. ■ **Independent practice** – you can work in private practice either for an organization or for your own business (discussed in detail in Chapter 17).	■ Within NHS there are children's mental health services **(CAMHS)** covering mild to complex mental health difficulties. ■ Mental health support teams **(MHSTs)** see children and young people in **schools** and **community settings** (if outside school hours). ■ **Residential settings** can provide therapeutic support from trained CBT therapists. ■ Some children's charities offer CBT. ■ **Independent practice** – you can work in private practice either for an organization or for your own business. There is a growing number of independent CBT therapists working in the private sector.

Aspect of CBT	Adults	Children and young people (CYP)
Common presenting problems	■ **Depression** – there are different presentations of depression, the most common being Major Depressive Disorder (MDD), but can be chronic, episodic or both. ■ **Anxiety disorders** – including: 　■ Generalized anxiety disorder (GAD) 　■ Obsessive Compulsive Disorder (OCD) 　■ Social anxiety 　■ Specific phobias 　■ Health anxiety 　■ Post-traumatic stress disorder (PTSD) ■ **Habit and tick disorder** – such as Tourette's syndrome, skin picking and trichotillomania (hair pulling). ■ **Substance misuse**. ■ **Personality disorders** – although the evidence base for its effectiveness is not as strong. Dialogical Behaviour Therapy (DBT) is often used as opposed to a more generic CBT approach. ■ **Neurodevelopmental conditions** – ADHD and autism. The evidence base isn't as robust, but CBT can be adapted.	■ **Separation anxiety** (common in younger children), which is attachment related. ■ Any **anxiety disorder**, but OCD and GAD are more commonly identified as specific anxiety disorders. ■ PTSD or other **trauma** (developmental). ■ **Bereavement**. ■ **Depression** (often co-morbid with anxiety in children). ■ **Neurodevelopmental conditions** including ADHD and autism.
Approaches used	■ A range of evidence-based CBT protocols in line with NICE guidelines and Roth & Pilling (2007) CBT competency framework. This includes both low- and high-intensity approaches. ■ A formulation-driven approach which uses CBT theory and skills to target beliefs and behaviours maintaining the current problem. This is often adopted for more complex presentations that do not respond to a protocol approach. ■ A transdiagnostic approach refers to the application of CBT interventions across a range of conditions where there is no specific diagnosis or there is comorbidity.	■ Some protocols used for adults have been adapted for use with CYP. The most common ones are behavioural activation (BA), exposure & response prevention (ERP) for OCD, and cognitive therapy for social anxiety. ■ Transdiagnostic approaches are common as they cover a range of presenting problems that may not be easily diagnosed as a specific condition. An example of the treatment of anxiety is the Coping Cat manual. The cognitive behavioural map (CBM) is another transdiagnostic approach for CYP and families. ■ Parent-led CBT.

Working with adults

Most CBT therapists working with adults will treat common mental health problems at a step 2 (mild to moderate) or step 3 (moderate to severe) level. This is primarily due to the growth of CBT within the NHS resulting from the initiation of the IAPT enterprise in 2008. Now called NHS Talking Therapies, these services provide short-term CBT for depression and common anxiety disorders (summarized in Table 3.1 above). Based on targets and outcome data, these roles are characterized by high-volume caseloads. If faithful to the best available evidence and national guidelines, then good recovery rates can be achieved. However, services often limit how many sessions are available for any single course of therapy, which can make the role very demanding and stressful. It is the most common route to train and develop as a CBT therapist and provides a broad range of presenting problems to build competence.

A day in the life of an NHS Talking Therapies CBT therapist

Typically, therapists will see five clients a day for a fifty to sixty minute CBT session. For a full-time therapist, this equates to an average of twenty-five contacts a week. This may vary across services. Once a month, one of the daily sessions will be replaced with a clinical supervision session. Time should be allocated for team meetings and training. In terms of daily management of their diary, the therapist is normally given autonomy to organize appointments and breaks to suit. Some services expect you to work at least one evening a week, so start times will vary. The example shown in Figure 3.1 is for a nine to five day when I worked full time in an IAPT service.

Figure 3.1 – Typical day in an NHS Talking Therapies role

Time	Activity
9 – 10am	Client 1 – Assessment session
10 – 10.30	Notes and assessment letter for GP Coffee at desk
10.30 – 11.30	Client 2 – treatment session 4 for OCD
11.30 – 12	Notes and other admin
12 – 12.45	Break
12.45 – 1pm	Preparation for afternoon clients and admin (phone calls, speaking to team leader)
1 – 2	Client 3 – treatment session 3 for GAD
2 – 3	Client 4 – treatment session 2 problem and goals
3 – 3.30	Notes for clients 3 & 4 and tea break
3.30 – 4.30	Client 5 – treatment session 8 for PTSD
4.30 – 5	Notes for client 5 and catch up on admin

This schedule can vary but it is notable that little time is allowed between sessions to read or fully decompress. Some therapists choose to put their appointments back-to-back and then write notes at the end of the day, whereas others will allow spaces as shown above.

CBT for adults in specialist services

Specialist services within the NHS cover a range of settings across secondary and tertiary care. They operate as teams, so CBT will be one of many therapeutic approaches and the CBT therapist will be part of a multi-disciplinary team (MDT). Examples of specialist services where CBT may be practiced include:

- Early Interventions in Psychosis (EIP) – which is aimed at first-episode psychosis in 18–35-year-olds. EIP services have been using CBT-informed approaches for decades, and the evidence base is growing for the use of adapted CBT for psychosis. Many mental health nurses in EIP services train in CBT.
- Eating disorder (ED) services also use a team approach, and CBT is one of the therapeutic interventions frequently used. Again, the evidence base for this client group is growing.
- Substance misuse services use CBT to help people with addictions to understand the connection between their behaviour, thoughts and emotions. When substance use is associated with emotional pain and traumatic experiences, then reducing the substance in favour of talking about thoughts and feelings can be overwhelming for this client group. This makes therapy engagement and commitment challenging, but CBT can be very effective.
- Physical healthcare services, where psychological support can supplement recovery. For example, oncology, stroke units, gastroenterology and pain clinics. These are often hospital-based jobs.
- Perinatal mental health – these services support women during and after pregnancy who have additional mental health needs. CBT is commonly used as a therapeutic approach and is gathering a growing evidence base.
- Psychological medicine – this is the intersection between physical and psychological health where medically unexplained conditions are explored. This includes non-epileptic seizures, fibromyalgia and some forms of unexplained paralysis and chronic pain. Often referred to as psychosomatic conditions, a common theme is emotional avoidance. CBT is used over a much longer period.

These roles often suit therapists with a core profession in mental health such as mental health nursing or clinical psychology, as it is sometimes stipulated in the person specification for the job, but not always.

A day in the life of a specialist CBT therapist in the NHS

The following is an example of typical day when I worked in a department of psychological medicine in a large teaching hospital. I had an honorary contract one day a week for six years when I was course director of the CBT programme in the same teaching hospital. This allowed me to maintain my BABCP accreditation as you must be in current clinical practice to be able to teach trainee CBT therapists. I was part of a team made up of psychiatrists, mental health liaison nurses, occupational therapists and doctors from associated services such as neurology and cardiology. Referrals would come from internal departments where no medical cause could be determined for a person's physical complaint, from the emergency department or from one of the nurses in the team if brief interventions and psychoeducation were not sufficient to improve a person's wellbeing.

Figure 3.2 – Typical day in an NHS tertiary care service

Time	Activity
9 – 9.30am	Briefing meeting with rest of team to discuss new referrals
9.30 – 10.30	Client 1
10.30 – 11.30	Clinical supervision
11.30 – 12	Write up notes
12 – 12.45	Lunch break
12.45 – 1pm	Prepare for next client (read notes)
1 – 2	Client 2
2 – 3	Write notes and read research papers
3 – 4	Client 3
4 – 4.30	Write notes and any actions from session
4.30 – 5	Debrief with colleague

Although this type of day looks less demanding than that of a practitioner in a primary care or NHS Talking Therapies role, the presenting problems are much more complex and so require more time to prepare and discuss within the team.

CBT in non-NHS settings

We have already established that CBT is not a new psychological therapy. Its clinical use precedes the introduction of the NHS IAPT initiative by decades, but the development of the evidence base has been hugely influenced by this movement. CBT is practiced in prisons and military settings as part of their mental health provision, the police force, university student wellbeing services and third-sector organizations such as mental health charities like MIND. Some of these roles are described in the stories below, including the pathways to working in these settings.

CBT in a prison service

Anna's story outlines her journey to becoming a CBT therapist in the prison service.

My undergraduate degree was in English Literature. I think this is where my love of analysing information started. Following graduation, I saw a talk at the job centre promoting the incredible work prison officers do, so I thought, why not? At the age of 22, I became a prison officer in a male prison. This is where my desire to help people and make sense of why people commit offences really started to grow.

I then transferred to another prison and changed roles from prison officer to facilitator. I facilitated groups helping men who had committed offences to make sense of their offending behaviour. This is where my passion for psychology and applying theory to practice began to grow. I was so lucky to be accepted onto a CBT course. I had a part-time placement in an IAPT service alongside my work in the prison. I started to make sense of CBT in relation to psychopathologies rather than risk factors related to offending. I learned so much working with people in IAPT services. I was then employed delivering therapy within prisons. I am now the clinical lead for midlands integrated therapy service. I love CBT and being part of an incredible forensic service that genuinely strives to make a difference.

Anna's story highlights how working as a prison officer developed her interest in therapy, which ultimately led to her becoming a successful CBT therapist and manager in a prison service. Below is a list of typical duties for a CBT therapist in a prison setting:

- Assessment and ongoing management of risk to inform support journeys.
- Assess the service user's suitability for high-intensity, step 3 interventions.
- Formulate and implement therapy plans that meet the needs of the individual.
- Carry out interventions relevant to individual client needs including 1:1 sessions and group work.
- Recognize the culture and systems of the different prisons in designing realistic interventions with achievable outcomes.
- Collaborative development of release plans appropriate to the individual's needs.
- To work as part of a team to ensure appropriate stepped care.

CBT for military personnel

A higher incidence of mental health problems has long been associated with military roles. A lot has been written about post-traumatic stress disorder (PTSD) in relation to repeated exposure to traumatizing events during deployment, but military staff are also more likely to experience depression, anxiety, insomnia and substance-use problems (Kelly *et al*, 2019). These problems can persist after leaving the military, and services have been developed to support the specific needs of veterans. CBT is an appropriate approach to treat these presenting problems (Liu *et al*, 2023). It may be within the service or in the community. In the British Army, CBT is often delivered by serving mental health nurses who have done additional training in CBT. Community-based services include charities such as Help for Heroes, which provide support to the armed forces community including psychological therapies. Many NHS services provide specialist psychological therapy support for veterans. You do not have to have a military background to offer CBT.

Sam describes his role as a CBT therapist in an NHS veterans service.

> *We tend to see trauma presentations, particularly complex trauma, as well as other clinical needs such as OCD, low self-esteem, and depression. I carry a clinical caseload of 16 clients, and we offer clients a choice of online or face-to-face sessions. We also do 'walk and talk' therapy, where we may see clients at the local beach, for example, to help support engagement with our service. Each Welsh health board has a veteran's service, and we regularly meet and collaborate together to discuss service requirements and expectations. Although I have never served in the armed forces, it is a personal interest of mine, and it is great to apply CBT to such a diverse and specialist population.*

Working with children

Therapists who choose to train via the CYP route will already have experience of working with children in different roles. This may be in education or youth work. Within these roles, you may notice issues relating to the young person's mental health and want to be able to work at a more therapeutic level.

A day in the life of a CYP CBT therapist

This role can be fixed in one base but most often it will require travelling between locations, such as schools, community centres and the team base. This means that the number of contacts per week will be less due to the logistics of seeing children and young people face-to-face. Each service will have its own expectations, but an average of three face-to-face contacts is normal, or four if children are based in the same school you are visiting that day, or you perform online sessions from the base. The example shown in Figure 3.3 is taken from when I worked for a mental health support team (MHST).

The diary will vary due to the schedule of each school. For example, some schools will not allow children to miss assemblies or certain classes during exam periods. The example above is for a full day of four contacts. However, you may often arrive at a school and the room you booked is no longer available or the child has not attended school that day, so the session does not take place or is reduced in time due to finding a safe place to work. For roles like this, you need to be flexible and tolerant of last-minute changes.

Figure 3.3 – Typical day of a CYP CBT therapist

Time	Activity
9.15 – 10.30am	Arrive at school 1 CBT session with CYP Book next appointment with school admin
10.30 – 10.50	Travel to school 2
11 – 12	CBT session with CYP
12 – 12.15	Travel to base
12.15 – 12.45	Write notes for sessions 1 and 2 Break
12.45 – 1pm	Travel to school 3
1 – 2	CBT session with CYP
2 – 3	CBT session with CYP
3 – 3.15	Travel back to base
3.15 – 3.30	Break
3.30 – 5	Notes for CYP 3 and 4 and catch up on admin

Transitioning between working with adults and children

I made this transition by choosing to do additional training on CBT for children and adolescents before working with children, but this is not necessary. Polly's story describes how she trained as an adult CBT therapist and moved into a CAMHS role.

Polly's story

I qualified as a CBT therapist within an adult IAPT service. After working with adults for several years, I then moved into a CBT therapist role within CAMHS. I don't have a core profession and at that time it was unusual to work within a CAMHS service without a core profession. I am a strong advocate for encouraging KSA applicants who are trained in CBT and passionate about working with young people to make the transition.

It is also possible to transition the other way if you are trained in CYP but want to work with adults. Some CYP training will teach you how to adapt NICE-recommended CBT protocols for adults, so you may already have knowledge and experience of these. You will certainly have core CBT skills and be able to work creatively and flexibly, so this will facilitate your transition to working with adults. Having a good clinical supervisor to support your transition is essential. Kara describes her move from working in CAMHS to an adult IAPT service, which is the reverse of Polly's story.

Kara's story

I trained as a mental health nurse and worked in CAMHS for many years. I did the CYP training and became a CBT therapist in my service once I completed the course. I found my CBT skills were very generic and I was working with the same presenting problems all the time. I fancied a change and wanted to see if I could adapt my skills to work with adults, so went to work in an IAPT service. This was a big change and I felt out of my depth at first but with good support from my supervisor and team leader, the transition is possible.

Working independently

Many CBT therapists will do some private work at some point in their careers. This may be for an agency or company, or they may set up a private practice. Chapter 17 explores this process in more detail, but here, Bea describes her role as an independent CBT therapist and owner of a successful CBT business.

Bea's story

I was a mental health nurse before training as a CBT therapist. I have been the director of my own private limited company (Creating Space Therapies) since 2016. I have steadily seen my private therapy practice grow, and now work full time as an Accredited BABCP CBT therapist and EMDR practitioner, CBT clinical supervisor, and usually have a client waiting list. I specialize in working with trauma, social anxiety and generalized anxiety. I split my week into client-focused workdays (four out of five days), dedicating one day to other tasks and activities.

Bea outlines some of the typical activities she engages in across her working work.

Figure 3.4 – Typical activities of an independent CBT therapist

Focus of day	Activities
Client focused	- Batch reading and responding to emails at a couple of intervals during the day. - Seeing three clients in the morning with short breaks in between. - Lunch, a short meditation practice ideally like the '3-minute breathing space' (doesn't always happen). - Seeing another three clients for my afternoon clinic. - Writing up session notes.
Admin and business development day	- Reviewing my policies and procedures. - CPD: this can involve listening to podcasts; attending workshops both online or in-person; reading articles and action plans. - Writing blog posts, social media, website development. - Networking.

Combining roles

A theme throughout the book is the flexibility of a CBT career. The stories above provide insight into specific roles, but you can combine roles to suit your circumstances and interests. Due to the broad and varied opportunities available to CBT therapists, you do not have to settle for a job that does not maintain your passion for CBT. You can work part time in more than one service or combine an employed position with private work. Later in the book we explore these options in more detail, but Alison's story gives a flavour of how a CBT career can provide this flexibility.

Alison describes her journey to become a CBT therapist, working predominantly with children, motivated by her own lived experience in early life. Although this account has been shortened, a reference to her book is given where you can learn more about her personal and professional journey and the remarkable impact she has had on the development of CBT for children.

Alison's story

I had a tricky childhood myself which ignited my passion for working with children. I had a range of caring roles supporting children initially as a nanny, then as an adviser before working in schools for several years, including teaching assistant (TA) roles at a senior level. In 2011, I trained to be a CBT therapist. I did a placement in school and had another placement with adults. Once I had graduated in 2012, I created my own job and worked on a self-employed basis working in schools with children, delivering CBT. Later, I started a limited company and worked privately, seeing children and adults in addition to staying in schools a few days a week. For the last 11 years, I have lived and breathed CBT, treating hundreds of children, young people and adults with a range of emotional needs. I also supervise trainee CBT therapists working with children and adults. I have personally trained in many additional third-wave therapies such as compassion-focused therapy, ACT, DBT and another modality EMDR, which I equally love.

I have created a CBT book that demonstrates to parents, adults working in schools, and trainee practitioners, easy strategies to gain a shared understanding of a young person's difficulties. The child-friendly cognitive behavioural map (CBM) is at the heart of it. It has taken 20 years to steer the ship to where I want to be. I have followed my heart and passion, doing something I feel passionately about to make a difference. Through my book, I can support young people with their emotions and equip them with strategies that help.

In terms of building a CBT therapist, Alison's story demonstrates the **qualities** of grit and determination required to move through the process of becoming a CBT therapist and beyond. It began with her own difficulties experienced as a child, which ignited her passion to want to work with children. Her journey shows her development of the **essential knowledge and skills** necessary to train as a CBT therapist. Her book (Triste, 2023) promotes the CBT approach using the cognitive behavioural map (CBM). She has never stopped learning new skills and remains inquisitive and resilient, which is a clear sign of the **personal resources** she uses to progress in her CBT career.

Take-home messages from CBT therapists

I asked people on my CBT Careers Facebook group what information would have been helpful to know before they started their CBT career journey. Figure 3.2 provides a summary of their tips and advice.

Figure 3.5 – Tips from therapists who have walked the journey ahead

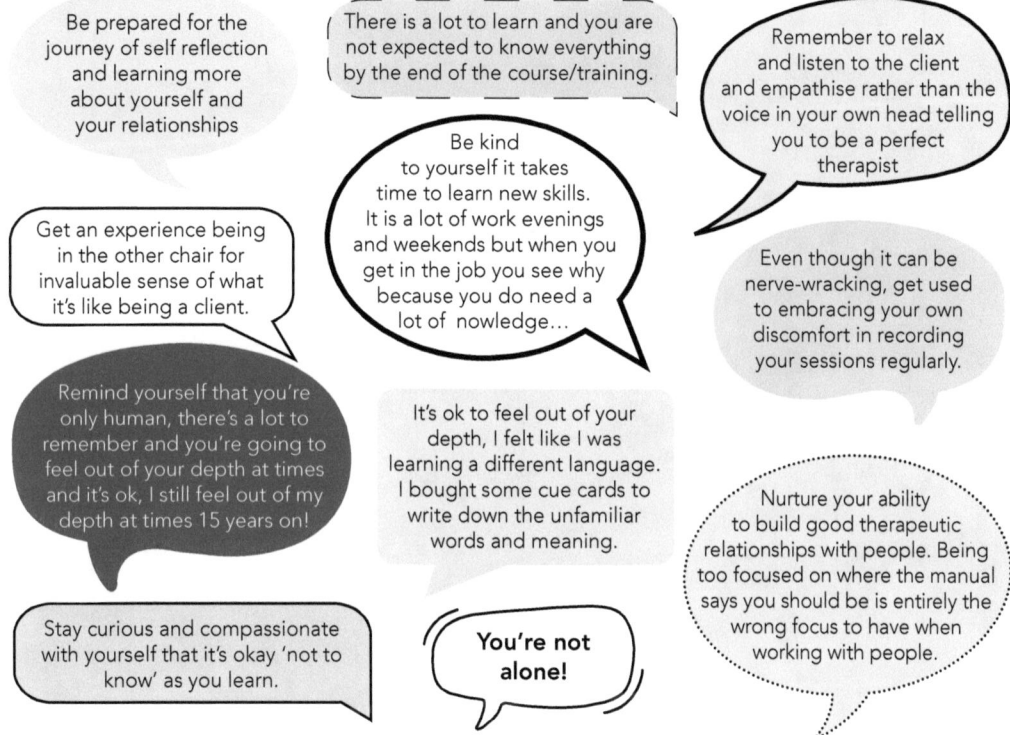

Summary

This chapter has outlined what a CBT career could look like and the different pathways you can take. It provides only a brief overview of the types of roles and services where you can apply CBT. Stories and outlines of a typical day in the various roles illustrate the possibilities available. As we work through the book, we explore even more career options once you have qualified and developed your clinical skills and knowledge.

Chapter 4
Diversity in CBT

The ongoing growth of CBT in the UK has led to a recognition that certain groups are not accessing services. It is reasonable to expect that most people receiving CBT are likely to be White, straight, able-bodied adults. This leaves significant numbers of people who are not accessing psychological therapies, including Black and ethnic minority groups, people with neurodiversity and other disabilities, and the LGBTQ community.

In addition to the challenges faced by those accessing services, these challenges can also be experienced by mental health professionals who identify with any of these groups. The workforce should reflect the population we are working with. Unfortunately, people from any of the protected groups identified in the Equality Act (2010), seeking a psychology career, can face barriers at every stage of their journey. There is a lot of rhetoric around equality, but we are far from seeing equity in healthcare and the career pathways leading to the full range of senior positions. However, CBT as a psychological therapy profession within the UK, is experiencing a shift towards a transcultural approach that attempts to address diversity at an individual, organizational, and political level. Although these changes take time, it is hoped that this will make CBT careers more inclusive.

Although a bigger set of issues than this chapter alone can cover in adequate detail, there are stories from people from diverse backgrounds who have lived experience of developing careers in CBT. These stories are inspirational and important for all of us to learn from and adopt a more open and inclusive approach to CBT for patients, trainees, and colleagues alike.

I am aware of my position as a White-British, straight, female CBT therapist writing about diversity from perspectives of which I do not share personal experience. I have lived experience of neurodiversity that I will share, but to illustrate some of the experiences of therapists from different ethnic backgrounds and from the LGBTQ community, I am grateful for a range of first-hand accounts provided by people at different stages of their CBT career journey to bring some of these issues to light.

What is equality?

Equality has become a broadly used umbrella term but alludes to a state of being equal in terms of status, rights, and opportunities. The Equality & Human Rights Commission states that no one should have poorer life chances because of the way they were born, where they come from, what they believe or whether they have a disability. Equality acknowledges that people from certain groups have historically faced discrimination on the grounds of race, disability, gender and sexual orientation. The Equality Act (2010) is the product of decades of legislation addressing discrimination of people from different groups within society. The Equality Act makes it illegal to discriminate on the grounds of the following **protected characteristics**:

- Age
- Disability
- Gender reassignment
- Marriage and civil partnership
- Pregnancy and maternity
- Race
- Religion or belief
- Sex (more broadly applied to gender)
- Sexual orientation

The law protects against discrimination in the workplace, in education, as a consumer, when **working in public services**, when buying or renting property, and as a member or guest of a private club or association. Clearly, this includes professionals working in public health and social services. Mental health is included as a disability, as are neurodevelopmental conditions such as autism, ADHD and dyslexia.

It is useful to consider psychopathology here. This is how we understand the lived experience of mental distress and how conceptualizations have changed over time in the UK. The medical model has been the most dominant, characterizing mental distress in terms of classified 'symptoms' and assuming universality of experience. Nursing adopted a broader biopsychosocial model (Engel, 1977) that recognizes illness and health are the result of an interaction between biological, psychological, and social factors. Mental health nursing philosophy extended this in the recovery model that places the lived experience of the person at the centre of care and treatment to increase social inclusion and reduce stigma (Repper & Perkins, 2003). This is directly relevant when discussing notions of equality as this includes the lived experience of the professionals, something that the CBT profession can learn from.

The BABCP recently produced their 'Equity, Equality, Diversity, and Inclusivity Statement' (EDI) in response to an independent diversity audit of the organization in 2020. This highlighted a predominance of a 'White voice', which has led to intentional changes that take account of the perspective of all members including minority groups. They have changed the core curriculum and accreditation requirements to reflect the need for specific training in equality, diversity and inclusion during training and as ongoing professional development. There are many projects and special interest groups (SIG) that will continue to develop the integration of the EDI aims. Equality will always be a moving target. It needs to be dynamic and intentional for active change to occur.

More recently, we have been made aware of unconscious bias to help us make implicit forms of discrimination explicit. Unconscious bias is when we use our previous experiences, beliefs, and assumptions about people to guide our decisions and judgements. This includes using stereotypes and assuming that people you perceive to be 'like you' are superior to those who appear different. This process is so subtle that it can even affect people committed to equality. This makes it complex and difficult to eradicate, but awareness is essential.

Reflexivity in CBT practice

Reflective practice is a hallmark of all good health and social care practice. Reflective models allow critical evaluation of practice, identifying strengths and areas for improvement. Robust models are normally cyclical and include Gibb's (1988) learning cycle and Kolb's (1983) experiential learning model. Reflexivity takes reflection to a different level, asking the question "What did I bring with me to this process (CBT practice and therapeutic relationship), and what effect did *my* involvement have?" Reflexivity allows us to be *inside* the analysis as opposed to merely standing back and reflecting. This sheds light on the similarities and differences shared by both therapist and client and how our identities and power processes can influence the therapeutic process. Etherington (2016) advocates the reflexive use of own personal experiences as a means for encouraging shared understanding and addressing issues of agency in the therapeutic relationship. This seems particularly important when working with people from diverse backgrounds, as the therapist may fall into the unconscious bias trap which is indicative of a power imbalance. How we manage that and reconcile these differences is open to be explored when we take a reflexive view of therapy. Krause (2022) outlines the case for placing culture, race and politics at the centre of any systemic therapy.

When considering cultural issues, it is notable that the literature tends to focus on diversity and how we can account for and manage differences between the client and therapist positions. Beck (2016) provides a model of transcultural CBT that includes diversity across ethnicities. It is important that we as therapists account for our own cultural background and recognize differences in world views between individuals, not privileging one over another. CBT can be misused if the therapist merely attempts to get the client to enter their world. Taking a reflexive approach would encourage the therapist to enter the client's world and the guided discovery would be two-way, leading to a more powerful collaboration. Identity is central to this process.

Language, identity and culture

Language plays a critical role in how we create culture. If we consider a social constructionist perspective, power and identity are constructed in discourse. This includes talk and texts in our everyday lives (Potter & Wetherell, 1987; Edwards & Potter, 1992). For many years, the 'collective' narrative has been one-sided and exclusionary, being told from the dominant standpoint which perpetuates an oppositional stance. This manifests in a 'them and us' position that plays down individual differences and homogenizes people according to their association with one group.

To realize inclusion, we need to adopt the language of inclusivity. It is not suggested that merely changing the pronouns from 'them' to 'us' is all it takes to address this institutionalized bias, but it is an important step. As CBT therapists, at all stages of career progression, there is a common motivation to want to help people using the CBT approach. This is a basic level of 'us', with a range of individual differences and lived experiences that enhance rather than divide CBT therapists.

A narrative approach encourages us to listen to stories to gain insight into the lives of people with different experiences to our own (McAdams, 2001; Adler *et al*, 2008). In his classic text Stigma, Goffman (1963) described stigma as extending to those working with people from marginalized groups. He called this 'honorary stigma'. For example, learning disability nurses can become stigmatized within the healthcare professions for working with people with learning disabilities, therefore receiving less status and opportunities within nursing. If we liken this to CBT and those who work with minority groups, the same struggles are apparent. Being from these groups adds another layer of stigma for the therapist or trainee, but it is also a means for connecting to people who may not otherwise access services.

As far back as 30 years ago, Meichenbaum (1993) described the shift in metaphors used in CBT over time from that of 'conditioning' to 'information processing' to 'narrative construction'. "The therapist also helps clients relate examples of their strengths, resources, and coping abilities to convey the rest of the story" (Meichenbaum, 1993, p204). He suggested that CBT therapists should learn ways to encourage clients to develop and transform their narratives. This view has been supported by many, most notably White and Epston (1990), Singer (2005) and Adler and McAdams (2007). The position adopted in this book aims to reiterate this message, relating these ideas to the theory and practice of contemporary CBT. The storied accounts provide insight into the lived experience of CBT therapists from different backgrounds to build a greater understanding of how we can contribute to the development of a transcultural CBT profession.

Addressing diversity

We live in an autobiographical age. There has been an ongoing movement in the UK to recognize people from marginalized groups. Rather than being invisible or ignored, people are sharing their experiences on social media which is an effective platform to reach a large audience. Of course, this is a double-edged sword as the negative responses from some people lead to cyber-bullying, trolling and hate crimes. Legislation is addressing these unacceptable behaviours on a larger scale than ever before. Putting the recommendations of the Equality Act (2010) into practice can serve to protect people, but not everyone wants to be protected as this highlights the perceived vulnerability that can perpetuate bullying and marginalization.

Compared to some other health professions, CBT is evolving at a rapid pace in terms of cultural awareness and attempts to move on from the 'traditional' practice which was largely informed by White middle-class therapists treating White middle-class patients. In addition to institutional changes such as the BABCP EDI statement, this diversity is partly due to the different pathways into a CBT career that attracts practitioners with a diverse range of backgrounds. As this diversity has grown, practitioners from marginalized groups have been able to use their lived experience to extend their CBT practice to underrepresented communities.

The helicopter view is a simple model used in business as a reflective tool to understand complex phenomena. The three levels are often referred to as micro, meso and macro. We can adapt this to help us consider diversity at three levels: the **individual** (client or therapist), the **local community** (service or geographical place), and the **bigger picture** (political, cultural, systemic context). This is shown in Figure 4.1 below.

Figure 4.1 – Helicopter view of diversity

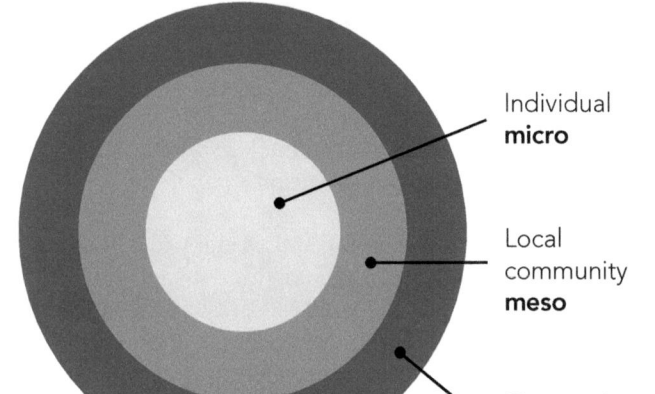

Diversity awareness must go beyond a mere recognition of minority groups. It is important not to homogenize a group identity. For example, being identified as part of a Black, Asian and Minority Ethnic (BAME) or LGBTQ+ community does not mean that all people share the same views or have had the same life experiences. There is a danger of unconscious bias occurring when these assumptions are made. Although the position that we should 'treat each person as an individual' can be criticized for not recognizing specific cultural factors, there must be a balance to recognize individual differences. This goes back to identity and the life-story approach espoused throughout this book. This requires listening to the lived experience of the individual and making sense of their emotional distress within the context of their culture. This is echoed by Lawton *et al* (2021) who suggest that effective CBT needs to consider culturally sensitive issues within the patient's accounts of personal lived experience.

Language relating to diversity is a sensitive issue because it is impossible to have terminology and labels that are universally agreed upon by people from different groups and backgrounds. Being mindful of this, I have chosen to use broad terms to discuss some of the issues relating to people who identify with some of the protected characteristics outlined in the Equality Act (2010). This discussion aims to present these issues within the context of the CBT profession from the perspective of therapists with lived experience. Not all minority groups are represented, as the stories provided are from a self-selected sample by invitation on social media. Individual beliefs and values will vary within groups, so it is accepted that the views expressed may not be fully representative, but these voices need to be heard for the development of more transcultural and inclusive CBT career pathways for all.

Racial diversity in CBT

Terminology for addressing racial diversity in the UK has orientated around the term 'Black, Asian and Minority Ethnic groups' (BAME), although this is now considered outdated. The BABCP recently adopted the term 'People of the Global Majority' (PGM) as a more inclusive term that recognizes representation beyond the UK. They provide the following definition and rationale on their website (BABCP Equity, Equality, Diversity & Inclusivity Statement):

"PGM refers to people who are Black, Asian, Brown, dual-heritage, indigenous to the global south, and or have been previously described as 'ethnic minorities'. These groups currently represent approximately 80 per cent (80%) of the world's population."

Despite this shift, it is recognized that the term BAME is still widely used by individuals, communities, and organizations. Within the NHS Talking Therapies services and the BABCP, there have been special interest groups tasked with addressing the gaps in psychological therapy provision for people from BAME communities. Some innovative and inspirational initiatives have led to positive outcomes. One such offering is the IAPT Black, Asian and minority ethnic service user positive practice guide (BABCP, 2019). In the same year, there was a special issue of the *Cognitive Behavioural Therapist* journal, also published by the BABCP. This addressed several issues across different groups.

Issues relating to race have long, historical, and political roots that have perpetuated racism and discrimination in all areas of daily life, including health, housing, education, employment and socioeconomic status (Nazroo *et al*, 2020; Hogarth, 2019). Racism goes beyond overt discrimination. It is often subtle or so embedded in organizations that it becomes institutionalized and often invisible, appearing in the form of unchallenged statements and slights which can offend. These are known as micro-aggressions and can operate at an unconscious level (Sue *et al*, 2007; Lago, 2011). These processes contribute to the consistent finding that people from BAME communities experience less favourable outcomes for CBT treatment than the White population and are more likely to disengage from therapy (Naz *et al*, 2019; Nazroo *et al*, 2020).

Lopez *et al* (1989) were among the first to address the need for cultural adaptation of therapy. They proposed the 'social cognitive framework' which highlights three stages: being aware of cultural issues, heightened awareness in therapy and cultural sensitivity. In terms of 'how' to address cultural issues in therapy, Bernal *et al* (1995), in their ecological validity model, suggest that it must be fully integrated at every level. This includes language, context, goals, content, methods and the use of appropriate metaphors and concepts that match the experiences of the person. Laungani (2004) identified four core dimensions of difference between Asian and Western cultures: individualism-communalism, cognitivism-emotionism, free-will-determinism and materialism-spiritualism. Despite these early attempts to address culture in therapy, Naheeml (2019) highlighted the persistence of an ethnocentric approach to CBT based on Western values. This is echoed by Huey *et al* (2023).

In their recent review of culturally adapted CBT, Naheem *et al* (2023) found a lack of consistency in terms of what elements are most important to adapt. Naheem *et al* (2009) produced the Southampton Adaptation framework, which was the first and one of very few to be studied using randomized controlled trials (RCTs), of which there are 22 to date. There has been significant stakeholder involvement, and it provides a robust bio-psychosocial-spiritual model for CBT. Integration has been challenging, which is echoed by Faheem (2023) who surveyed staff in NHS Talking Therapy services to assess cultural competence, concluding it to be a 'poor show'. In a reflexive thematic analysis, Faheem identified three themes: encountering cultural dissonance in therapy, challenges in making cultural alterations, and identifying cultural competency needs. This was attributed, in part, to a lack of 'meaningful' training (Clegg *et al*, 2016). Lawton *et al* (2021) suggest that the BAME service user positive practice guide (PPG) (BABCP, 2019) audit tool provides a means for developing culturally adapted services.

CBT therapist perspective on racial diversity in CBT

In terms of integrating cultural awareness, the literature has focused on the micro (individual) and macro (political) levels of the helicopter view. We need to focus on the middle level, which is the local environment therapy takes place in services. This includes an examination of issues relating to the workforce. Less has been written on the experiences of healthcare practitioners from BAME communities. Fernando (2017) provides a detailed historical account of institutionalized racism within British psychiatry and clinical psychology that demonstrates the longevity of the problem and how slowly things have progressed. Fernando describes his own experiences of glass ceilings for promotion and career progression for non-White professionals. This is reiterated in a recent collection of narrative accounts by clinical psychologists from racially minoritized backgrounds at all stages of career development (Farooq *et al*, 2022; 2023). These lived experience accounts are a necessary way to bring equality legislation to life or else racial matters can remain an abstract construct at an intellectualized level. This is what has thwarted change.

Carlo shared his CBT career journey and experiences as a Black CBT therapist in the NHS.

Carlo's story

Carlo described growing up in a poor area with rich cultural diversity. His parents are from Barbados, where mental health is not recognized like it is in the UK. He remembers recognizing the trauma experienced by young Black men and a strong desire to want to make a difference. He was the first in his large Caribbean family to go to university. He thought he wanted to study business but changed his mind when he discovered psychology and criminology. He volunteered for two years in mental health settings and tried to get on the doctorate programme in clinical psychology but found it extremely hard. He found Black people were working at a support level, but not many in higher positions or in clinical psychology. He also describes colourism within services, where discrimination is worse for people with darker skin. He had a care-coordinator role as an assistant practitioner before training as a PWP in IAPT. After working as a senior PWP, he did his high-intensity training and has been a qualified CBT therapist for the past five years.

Carlo states that his experiences overall have been positive. He reflects, however, that across four teams (totalling 130 practitioners) there were only three other Black males. He found more diversity on CBT training courses. He describes how he sometimes feels like a unicorn as a Black male in services. He has a strong drive to want to represent Black people, but recognizes that, as a minority therapist, you can end up taking on more work. He values being a mentor to trainees and therapists from diverse backgrounds and summarizes his advice:

- *Remember that your experiences are valuable and helpful to others.*
- *There are BAME SIGs, policies and support to guide you.*
- *Be a mentor or seek a mentor.*
- *If you experience barriers, then look for structures to address them in your way.*
- *There are different levels of action, so do what you are comfortable with.*

I also spoke to Tasha about her experiences of being a Black woman and CBT professional.

Tasha's story

Tasha was a social worker working with adults when she became interested in CBT. She did not have enough mental health experience to do the high-intensity training so became a PWP first. she has currently completed her high-intensity training. Tasha works in a geographical area where there are very few Black people. She values her diversity being recognized in clinical supervision when asked for her opinion from 'a Black woman's perspective'. She does not like the term 'colour blind' as she does not wish to be 'washed away'. Although she recognizes that stereotypes and biases occur for minority therapists, like Carlo, she states that her personal experiences on her CBT career journey have been positive.

There is an absence of voices from therapists of different ethnicities, but the stories presented here are from a self-selected sample. Selina is from a South-Asian background and her story is presented below when we discuss intersectionality.

Spiritual diversity in CBT

Spirituality is an umbrella term that addresses beliefs across, and independent of, religious and faith groups. These will vary in terms of how emotions are viewed and beliefs regarding personal autonomy. To gain an understanding of the context of a person's presenting problems it is necessary to explore such beliefs (Cook *et al*, 2009). Waller *et al* (2010) state that "it is necessary to decide if the spiritual issue being raised is a source of mental distress, a resource for good mental health or a red herring that is not for addressing in therapy" (Waller *et al*, 2010, p95).

Religion and spiritual beliefs have been viewed as compatible with a CBT approach due to the emphasis on lived experiences, belief systems and identity (Hathaway, 2013; Hays, 2006). There has been a growth of religiously integrated CBT (RICBT) approaches that address the religious beliefs of clients. Early approaches targeted more mainstream religions such as Christianity (Stanley *et al*, 2011) but more recently research has extended the evidence base for RICBT for other religious groups including Muslims (Beshai *et al*, 2013). Sabki *et al* (2019) developed an Islamic-informed CBT (IICBT) intervention based on verses from the Quran and Hadith to help depressed Muslim patients in Malaysia.

CBT perspective on spirituality in CBT

Jodie has kindly shared her story of being a converted Muslim and some of the issues she experienced when working in the NHS. She now specializes in Islamic CBT in her own private practice and shares some advice for using CBT with Muslim clients.

I started in the NHS only two weeks before I converted. I was unfortunately told that God had no place in therapy after I brought up, in supervision, a client wanting to talk about God. I found it difficult to be idiosyncratic with clients but only secularly, especially when they didn't want that. I found most colleagues didn't understand Islam or being Muslim, including asking if I have an alcoholic drink at Christmas. There was no aggression or conflict, but a lot of ignorance. I went into private practice full time. I now specialize in faith-based approaches for Muslim clients.

Systemic issues – *for many Muslims, their family are a huge part of their lives. Thinking more flexibly about how to tackle systemic issues is very important. Cutting ties with family is rarely permitted – in cases of abuse this is permitted, obviously, however many people still feel unable to end relationships.*

Shame – *unfortunately some people have learned our religion in a way that is shame based. Having tools to work with shame, I particularly like compassion-focused work for this, which is very important as shame can become a significant barrier to change.*

Gender – *generally, men and women would want a therapist of the same gender as it would be seen as inappropriate for many to work with someone of the opposite sex.*

Jodie also suggests learning the basics about a religion but also asking the person, as they are the expert on what they believe.

Gender and sexual identity diversity in CBT

It is important to state that gender and sexuality are not the same. This discussion will include research and issues affecting each and/or both, as there can be overlap, or intersectionality, and both relate to a person's identity. Grimmer (2021) uses the term 'gender, sexuality, and relationship diversity (GSRD)' to include people who identify as gay, lesbian, bisexual, transgender, queer/questioning, and intersex (LGBTQI), among other possible identities. In the UK, 'LGBTQ+' is the term most used to describe the range of sexual and gender identities (Foy *et al*, 2019).

The UK Royal College of Psychiatrists defines transgender and gender-diverse people as "individuals whose gender identity and/or gender role do not conform to the sex assigned to them at birth (cisgender). While the term 'transgender' is commonly accepted, not all gender-diverse people self-identify as transgender, or with the binary concept of gender that is common to most cultures" (RCP, 2018, p2). This definition has been developed in response to gender equality movements to increase inclusion and understanding of gender diversity in healthcare (Bouman *et al*, 2017a & b; Richards *et al*, 2016; Saewyc *et al*, 2017).

It is widely recognized that people identifying as LGBTQ+ experience a disproportionate burden of mental health problems compared to heterosexual people (Meyer, 2003; Plöderl & Tremblay, 2015; Semlyen *et al*, 2016). For transgender people, the risk of poor mental health is even greater, with higher rates of suicidal ideation reported (Testa *et al*, 2017). This is associated with higher levels of stress caused by stigma and discrimination within a hostile homophobic and transphobic culture (Meyer, 2003; Meyer & Frost, 2013; Carvalho *et al*, 2022).

Pachankis & Goldfried (2004) define homophobia as "an extreme, negative reaction on the part of both heterosexual and homosexual persons to homosexual individuals and homosexual behavior" (p228) and heterocentrism as "the systemic attitudes and assumptions that operate in a society that understands itself, by default, as purely heterosexual" (ibid, p. 228). This can lead to internalized homophobia by the individual that manifests in shame and fear of disclosure. As an LGBTQ+ identity can often be concealed, Pachankis (2007) suggests that the individual will need to assess the potential threat of disclosure within the context of the social and cultural environment. This adds to the burden of stress due to heightened hypervigilance. Foy *et al* (2019) distinguish between homophobia and biphobia. Bisexual people are likely to experience higher levels of stigma and discrimination as their identity can be stereotyped and misunderstood by both the heterosexual and homosexual communities, leading to double discrimination (Balsam & Mohr, 2007; Bostwick & Hequembourg, 2014; Dyar & London, 2018; Foy *et al*, 2019).

In terms of minority stress, there are specific issues relating to people from sexual minority groups including the risk of internalized homophobia or biphobia, the threat of being "outed" without consent, and increased vigilance for hostility (Grimmer, 2021). This may explain the fear related to accessing services. Under the Equality Act (2010), sexual orientation has been recognized as a protected characteristic so people should not be discriminated against within the national health and social care systems. Attempts have been made to address previous barriers such as heteronormative language and imagery through sexuality monitoring of patients and practitioners and mandatory LGBTQ+ equality training (NHS Equality & Diversity Council, 2015). Despite this, LGBTQ+ people report less favourable experiences and outcomes from psychological therapy treatment (Elliott *et al*, 2015; Rimes *et al*, 2018).

There has been a movement towards adapting CBT for the LGBTQ+ community. Hall *et al* (2019) introduced an eight-week CBT group programme called 'Being out with strength' (BOWS) to reduce depression in LGBTQ young people, and Skerven *et al* (2019) proposed the use of dialectical behaviour therapy (DBT) to address internalized stigma and shame. Carvalho *et al* (2022) describe the factors essential to developing affirmative CBT for gender and sexual minorities (GSM):

1. Acknowledge and validate the strengths, resilience and autonomy of the person.
2. View same-sex attraction and gender diversity as variations in positive human experience, rather than a pathology.
3. Seek to understand the developmental and cultural background of the person.
4. Acknowledge sources of minority stress as core contributors to psychological distress.
5. Therapist self-examination and reflection on personal attitudes relating to gender and sexual identity diversity.

Affirmative CBT interventions specifically acknowledge and target symptoms relating to minority stress. This includes building resilience and assertiveness and encouraging connection to the GSM community to reduce isolation and build or maintain a positive view of their identity.

CBT therapist perspective on LGBTQ+ in CBT

During an interview with Daisy, the BABCP LGBTQ+ special interest group chair, she shared her perspective on being a CBT therapist from the LGBTQ+ community. First, she stated that assumptions about sexuality are often made by colleagues and clients, but being 'out' and self-disclosing sexual identity is a personal choice. She is open about being lesbian. We discussed the use of language and how no terms or phrases are universally accepted, so it is important to express your preferred terms and encourage other therapists to explore sexual identity with all clients as standard practice. This requires the use of affirmative language. Some staff are hesitant to ask about sexuality due to fear of offending or embarrassing a client, but sex and sexuality should be part of the formulation as this relates to identity and can impact mental health. There has been a lack of training in services, but this is changing.

Daisy is an LGBTQ+ activist and has made substantial changes at the macro (political) level including setting up the BABCP LGBTQ+ SIG and introducing the National Network for LGBTQ+ champions within NHS Talking Therapy services. These provide LGBTQ+

therapists an opportunity to share lived experiences and inform the development of more inclusive services. However, Daisy warns that staff who consciously volunteer may find themselves doing additional work in their own time and at their own financial expense. Even staff who are 'out' but do not volunteer may be approached on issues relating to LGBTQ+, just based on their identity, which is a protected characteristic. Such exploitation, even if unconscious, will add to existing minority stress. This can be difficult when the therapist is passionate about supporting their community, but personal boundaries must be respected by the organization.

Daisy provides the following tips:

- CBT training is demanding but rewarding.
- There should be no barriers to becoming a CBT therapist.
- There is a general lack of training on the specific needs of the LGBTQ+ community but this is changing.
- Join special interest groups or become an LGBTQ+ champion in your service.
- There is a gap in the literature on the experience of lesbians, bisexual men and women and the voice of transpeople.
- People need to be aware of the difference between gender and sexuality.

Daisy also highlighted the need to consider intersectionality in CBT services, which leads us to Selina's story.

Intersectionality from a CBT therapist's perspective – Selina's story

So far, we have discussed diversity as it relates to individual protected characteristics. However, intersectionality occurs when you identify with more than one protected characteristic, which increases the likelihood of discrimination and stigma. Selina provides her account of being a bisexual woman from a South-Asian background.

When I was younger, I always imagined myself becoming a teacher. I tried three times to get on the PGCE course but as fate would have it, I was unsuccessful. Coupled with my experiences at university, I eventually trained as a cognitive behavioural therapist and have now worked within NHS Talking Therapies for over ten years. It was during my bachelor's degree in Manchester that I developed a crush on my best friend and fell in love. Fall I did, as sadly this love was unrequited. I forgot to mention that my best friend was female, like me, and coming from a South-Asian background, the notion of being anything but heterosexual was overwhelming for me. What would people think? What about my dream Indian wedding? What would I do after university? How would my family cope? I felt so isolated and could not find my voice to speak up and recognize I needed help.

In 2003, I had a breakdown and was diagnosed with depression and psychosis. The reason I am mentioning this is that my lived experience of mental illness, trouble accepting my sexuality and coming from a minority background, very much led me to my training in cognitive behavioural therapy and the work I do today. Out of a difficult ten years of my life, I, like many, wanted to create a positive narrative and use my experiences to support others. At the time, mental illness was rather stigmatized, especially for minority communities, so I was fortunate to be a part of campaigns such as Rethink's 'Time to Change' and Stonewall's 'It Gets Better' campaign. I am very proud of these achievements.

During my training in cognitive behavioural therapy, I reflect now that I was still recovering from my illness and there was a part of me still struggling to connect with the course material. A lot of the material was not touching upon issues related to race or sexuality. Coincidentally, one of my course lecturers was a lesbian and I remember feeling some comfort in this and remembering that representation matters. Role models matter. I will touch upon this further when I explain my top tips for working with minority distress and sexuality.

Currently, I am in a leadership role within NHS Talking Therapies and I co-chair the service's LGBTQIA + working group. I have been a co-chair for a gender and sexual orientation and sexual identity group for a local NHS Trust previously. I am passionate about the need to better understand those who may be struggling with their sexual orientation and or mental health. I often use the phrase 'minority distress' when discussing such themes. NHS England and the LGBT Foundation are currently putting together a Positive Practice Guide for NHS Talking Therapy services working with the LGBTQIA + community. I look forward to reading it when it arrives. Meanwhile, the issues faced by the LGBTQIA + community are very relevant today. The UK Prime Minister Rishi Sunak recently said at the Conservative Party Conference in Manchester that "men and men and women are women… it's common sense". Alluding to people not being able to choose their gender, greatly sets the trans community back several years. Rather than debate the view of trans people and politics, the important point to raise is that the stressors and challenges faced by the LGBTQIA + community are real and present.

It is vital that people understand minority distress when working with patients from these communities. To help, here are some top tips that I feel would help clinicians working with the LGBTQIA + population:

1. Always be person centred and idiosyncratic in your approach. It is important to see one individual who is LGBTQIA + as one person who is LGBTQIA + .
2. Aim to understand the language used by these communities. Respect people's pronouns and, if unsure about anything, ask!
3. Look for positive role models for patients to look up to. Representation matters and believing that it is OK to be themselves is useful in therapeutic work.
4. Be aware of the economic/social/political climate someone has come from and how this may have impacted their views on sexuality and the challenges they have faced.

5. *Equally, never assume that a person from the LGBTQIA+ community has struggled with their sexuality. Though this was my experience, some people never question themselves as anything but themselves and are comfortable with this.*
6. *Link with local and national charities that can help the LGBTQIA+ community with things like sexual health etc.*
7. *When relevant, work on that individual's identity and what it means to them. Help build confidence.*
8. *If you work in a service, encourage outreach work to these communities.*
9. *Training. Many organizations and charities now offer training on LGBTQIA+ language and are there to help educate people who may be unclear or need support.*
10. *Finally, be open, non-judgemental and treat every LGBTQIA+ person you interact with no differently to how you would treat a non-LGBTGIA+ individual. If you find yourself triggered or struggling with a clinical presentation, take it to supervision.*

Selina's story is powerful and inspiring. She outlines her many challenges and how she overcame them to develop her career in a meaningful direction based on her values and identity. Her advice is authentically based on her lived experience and serves as essential learning for all therapists and service managers.

Disability, neurodiversity and CBT

Disability is defined in broad terms within the Equality Act (2010) as a physical or mental impairment that has a substantial and long-term adverse effect on someone's ability to perform daily activities. This includes difficulty concentrating and problems with sleep, causing fatigue. Not often viewed in terms of diversity, having a long-term health condition requires resilience to deal with adversity. People living with long-term health conditions face many barriers to employment. The Equality Act (2010) requires employers to make reasonable adjustments to make the environment and workload more appropriate to the needs and capacity of the person. Being a CBT therapist or trainee is extremely demanding, so it is essential to reduce these demands as much as possible. CBT can be used for long-term health conditions (Kinsella & Moya, 2021).

Neurodiversity has been receiving more attention in recent years. Previously viewed more as a concern for children and young people, predominantly males, it is now recognized that many people have only been diagnosed with autism and/or ADHD as adults. Women have been a silent population, but this is changing with updated research, training and storied accounts by adults on social media. Identifying with autism and/or ADHD can open opportunities to learn how to manage daily difficulties associated with these life-long conditions. If you are neurodiverse and working as a CBT therapist or thinking of doing the training, there may be some issues that impact you. As a woman diagnosed with ADHD, later in life, I am very aware of some of these challenges and how I manage them in my therapist role.

CBT therapist perspective on disability and neurodiversity in CBT

Disability is clearly a broad category. The first account is provided by Natalie, who describes her experiences as a CBT therapist with a long-term physical health condition (LTHC) and chronic pain.

I volunteered to become the LTHC 'champion' during my time as a PWP. I have a chronic pain condition myself and felt that my personal experience would be beneficial to this client group. I was a participant in a pain-management group which used a combination of acceptance and commitment therapy (ACT) and CBT. My passion for ACT developed very quickly from that point and I began a process of self-learning the principles and applying ACT to myself. I went on to support a CBT therapist to run an ACT-based LTHC group and thoroughly enjoyed this type of work. My own experience of chronic pain and how much ACT helped me to live my best life has motivated me to help others. I enjoy seeing the significant difference therapy can make to someone's life by helping them manage pain more effectively and how they gradually learn how to accept their pain or illness.

Natalie's story illustrates how she discovered ACT through her work as a CBT therapist and applied it to herself. This is a great example of using a CBT from the inside-out approach, with ACT to help her live her best life. Her positive experiences have influenced her practice and desire to help others with LTHC and chronic pain in her successful independent practice. More of Natalie's story is shared later in the book.

The next story is my own lived experience account of being a CBT therapist with ADHD.

Even before my diagnosis, I was aware that daily life seemed more demanding for me than for most people. A racing brain, energetic, loud and excitable but with a tendency to snap in a moment. Now it makes sense that the hyperactive brain is more aroused more of the time, and there is an excessive flow of adrenaline making me prone to act on my impulses before the frontal cortex allows me to think things through. Self-control is central to daily functioning as I don't always trust myself to stay on task. Over the years, I developed strategies without realizing. Naturally disorganized, I must work hard at creating order and structure at work. Having systems in place that require little thought works best and this requires repetition to the point of automation. For example, when learning a new online records system, I will need to focus extremely hard for the first few times until I can do it almost on autopilot. Timing tasks helps to stay realistic when planning my diary. For example, I can only concentrate on writing clinical notes for ten minutes at a time. To manage this, I need to organize my environment to reduce distractions. This technique also works to overcome procrastination. Planning regular breaks to 'decompress' also helps to reduce my brain arousal.

CBT is a helpful approach for managing ADHD symptoms. Specific protocols have been presented but the current evidence base is not as robust as for other conditions. Research by Spricht *et al* (2012) led to the development of a manualized CBT protocol for adult ADHD by Safren *et al* (2018). They identify three main areas to help people with ADHD: organizational skills, reducing distractibility and addressing unhelpful thoughts. I specialize in CBT for ADHD and have developed a maintenance cycle for ADHD called the threat-demand cycle. This is the idea that every demand presents as a threat, then, when on threat alert, everything seems like a demand. This cycle can be perpetual for someone with ADHD.

I have produced a series of guides (downloadable from the Resources page) which can be used by therapists, supervisors, managers and colleagues to help manage symptoms in the workplace:

- **ADHD & CBT: A self-help guide to the effective use of CBT for ADHD** – A 25-page guide which outlines symptoms, assessment, lived experience perspective and how to use CBT to manage symptoms. This is an overview but is useful for people who suspect they may have ADHD or supervisors, managers and colleagues of a CBT therapist with ADHD.
- **CBT & ADHD: A guide to effective use of CBT for ADHD (Practitioner's guide)** – A 15-page version of the previous guide, which covers similar material and aims to help practitioners understand the nuances of working with people with ADHD.
- **ADHD procrastination guide** – A 15-page guide that provides strategies for monitoring and overcoming procrastination. It is useful for clients and staff as a self-help tool.
- **Managing emotions with ADHD: A guide to effective use of CBT** – A 15-page to effective use of CBT. This is a 15-page guide that outlines some of the main difficulties faced by people with ADHD in relation to emotional regulation.

All these guides build on the evidence base but incorporate my lived experience to include the nuances of ADHD which are not always highlighted in the literature.

Figure 4.2 – Threat-demand cycle of ADHD

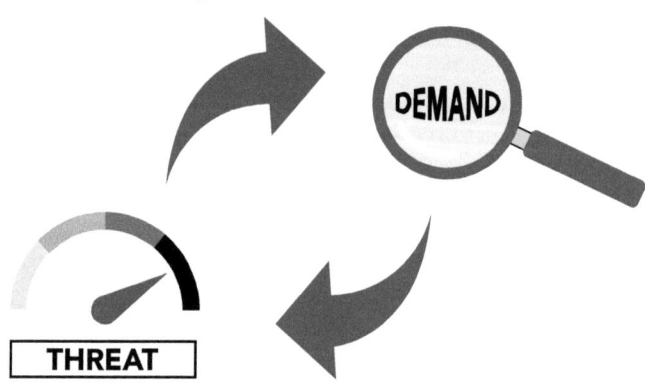

Addressing the needs of a diverse CBT workforce

A common thread relating to any position of diversity is **maintaining identity**. At an individual (or micro) level, this involves knowing what your needs are and how to get them met. The macro level provides research, policy and legislation relating to equality to protect individuals on the grounds of identity factors. It is the task of psychological therapy services to integrate the macro and micro levels to provide inclusive services for staff as well as clients.

From the discussions and shared accounts presented in this chapter, some steps to creating a service based on equality and diversity are summarized below.

- Audit – outcome data, staff mix.
- Language and resources.
- Psychologically safe spaces for staff to express their concerns and needs.
- Training on inclusion.
- Embedded in clinical practice – supervision, asking questions about identity as standard practice.
- Opportunities for career progression for all.
- Zero tolerance of discrimination.
- Special interest groups for professionals.
- Peer support.
- Champions.
- Mission statements by services to maintain accountability.

Summary

This chapter has addressed diversity in CBT. The perspectives of different therapists was provided in storied accounts of their lived experiences. Although the chapter and stories do not cover the full range of minority groups, it is intended to show how the CBT profession is becoming more inclusive. However, the wider literature suggests there is still a long way to go for equality to be fully realized in services. Some broad conclusions and tips were summarized at the end in terms of organizational responsibility to minimize discrimination and bias.

Chapter 5
CBT career roadmap: Pathways to becoming a CBT therapist

One of the strengths of the CBT career trajectory is that there is more than one route to becoming a CBT therapist. On average, this journey can take around eight years, so understanding these different routes and which one best fits your background, qualifications and experience is essential to navigating through the process. Without a clear understanding of these pathways, it is possible to get stuck or pursue academic courses that may not provide the best chances for progression to CBT training. It is important to have this advice at school and college levels so that students can make more informed choices before applying for university courses relating to psychology.

Using the roadmap shown in Figure 5.1, this chapter covers a range of situations before CBT training and how to move forward in your journey towards accreditation.

Pre-degree level

Before choosing a degree course, you need to know what options are available that lead to a clinical career in the mental health field. The most popular degree choice for people interested in mental health is psychology. If you are totally committed to this choice, then you can move to the section aimed at psychology graduates. However, there are other pathways that will increase your career opportunities while gaining the psychology knowledge that you are passionate about.

Core professional training degree

One of the fundamental requirements for CBT training is a core profession in the mental health field. This provides the necessary psychological theory and clinical skills on which to build as a CBT therapist. Core professional training is normally a three-year undergraduate degree which provides a clear career pathway on completion with job opportunities as soon as you qualify. You will also become registered or accredited within that profession.

Without a core profession, the other starting point is often a psychology degree. It is important to recognize the limitations of having a psychology degree alone due to the high number of graduates without clinical experience or applied psychology skills. The pathways to CBT training without a core profession are likely to take longer as you will need to gain the relevant clinical skills and, due to the competition, this market is already saturated.

Figure 5.1 – CBT career roadmap

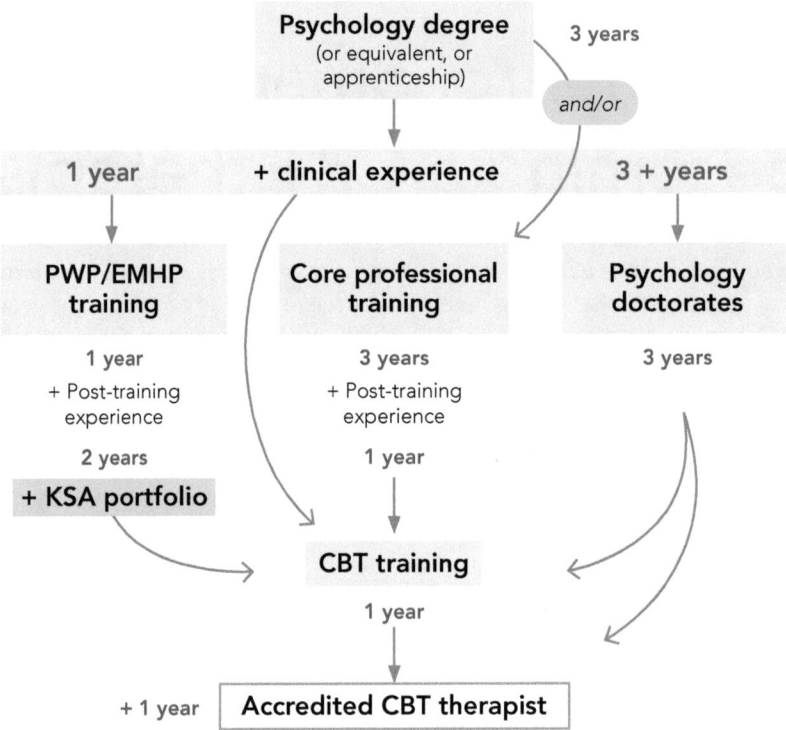

If you are studying psychology at GCSE or A-level in the UK educational system and are passionate about pursuing a clinical career in psychology, then consider applying for a core professional degree. The academic focus of a core professional training programme is psychology-based and this knowledge is applied to the clinical area of that core profession. This means that you are applying psychology theory to practice throughout the degree. On completion, you are a qualified mental health professional, which provides so many more career options. If becoming a CBT therapist is your goal, then entering training is much easier with a core profession in mental health.

The options for core professional training that are recognized by the British Association for Behavioural and Cognitive Psychotherapies (BABCP) are listed in Table 5.1 with details of the professional bodies that register or accredit practice.

More details on these core professions can be found by accessing the individual professional bodies. This research will broaden your understanding of the different professions that make up the mental health field and may inform your career choice. It is important to have the bigger-picture perspective to remain open-minded and flexible in your thinking. The commitment to one pathway, like the pursuit of a pure psychology degree, can give you tunnel vision and close off other options.

Remember that you can still access CBT training without a core profession, and we will discuss this separately.

Table 5.1 – Core professions in mental health recognized by the BABCP

Core profession	Required level and professional body
Arts therapist	Qualified and registered with the Health and Care Professions Council (HCPC)
Counselling	Accredited with recommended professional bodies (see BABCP website)
Medicine	Psychiatrist or GP
Nurse	NMC registered mental health nurse or learning disability nurse
Occupational therapy	Qualified and registered with the HCPC
Psychotherapy or psychotherapeutic counselling	Registered with the United Kingdom Psychotherapy Council (UKPC)
Social work	Qualified and registered with UK regulated body
Postgraduate doctorate in clinical or counselling psychology	Qualified and registered as HCPC practitioner psychologist
Educational psychology	Qualified and registered as HCPC practitioner psychologist
Health psychology	Qualified and registered as HCPC practitioner psychologist
Forensic psychology	Qualified and registered as HCPC practitioner psychologist

The core professions most accessible at degree level

Clearly, some of the core professions listed require more than an undergraduate degree, so we will focus now on the most accessible options for a first degree.

Nursing

Not all nursing degrees lead directly to CBT training. The reason that only mental health and learning disability nursing are considered core professions in mental health is due to the proportion of psychology-related content. The curriculum provides essential knowledge and skills including psychopathology and therapeutic approaches to support people with learning disabilities and/or mental health problems while on clinical placements.

During training, you will learn clinical skills on placements in a range of settings for people with different mental health or learning disability needs. Some examples of typical placements are provided in Table 5.2.

Table 5.2 – Common placements during mental health and learning disability nursing training

Mental health nursing	Learning disability nursing
<ul><li>Assessment units in mental health hospitals</li><li>Hospital wards working with people experiencing acute mental health problems</li><li>Community mental health teams</li><li>Crisis intervention services</li><li>Forensic units for people with a mental health problem who are in the legal system</li><li>Services for people with dementia and associated mental health needs</li><li>Child & Adolescent Mental Health Services (CAMHS)</li><li>Eating disorder services</li></ul>	<ul><li>Community intellectual disability teams</li><li>Child & Adolescent Mental Health (CAMHS) intellectual disability teams</li><li>Schools for children with learning disabilities</li><li>Residential settings for people with complex health needs</li><li>Assisted independent living</li><li>Community projects to increase social inclusion</li><li>Forensic services for people with learning disabilities</li></ul>

On completing training, you will receive a bachelor's degree in that field of nursing and registration to the Nursing and Midwifery Council (NMC). Due to the variety of clinical experience gained on these nursing courses, you will have many options as a qualified nurse and will have good earning potential.

Social work

A degree in social work provides knowledge informed by sociology, psychology and politics, which is applied to several different client groups requiring help. This includes children who are at risk of harm or neglect, and vulnerable adults who have mental health problems or limited capacity to make decisions concerning their safety and rights. You gain clinical skills through a variety of placements over the course of the degree. Social Work England (2023) updated their guidance on practice placements. They describe statutory placements that take place within local authority settings or within the private, voluntary, and independent (PVI) sector and include:

- Local authority residential settings for children
- Adoption and fostering services
- Therapeutic interventions for sexual abuse
- Older adult services
- Schools
- Hospices
- Healthcare facilities and hospitals
- Substance-use clinics
- Community service organizations
- Child welfare agencies
- Interpersonal violence crisis centres
- Mental health organizations

During training, you will only have the opportunity to work in a small number of these settings, but some courses allow choice regarding placement preference. If not, then, on completion of training, there are opportunities in all areas of social care as, like all public services, they are vastly under-resourced.

Occupational therapy

An occupational therapy degree focuses on the knowledge and skills necessary for helping people with a range of physical, psychological and emotional difficulties to maximize daily functioning. This includes people with disabilities, long-term physical conditions, trauma and other mental health difficulties impacting daily life.

The curriculum covers theory from psychology, sociology, social policy and ergonomics (environmentally driven design to increase user benefit). Clinical skills are gained from working with different client groups in various settings including:

- Post-operative surgery wards in hospital
- Community mental health teams
- Stroke rehabilitation units

- Mental health wards following a crisis or severe change to mental health status
- Early intervention teams
- Employment services to help people back to work following an accident or illness
- Learning disability teams

On completion of training, you will register with the Health and Care Professions Council (HCPC) and the Royal College of Occupational Therapists (RCOT).

Comparing content of a psychology degree and common core professional degrees

To weigh up the differences between a psychology degree and core professional training degrees, it is useful to compare the content and learning methods used. Table 5.3 does not cover all degree content as specific courses may vary in their curriculum. However, it gives a snapshot of theoretical content and learning methods offered. Mental health and learning disability nursing have been combined as the content shown is broad. Within each field of nursing, there will be additional content relating to the specific client group.

The table demonstrates some clear differences between a psychology degree and the three core professional training degrees. Firstly, a psychology degree will not provide skills that are transferable to a clinical role. This is because it is a purely academic course. The core professions are divided equally between theory and practice, with skills acquired through the completion of supervised clinical placements. This teaches the basic therapeutic skills necessary for any psychological intervention and can be developed later during CBT training.

Another major difference between graduating with a psychology degree and a core professional degree is your **identity**. With a core profession, you immediately identify as a mental healthcare professional with applied psychology knowledge and skills, whereas a psychology degree will lead to the identity of a psychology graduate. This will require further work experience and training to enable you to identify as a practitioner.

Table 5.3 – Comparing psychology degrees with core profession training degrees

	Psychology degree	Mental health and learning disability nursing	Occupational therapy	Social work
Theory (may vary)	Branches of psychology: ■ Cognitive ■ Developmental ■ Social ■ Clinical ■ Occupational ■ Health	■ Ethics & professional practice ■ Biopsychosocial model of care ■ Mental health legislation ■ Psychopathology ■ Social inclusion & equality	■ Ethics & professional practice ■ Biopsychosocial model of care ■ Psychopathology ■ Social inclusion & equality ■ Environmental effects on health and wellbeing	■ Ethics & professional practice ■ Biopsychosocial model of care ■ Social policy ■ Social inclusion & equality ■ Mental health law ■ Psychopathology
Skills	No	■ Communication ■ Therapeutic relationship ■ Needs assessment ■ Mental health assessment ■ Goal setting ■ Risk assessment & management ■ Safeguarding ■ Treatment plans ■ Reflective practice	■ Communication ■ Therapeutic relationship ■ Needs assessment ■ Goal setting ■ Risk assessment & management ■ Safeguarding ■ Treatment plans ■ Reflective practice	■ Communication ■ Therapeutic relationship ■ Needs assessment ■ Goal setting ■ Risk assessment & management ■ Safeguarding ■ Care plans ■ Reflective practice
Methods	■ Lectures ■ Coursework ■ Dissertation ■ Exams	■ Lectures ■ Clinical placements ■ Clinical supervision ■ Self-guided study ■ Course work ■ Dissertation	■ Lectures ■ Clinical placements ■ Clinical supervision ■ Self-guided study ■ Course work ■ Dissertation	■ Lectures ■ Clinical placements ■ Clinical supervision ■ Self-guided study ■ Course work ■ Dissertation
Leads to a professional job on completion?	No	Yes	Yes	Yes

N.B. There is a downloadable version of this table on the Resources page

Psychology graduate

You may already have a psychology degree and want a clinical career in mental health. In this section, we consider some pathways to achieve this. The journey from this point will be long and challenging as it is an extremely competitive field. You are likely passionate about psychology and helping people, so the decisions you make need to satisfy these fundamental needs. Each step of your journey should be seen as valuable and not a compromise if you have one goal in mind. Try to remain open-minded as, despite the competition, there will always be demand for your skills and passion.

Psychology doctorates

The most common pathway chosen by psychology graduates is clinical psychology. This is a doctoral programme across three years leading to the title of Doctor of Clinical Psychology (DClinPsy), registration with the Health and Care Professions Council (HCPC) and Chartered status with the British Psychological Society (BPS). It is also recognized as a core profession in mental health by the BABCP. The training includes a combination of academic study, clinical skills and research leading to a thesis on a chosen subject. There are two other applied psychology doctorates aimed at supporting people with mental health needs: counselling psychology and forensic psychology. All three programmes share common features in terms of requirements, methods of teaching and components of the course, but the client populations differ. Clinical psychologists work with clinical populations experiencing pathological mental health conditions, identified through diagnosis. Counselling psychology addresses emotional and social issues causing stress in everyday life including bereavement, sexual and domestic abuse and relationship problems. Forensic psychologists work with people who have mental health conditions and have either committed a crime or are in the criminal justice system awaiting trial.

CBT is one of the approaches used by clinical and counselling psychologists and is also commonly used in forensic psychology. In some clinical psychology courses there is sufficient content relating to CBT theory and practice to meet the minimum training standards (MTS) for accreditation with the BABCP. Training includes other psychological approaches to treating mental health conditions which broadens the scope of the role. Clinical and counselling psychologists often adopt an integrative approach to psychological therapy, but some choose to identify with one approach such as CBT.

To gain the relevant clinical experience to access the doctoral programmes, you will normally need to demonstrate two to three years in clinical roles. In some cases, people will have many more years of clinical experience and still find it hard to be accepted onto a course. The most common clinical role that graduates will apply for is the psychology assistant (AP) role. Due to the competition for places on courses, AP posts are also fiercely competitive. Chapter 6 explores gaining clinical experience at all levels of the CBT career journey.

Table 5.4 compares some of the features of the three doctoral pathways with the CBT therapist role.

Table 5.4 – Comparing psychology doctorates with CBT therapist role

	Clinical psychologist	Counselling psychologist	Forensic psychologist	CBT therapist
Client populations	People with a range of mental health conditions People with learning disabilities All ages across the lifespan	Anyone experiencing problems in everyday life causing stress and distress Couples and families	People with mental health problems who have committed or are at risk of committing criminal offences	People with a range of mental health conditions All ages across the lifespan Couples N.B. CBT can be adapted for people with learning disabilities (also known as intellectual disabilities).
Presenting problems treated	Depression Anxiety disorders including: ■ Generalized anxiety disorder (GAD) ■ PTSD ■ Panic disorder ■ Health anxiety ■ Social anxiety ■ Obsessive compulsive disorder (OCD) Substance misuse Addictions Eating disorders Personality disorders Psychosis Neurodevelopmental problems such as: ■ Autism ■ ADHD ■ Learning disabilities	■ Depression ■ Anxiety ■ Health issues ■ Bereavement ■ Trauma ■ Domestic abuse ■ Sexual abuse ■ Relationship problems ■ Identity issues ■ Bullying ■ Workplace stress	■ Personality disorders ■ Psychosis ■ Depression ■ Anxiety ■ Trauma	Depression Anxiety disorders including: ■ Generalized anxiety disorder (GAD) ■ PTSD ■ Panic disorder ■ Health anxiety ■ Social anxiety ■ Obsessive compulsive disorder (OCD) Substance misuse Addictions Eating disorders Personality disorders Psychosis Neurodevelopmental problems such as: ■ Autism ■ ADHD Learning disabilities N.B. Some of these presenting problems will require further specialist training and some have a weaker evidence base

Settings	Hospitals NHS secondary care Community teams Private practice	NHS secondary care Community teams Hospitals Private practice	Prisons Mental health hospitals Secure forensic settings	■ NHS psychological therapy services ■ NHS psychology services (Tier 4) ■ Hospitals ■ Community teams ■ Prisons ■ Private practice N.B. Due to diverse backgrounds of CBT therapists, you can apply it in several settings
Approaches	A range of psychotherapeutic approaches, including: ■ CBT ■ Psychodynamic ■ Integrative counselling ■ Dialectical behaviour therapy (DBT) ■ Schema therapy ■ Acceptance and commitment therapy (ACT) ■ Compassion focused therapy (CFT) ■ Mindfulness-based cognitive therapy (MBCT)	A range of psychotherapeutic approaches, including: ■ CBT ■ Psychodynamic ■ Integrative counselling ■ DBT ■ Schema therapy ■ ACT ■ CFT ■ Mindfulness	A range of psychotherapeutic approaches, including: ■ CBT ■ Psychodynamic ■ Integrative counselling ■ DBT ■ Schema therapy ■ ACT ■ CFT ■ Mindfulness	CBT is the principal approach but is an umbrella term. A CBT therapist may use: ■ Behaviour therapy ■ Cognitive therapy ■ Cognitive behavioural therapy ■ Schema therapy ■ ACT ■ CFT ■ MBCT
Can diagnose mental health problems?	Yes	Yes	Yes	Yes

Although the doctoral programmes are very popular, they may not appeal to all psychology graduates pursuing a clinical career. The competitive nature, high entry requirements and length of time it takes to gain adequate clinical experience can be off putting. Other options lead to satisfying clinical careers.

Reflection point

What is it about mental health that attracts you? Is there a particular career pathway that you are pursuing? Would being a CBT therapist satisfy your career needs? Do your own pros and cons list of pursuing a CBT career.

Postgraduate professional training

An alternative to the doctoral pathways is to do an applied postgraduate degree that leads to a clinical role. This not only serves to impart relevant experience and knowledge for pursuing a clinical career, but it will also provide a professional identity to build on. Having a psychology degree alone will only allow you the identity of a psychology graduate, and waiting for many years to become a clinical, counselling or forensic psychologist will keep you in this place.

We have already considered some core professions and the information applies to you. A three-year training is likely to be the same amount of time you will need to demonstrate relevant clinical experience in other roles such as assistant psychologist posts. However, as a graduate, it is possible to complete core professional training at master's level on fast-track programmes. These are normally two years instead of the full three at bachelor's level. Some examples are provided below, but availability will vary around the UK.

Graduate Entry Nursing (GEN) in mental health nursing: This is a two-year master's programme that combines academic study and practice-based learning in a shortened course. Due to the time frame, it is intensive and you need to be very motivated for self-directed study and settle into clinical placements quickly. On completion, you will be a Registered Nurse (MH) with the Nursing and Midwifery Council (NMC) and graduate with a master's degree.

Master's degree in occupational therapy: It is also possible to access OT training at master's level with a psychology degree. Again, this is a more intensive training but leads to registration with the Royal College of Occupational Therapists (RCOT) after two years.

Master's degree in social work (MSW): This is a two-year programme leading to a professional qualification in social work and registration with the Health and Care Professions Council (HCPC).

Clinical Associate in Psychology (CAP): This is an alternative qualification which is offered to psychology graduates as an apprenticeship for eighteen months and leads to a master's degree. It is funded by the NHS, so you earn a salary during training that is increased on completion of the award. A clinical associate in psychology supports people with mental health problems in different settings using a range of psychological approaches. You can go on and specialize in an area of mental health with further training. This role provides the perfect blend of theory and practice to progress into CBT training.

In Scotland, there are two established programmes for clinical associate training leading to master's degrees: an MSc in psychological therapies in primary care, and an MSc in applied psychology for children and young people. These programmes are supported by NHS Education for Scotland (NES) and the Quality Assurance Agency (QAA) for Higher Education in Scotland (HES). As with the CAP apprenticeships in England, trainees earn a salary during training which increases once qualified.

Sarah's story

Sarah's story details the challenges of pursuing a clinical career as a psychology graduate. This led to her gaining a core profession as a social worker before moving on to CBT training and an extremely successful career in a relatively short space of time.

I have always been fascinated by people and human behaviour, including what makes us who we are. I studied psychology as an A-level and then went on to complete a psychology degree. Despite finding this very interesting, I also found it hard and I failed my second year. I went back and continued with the degree, eventually getting a 2:1, which felt like a huge achievement. I knew this was the career that I wanted to progress with and around twelve years ago I officially started my career working in mental health as a support worker in a forensic mental health unit. I had the opportunity to gain front-line experience and was able to have some ad hoc supervision with the psychology team, but also to observe and then co-facilitate groups.

I felt ready to progress with my career and started to look for an assistant psychologist job. This was probably one of the most disheartening experiences of my career! So many applications and so many knockbacks. I eventually got an interview and got a position within an IAPT service, and my role was like one of a PWP. I started learning about CBT, and instantly saw its place. I did this role for a few years, before having my son. I then started to get that feeling of wanting to progress further. I missed being part of a multi-disciplinary team (MDT) and working with people with severe and enduring mental health difficulties. I was offered a place on the postgraduate scheme to train as a social worker. I progressed as a social worker in a community mental health team. I missed psychology and still had a passion for CBT, but I didn't feel like IAPT was for me, so in 2018 I applied for the training in a CAMHS team and was successful.

Moving forward to now, I am head of psychological therapies for The Priory Group, and in an inpatient unit across a specialist eating disorder unit and acute wards. I am trained in Dialectical Behaviour Therapy (DBT) and other specialist CBT interventions. I have opened a specialist private multi-disciplinary mental health practice with a close friend and colleague who is a consultant psychiatrist, and we have a varied team of mental health professionals.

There are two things in my story that I want to get across. First, CBT training is diverse. It opens so many doors, including working in a variety of settings and completing further training. Secondly, anything can be possible, so just keep going. Pursuing a psychology career is frustrating. Success rates for getting onto the doctorate are low. CBT training is becoming more and more competitive, and people are getting places with vast experience and training. But I am someone who failed a year in my degree and am now working in my dream role. Remember what we say: whatever you choose to focus on will grow and you will get there!

Sarah's story is one of hope, and of determination to follow your passion. Thinking creatively helped her to move through the process while maintaining job satisfaction at every stage of her journey.

Low-intensity CBT training pathway (PWP, CWP, EMHP, EPP)

In addition to specific, core professional training programmes, psychology graduates can also access the range of low-intensity CBT training options detailed below. Most CBT training courses are aimed at treating adults with common mental health problems. This reflects the demographic needs of the population. However, there are a growing number of courses that address the needs of children and adolescents. These courses are often referred to as children and young people (CYP) and are offered at both low- and high-intensity levels. All these roles provide training at postgraduate level, but it is possible to do them at graduate level without a first degree. In these circumstances, you will need to demonstrate the ability to work at a degree level.

Psychological wellbeing practitioner (PWP)

The role of the psychological wellbeing practitioner (PWP) was introduced as part of the Improving Access to Psychological Therapies (IAPT) initiative (now known as NHS Talking Therapies), launched in 2008 in England. It fits into the stepped-care model at step 2, which is the provision of low-intensity CBT for mild to moderate mental health conditions including anxiety and depression.

Children and young people's wellbeing practitioner (CWP)

This is the equivalent of the PWP role but for children and adolescents. You will provide evidence-based interventions for children and young people with mild to moderate mental health difficulties. Part of the role is signposting children and young people to appropriate mental health and community services and referring those with more complex problems to the right mental health support. Once qualified, you may work in community-based CAMHS teams, primary care or mental health support teams (MHST) offering psychological therapies to children and young people in schools and working with their families as part of the wider systemic context.

Education mental health practitioner (EMHP)

This is a relatively new role introduced in response to recent legislation relating to mental health support for children and young people. It is an integral part of the mental health support team (MHST) model in the UK. Training to become an EMHP is at postgraduate diploma level, whereas PWP and CYP training is for a postgraduate certificate. The EMHP role is very focused on educational settings, working with schools and colleges to support the young person, whereas the CWP role can be practiced across different settings.

Enhanced psychological practice (EPP)

In Scotland, the enhanced psychological practice (EPP) programme is equivalent to the PWP programme in England. It is taught at the postgraduate certificate level and focuses on the application of evidence-based psychological therapies for mild to moderate mental health problems. There are options to work with adults (EPP-A) or children and young people (EPP-CYP).

Following training as a low-intensity CBT therapist, you will need to practice for two years before you are eligible to apply for high-intensity CBT training. The low-intensity role is diverse and there are many career progression opportunities, so you may decide to remain in this role for longer than two years. This was the case for Faz.

Faz's story

I graduated in 2005 with my psychology degree and started my MSc in research methods the following year. I gained clinical experience in support worker roles in various NHS settings. In 2009, I started my PWP training. I worked in low-intensity CBT for over four years and progressed into senior PWP roles. I went on to do the high-intensity CBT training which gave me a broad range of knowledge and skills to work across low- and high-intensity CBT roles. This has included management, lecturing on a CBT course and private clinical practice. I am an accredited CBT practitioner with the BABCP and have completed full EMDR training. My PWP background provided a strong foundation to build my CBT career.

Complete career change

There are many reasons why you may be contemplating a career change to become a CBT therapist. Your career may not have lived up to expectations, or you may have achieved all you want and have lost direction. The main reason people choose a career change is that their current role does not align with their values. These may have changed over time. For example, they may have been drawn to a particular career as it provided high earning potential, but it does not satisfy their need to help others. Or they have always wanted to work in mental health but became side-tracked into another direction and now want to re-engage with their values and career goals.

Reflection point

Why are you considering a career change? What is it about CBT that attracts you? Are there other options that would satisfy your needs? Draw up a list of the pros and cons of pursuing a CBT career.

Whatever the reason and circumstances, it is possible to make this transition. The time it takes will depend on your specific experience and qualifications to date. The information in this chapter has outlined some options that still apply, regardless of age and background. The pathway should match your personal experiences, qualifications and preferences.

If you are seeking a career change and do not have a first degree, there are other options available. There are courses provided at colleges specifically aimed at people who have not studied at degree level and want to progress to a career in health and social care. These are known as 'access courses', and you can check at your local colleges to see what they offer. Other pathways include apprenticeships as described above in the section on low-intensity CBT training. No matter what your current situation, there is a pathway that will help you move towards a career as a CBT therapist.

Summary

This chapter has presented a CBT career roadmap, and each of the various pathways has been considered. The map should help you to navigate your journey in terms of academic qualifications and professional training. The next chapter provides information on relevant clinical experience to help prepare for training.

Chapter 6
Gaining relevant clinical experience

Clinical experience is necessary before embarking on a career in mental health. This is regardless of pathway. You will not access a clinical training programme with academic qualifications alone. It can be difficult to find suitable placements or voluntary positions if you are not sure what counts as relevant experience. Arguably, any experience in a caring role is useful because, at the very least, it will allow you to decide whether healthcare or mental health is an area you want to commit to. Theory and practice can be very different, so it is important to gain a realistic perspective.

The relevance of the clinical experience becomes more important as you move along your career journey. Once you decide the pathway you want to follow, the experience you gain should be relevant to that specific professional or therapeutic role. Roles where you are actively providing therapeutic support rather than basic care needs alone will be considered more relevant to a psychological therapy career. The greater the variety of clinical skills learned the better for your chances of progression to a professional role.

This chapter covers issues relating to clinical experience across the different stages of your career journey. Each experience provides insight into mental healthcare provision and tips are provided to help you access work experience opportunities. Recognized policies and frameworks relating to key clinical skills from different core professions are used throughout the chapter, but we will begin by considering how we understand mental distress through a discussion of psychopathology. This will help you to contextualize your work experience in relation to the model of mental health guiding the different clinical service settings. Understanding mental health problems is also part of Roth & Pilling's (2007) **generic competencies** in their CBT competency framework, which will be referred to throughout this chapter. These skills are prerequisites for the basic CBT competencies necessary to develop as a CBT therapist.

Psychopathology

Before embarking on a career pathway in mental health, we need to make sure we understand the meaning of mental distress. The term 'psychopathology' originates from the Greek words "psyche" (soul) and "pathos" (suffering). Later, Latin translation led to the more current definition 'psycho' – of the mind – and 'pathology' the study of disease or illness. In broader terms, it is how we understand mental distress and there is more than one model or theory to explain this phenomenon. In most psychology textbooks psychopathology is referred to as 'abnormal psychology', with abnormal being defined as statistically rare or 'deviant' from the norm. These terms are clearly abhorrent and stigmatizing. The language we use to describe and make sense of mental health problems is important, so we need to be mindful of this, especially when working as mental health professionals.

There are different models of psychopathology, and a brief overview of some of them is presented below.

Biological model

This has been the dominant approach to mental health since the development of medicine and biological sciences. Science seeks to explain phenomena in objective terms, producing laws that can be generalized. This has led to the categorization of lived experience of mental health problems into symptoms and diagnoses in manuals such as the Diagnostic and Statistical Manual of Mental Disorders (DSM) and the International Classification of Diseases (ICD). It has also led to developments in pharmacological treatments for some of these conditions, which have had a profound effect on the quality of life of many people with severe mental health problems.

This model has the most support for serious mental health problems that have been shown to have a biological basis. Considering common mental health problems, such as depression and anxiety, it is impossible to be entirely objective when trying to make sense of someone's emotional experience. Interpretation will always play a role, and our own backgrounds, beliefs and personal experiences will guide our different interpretations. The alternative models that follow attempt to address some of these shortfalls.

Biopsychosocial model

Developed by Engel in the 1970s, this model suggests that any disorder (physical or psychological) needs to be understood in terms of biological, psychological and social factors. More recently, there has been a renewed emphasis on the importance of neurological processes in influencing mental health. From this perspective, individual differences in life experiences and culture can be considered, and a holistic approach to treatment adopted.

Figure 6.1 – The biopsychosocial model

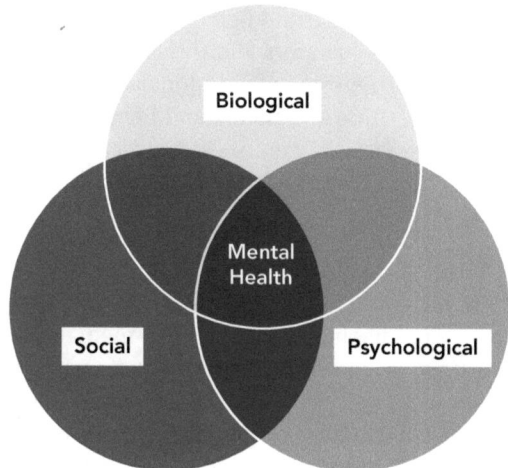

Humanistic

Sometimes referred to as existential humanism, a humanistic approach seeks to understand the human experience. Relational processes are central to this approach. There is a focus on personal growth, which gives rise to positive psychology. Internal experience is given a language to explore and understand issues affecting the person's psychological health, including attachments, identity, and loss. Expressing emotional distress is the focus of therapy, which is done within a safe and empathetic therapeutic relationship.

Social constructionist approach

This is the view that mental distress is a social construct given meaning in discourse. Issues of power and identity are made relevant in the talk and texts between health professionals and people experiencing mental distress. This emphasizes language as a means for constructing notions of mental health problems in our everyday conversations and interactions. This view departs from the positivistic paradigm of science, to adopt a relativist position that values individual differences.

Behavioural approach

Behaviourism is based on learning theory, which aims to explain behaviour in terms of conditioning. There is an emphasis on reinforcement as the mechanism of change. This takes two forms – classical conditioning, where negative reinforcement is the main driver (avoidance of the feared object or stimuli), and operant conditioning, where positive reinforcement (rewards) and punishment are the primary drivers for change. Mental distress is understood as being the result of conditioning.

Cognitive behavioural model

Combining theory from cognitive science and behaviourism, the cognitive behavioural model recognizes the role of both behaviours and thoughts (content and processes) in maintaining emotional difficulties. Patterns of emotional distress are understood in terms of a vicious cycle of physical sensations, thoughts and behaviours occurring within a specific context. Breaking the cycle is the aim of CBT treatment. This can be done at a cognitive and/or behavioural level. It uses a biopsychosocial framework.

Historical perspective

Early understandings of mental distress were largely based on supernatural causes, such as spirits or demons. The person displaying any signs of mental distress would often be feared or revered, and drastic measures were used in an effort to control or eradicate the problem. This led to torture and death based on society's beliefs at the period in history. Little more than a century ago in the UK, the Idiots and Lunacy Act legislated that people with mental ill-health or learning disabilities should be locked away in institutions to protect wider society.

Culture and mental distress

The experience of mental distress is not universal. Culture is part of the social influences that affect how we think about and feel emotions. This includes cultural values and rules related to expressing internal mental experiences.

A guide to understanding psychopathology is presented on the Resources page.

> ### Reflection point
>
> What is your understanding of mental distress? What has influenced your understanding? Reflect on the issues raised above.
>
> Read around the subject using a diverse range of texts from different fields to get a broad perspective. Talk to mental health professionals about their position on psychopathology and how this relates to the treatment approaches they use.
>
> Write a list of different terms for mental distress through time and across cultures. Write a personal position statement on your view of psychopathology.

Understanding mental health in practice

In the first instance, it is important to gain an understanding of mental distress by talking to and supporting people with lived experience. This could either be in an informal or voluntary role, or in a paid position. This will give you an opportunity to learn about:

- Different presenting problems
- The impact of living with a mental health problem on the person and their family
- How to build a therapeutic relationship based on respect and empathy
- Different models of care and treatment

Remember, you do not need to commit to one pathway. A broad range of experience will allow you to view the bigger picture and decide which area of mental health you are attracted to. The more you talk to staff who work in a mental health role the more you will learn about the different roles. Most importantly, the more life stories you hear of people with lived experience of mental distress, the greater insight you will build.

When deciding what paid or voluntary role to approach, do not be judgemental. Mental health and learning disability care jobs can be judged negatively as demeaning or belittling. Care work is unfairly viewed as mindless and manual, insinuating that it is beneath graduates or people with high academic achievements. Goffman (1963) identified a phenomenon called 'honorary stigma', which refers to the idea that those working with people from stigmatized groups face stigma themselves. Unfortunately, this still exists and has recently been explored by mental health social workers who were found to play down their role for fear of judgement from colleagues in other areas of social work (Tucker & Webber, 2021).

All caring jobs are valuable. It is what you bring to your job and learn from it that makes the difference.

We now turn to some key care skills that you should focus on when engaging in any clinical role.

Knowledge of ethical principles

For all health and social care practitioners, it is essential to follow a code of professional conduct based on sound ethical principles. The government developed principles of ethics for healthcare based on a report by Lord Nolan in 1995. There are seven principles for public life, sometimes referred to as the Nolan principles:

1. Selflessness
2. Integrity
3. Objectivity
4. Accountability

5. Openness
6. Honesty
7. Leadership

Although these are aimed at healthcare regulators to maintain ethical standards within organizations, anyone providing healthcare at any level needs to work to ethical principles. One of the most influential ethical frameworks in the medical field was introduced by Beauchamp and Childress (1979). It has been through some revisions (Beauchamp & Childress, 2013), but the principles remain the same. Often referred to as the four pillars of medical ethics, they should be used in clinical decision-making:

- Respect for autonomy (giving choice)
- Beneficence (doing good)
- Non-maleficence (doing no harm)
- Justice (being fair)

Gillon (1994) states that it is hard to argue against these four principles and suggests that the scope of this framework enables healthcare workers from disparate backgrounds to have a shared moral compass to guide clinical practice. Within nursing, these four principles are extended to include accountability, fidelity and veracity to make up the seven principles of nursing ethics. Another example of the integration of the four pillars of medical ethics is provided by Varkey (2021), who has incorporated these ethical principles, along with professional and clinical expertise, into his recent model of patient care.

Every core profession will have a professional code of conduct to guide ethical practice. In CBT we have the BABCP's standards of conduct, performance and ethics. Even if you are not a qualified CBT therapist, as a member of the BABCP you are expected to uphold these standards in any clinical role. There are fifteen standards as follows:

1. You must act in the best interests of service users.
2. You must maintain high standards of assessment and practice.
3. You must respect the confidentiality of service users.
4. You must keep high standards of personal conduct.
5. You must provide (to us and relevant regulators and/or professional bodies) any important information about your conduct and competence.
6. You must keep your knowledge and skills up to date.
7. You must act within the limits of your knowledge, skills and experience and, if necessary, refer the matter to another practitioner.
8. You must communicate properly and effectively with service users and other practitioners. As part of this process, you must tell people who use your service how they can complain about you and your practice to BABCP and any other regulatory bodies you are accountable to.

9. You must effectively supervise tasks that you have asked other people to carry out.
10. You must get informed consent to give treatment (except in an emergency).
11. You must keep accurate records.
12. You must deal fairly and safely with the risks of infection.
13. You must limit your work or stop practising if your performance or judgement is affected by your health.
14. You must behave with honesty and integrity and make sure that your behaviour does not damage the public's confidence in you or your practice. In addition, you have a professional responsibility to be open, honest and transparent with clients, patients or service users when something goes wrong. This responsibility is the professional 'Duty of Candour'.
15. You must make sure that any advertising you do is accurate.

Understanding ethical principles and specific codes of conduct will ensure you are working to a high professional standard in all caring roles.

Building a therapeutic relationship

Working with people in a care capacity requires a good therapeutic relationship. This is directly related to the previous section as we have a moral and professional duty of care to treat people with dignity, respect and fairness. The therapeutic bond provides a connection based on trust to foster a secure space for care and therapeutic interventions. Regardless of theoretical or therapeutic approach forming this connection is essential to any caring role. Carl Rogers wrote extensively on the therapeutic relationship. Within his person-centred approach, to psychotherapy, he identified three key requirements for an effective therapeutic bond: **empathy**, being **authentic**, and showing **unconditional positive regard** for the person (Rogers, 1951). This refers to being non-judgemental. These characteristics have become central features of the foundations on which to build a therapeutic relationship.

CBT has been associated with structure and skills which some believe make it mechanical. There has been a stereotype that CBT therapists are more concerned with measuring symptoms and providing interventions from manuals rather than focusing on the therapeutic relationship. This is entirely untrue. Without a strong therapeutic bond, it would not be possible to engage the person to commit to CBT (Leahy, 2001; Leahy, 2008; Gilbert & Leahy, 2007). Early work by Aaron Beck highlights the necessity of the therapeutic relationship, as it is based on collaboration between therapist and client. Goals and interventions need to be agreed upon within the therapeutic bond for CBT to be effective (Okamoto & Kizantzis, 2021). The book by Gilbert and Leahy (2007), *The Therapeutic Relationship in the Cognitive Behavioural Psychotherapies*, is a recommended read on this subject.

Core care skills

NHS England published the '6Cs' in a policy document called *Compassion in Practice: Nursing, midwifery and care staff – our vision and strategy* (NHS England, 2012). This has become synonymous with core values necessary to work in a caring role across health, mental health, and social care settings. The 6Cs stand for:

- Care
- Compassion
- Competence
- Communication
- Courage
- Commitment

Some of these values were discussed as core qualities in Chapter 2 on building a CBT therapist. We will focus on compassion, communication and competence in more detail below, with particular regard to clinical experience gained before professional training.

Compassion

The compassion in practice policy (NHS, 2012) defines compassion as follows:

> "Compassion is how care is given through relationships based on empathy, respect, and dignity – it can also be described as intelligent kindness and is central to how people perceive their care."
> (NHS England, 2012, p13)

This is an interesting definition. which includes values and qualities made relevant within care relationships. The term 'intelligent kindness' was developed in response to high-profile cases of cruelty in healthcare settings. It emphasizes the conscious effort and skills required to be a compassionate carer (Campling, 2015). It views compassion as interactive between service users and carers. When gaining work experience, it is important to have a clear understanding of what compassion means and how to demonstrate it in practice.

> ### Reflection point
> How would you describe compassion? What skills demonstrate that you are compassionate? How would you present this on your CV?

Communication

It sounds simple to say that communication skills are essential when working in a clinical setting. However, we need to understand what specific skills are necessary for working in a mental health role, how to use them competently, and the evidence base on which they are based. The notion of active listening is a key skill in therapy. It goes beyond listening to demonstrate your understanding of what you have heard, reflecting to the person and retaining the information for later. In CBT, this is part of the process of summarizing and providing feedback necessary for guided discovery.

Communication is an integral part of the therapeutic relationship. Creating a safe space for the person to speak openly when vulnerable is a skill that goes beyond words. In his influential book *The Skilled Helper* (Egan, 1975), Gerard Egan introduced a communication model for healthcare professionals that pays particular attention to non-verbal communication. The acronym SOLER incorporates the key skills needed to be an active listener:

- Sit squarely
- Open posture
- Lean in
- Eye contact
- Relaxed state

Stickley (2011) updated Egan's model to include touch and intuition when communicating in a therapeutic context. He uses the acronym SURETY (sit at an angle, uncross arms and legs, relax, eye contact, touch, and use your intuition). Touch is a controversial issue in health and social care; Quiddington (2009) describes it as a boundary issue that needs to be treated carefully. The main consideration is that you must always maintain the ethical standards of care set out in the professional code of conduct. O'Lynn and Krautscheid (2011) distinguish three types of therapeutic touch: instrumental, protective, and expressive. It is the expressive type of touch that Stickley refers to in his SURETY model of communication. Sharples (2013) suggests that expressive touch shows the person that you are there for them and that you care, especially at times when they are extremely distressed and find it difficult to hear your words. Therapists are not robots. Showing concern and empathy can extend beyond words in a professional way while being authentic and human (Stonehouse, 2017).

Competence

The 6Cs identify competence as an essential part of a caring role in healthcare. Any work experience you engage in should build competence in clinical skills. How this is defined and measured will vary. Competence can be assessed formally and informally.

NHS Health Education England (HEE) in partnership with Skills for Care and Skills for Health have produced the Care Certificate Framework. This is aimed at non-regulated workers such as healthcare assistants, mental health support workers, nursing assistants and other supporting roles to a regulated core profession. It provides standards of care to give workers the necessary introductory skills, knowledge, and behaviours to provide compassionate, safe and high-quality care and support.

The certificate covers fifteen standards of care:

- Understand your role
- Your personal development
- Duty of care
- Equality and diversity
- Work in a person-centred way
- Communication
- Privacy and dignity
- Fluids and nutrition
- Awareness of mental health, dementia and learning disability
- Safeguarding adults
- Safeguarding children
- Basic life support
- Health and safety
- Handling information
- Infection prevention and control

This programme is open to a wider workforce than just the NHS and consists of a comprehensive online learning programme. There are workbooks for each standard, and these are freely accessible to all on either the NHS Health Education England, Skills for Care or Skills for Health websites.

Regardless of whether you are working in a setting that provides the Care Certificate or not, you can use this framework to guide your personal learning goals. If you are working in a more therapeutic role, then you can use the Roth & Pilling (2007) generic competencies as a guide to skill development. The full framework can be accessed on the University of Central London website on their psychology and language science page (see Appendix 1). The generic competencies are summarized below:

- Knowledge and understanding of mental health problems
- Knowledge of, and ability to operate within, professional and ethical guidelines
- Knowledge of a model of therapy, and the ability to understand and employ that model in practice
- Ability to engage the client
- Ability to foster and maintain a good therapeutic alliance, and to grasp the client's perspective and worldview
- Ability to deal with the emotional content of a session
- Ability to manage endings
- Ability to undertake a generic assessment
- Ability to make use of supervision

Although each clinical role you undertake may not allow you to cover all these competencies, it is useful to know them in order to guide your clinical skill development before any CBT role or training.

CBT work experience

Although we have emphasized the importance of gaining relevant work experience, when it comes to CBT this is not easy. There are many barriers to getting access to live clinical work. This is for a good reason and is related to patient confidentiality and a general reluctance to allow untrained people to sit in on therapy sessions without a specific role. So, you need to think creatively about what work experience might look like, and how to get the most from it. Be open to contacting people and organizations.

A key to successful work experience is networking. Be active in making connections and asking questions.

- Write a letter describing your interest in gaining relevant work experience in the mental health field (see eFigure 6.2 for an example).
- Work experience is a fact-finding exercise, to clarify your understanding of the nature of the work you are interested in. It should never be just a tick-box exercise. You should enjoy the experience and need to be fully committed.
- Work experience may not be a long period of time. A focused insight experience can give you a clear idea of the job role and can lead to more substantial work experience opportunities through the networking you have started.

Figure 6.2 – Example of a draft letter regarding work experience

What to include in your letter

Dear **[person or organisation]**

I am interested in a career in the mental health field and would like to gain some relevant work experience. This will help me decide on degree **[or other training]** choices moving forward.

Include a photo

I am contacting you because **[show knowledge of the person or organisation]**

I would like to understand the role of the professionals working in your organisation and gain some knowledge and skills in supporting people **[name the appropriate client group in that setting]**.

[Say something about yourself and state what you can offer to the organisation while you are there]

[Demonstrate a professional attitude] I am a good listener and work well in groups or independently. I am trustworthy and respect confidentiality, so I will not share any details of my experience outside the organisation.

Thank you for your time. I look forward to hearing from you.
My contact details are below.

Think creatively about work experience

Most people try voluntary organizations for work experience first (see list below). Be mindful that these organizations will be contacted regularly and may not offer opportunities to everyone. However, these organizations can be accessed at all stages including pre-university for college students considering mental health as a career option. The list is not exhaustive so do your own research. Each of these organizations has specific information about volunteering opportunities on their websites:

- Open door charity
- MIND
- Scope
- Mencap
- Childline
- Samaritans
- International medical corps
- National Citizens Service (NCS)

If it is wider mental health experience you are interested in, then consider the core mental health professions such as occupational therapy (OT), mental health or learning disability nursing, social work, art therapy, and clinical or counselling psychology.

It is worth targeting organizations and services in your area to see if they can offer any opportunities. Consider self-employed mental health practitioners such as CBT therapists or applied clinical psychologists, as these are the jobs you want more insight into. You can find details on therapist directory sites such as *Psychology Today* or *Counselling Directory*.

Set some goals for the placement. Stating this to organizations shows initiative and will demonstrate to the employer that you are prepared and have realistic expectations for the work experience.

> **Reflection point**
>
> What care skills do I already possess? How can I build on these?
>
> What do I want to learn from a work experience placement? Formulate this as a set of goals.

Read, research and network

Do your homework before contacting an organization. Make sure you understand what they do and the client group they serve. Read up on mental health. What does psychopathology mean? What are the different ways to think about mental health? Join social media groups to learn more.

A note to employers

Even in clinical roles, it is possible to offer work experience to A-level and undergraduate students. Think back to your early career days and how you discovered your passion for working in the mental health field. We can tell our stories and show our skills without compromising confidentiality. Here are some ideas:

- Provide an overview of MH services and how CBT fits in (IAPT, secondary care, private)
- Describe and model a typical day in the life of a CBT therapist
- Give psychoeducation on the CBT model
- Do role-plays
- Go through anonymized cases
- Note-writing exercises
- Organize insight visits to other services, if appropriate
- Provide homework tasks – CBT from the inside out
- Guided study tasks

If the organization has not offered placements before, candidates can use the list above as suggestions for clinical-orientated tasks. They also make good goals for any clinical work experience and can be added to a letter when seeking work experience opportunities.

Summary

All work experience in clinical settings is important, but you need to approach each experience with a plan and specific goals to build your clinical skills. This chapter has provided some key concepts to help you approach any work experience opportunity with a clear idea of the skills and knowledge required to work in any mental health professional role. This will help you to focus your work experience to maximize opportunities to move forward in your CBT career journey.

Chapter 7
The Knowledge, Skills and Attitudes (KSA) route: building your portfolio

If you want to become a BABCP accredited CBT practitioner in the UK without a core profession in mental health, then you will need to complete a KSA portfolio. The aim of this is to demonstrate equivalence to a core profession in terms of key knowledge (K), skills (S) and attitudes (A). The thought of completing this portfolio often instils anxiety as it is viewed as a massive undertaking which adds to the threat of the task. In fact, if you are at the stage of completing a KSA portfolio either for entering a level 2 accredited CBT course or for individual practitioner accreditation later, then you already meet the criteria for the KSA. Passing it only requires you to express this clearly in the portfolio.

There are two distinct types of KSA portfolio. One is associated with training and is a requirement to enter a BABCP level 2 accredited course in the UK. This means that, on completion of the course, you can apply for practitioner accreditation immediately as you will meet all the minimum training standards (MTS) set by the BABCP. The other type of KSA portfolio can be completed by non-core professionals who did not complete a level 2 accredited training course but have made up all the MTS in their own time. The contents of the KSA are the same but there is a slight difference in expectation between the two. More details on applying for individual accreditation via the second route will be included in Chapter 11 on accreditation. Information here is relevant to both types of KSA.

This chapter aims to motivate you to start the portfolio and gives some advice on how to approach the task. There are some brief notes regarding each criterion, but it is not intended to be used as a checklist for what you should include. The KSA should document *your* individual academic and clinical experiences, so each portfolio is unique. Rather than providing answers, I hope that it will encourage you to ask yourself some useful questions that will guide your writing.

Chapter 7 The Knowledge, Skills and Attitudes (KSA) route: building your portfolio

Make the KSA your friend

The thought of doing a KSA portfolio tends to instil fear. This is often driven by uncertainty as to how to do it or about your competence in completing it to a high-enough standard to pass, and fear of failure and what that would mean for your future. So, it will feel like there is a lot at stake in terms of getting it right. The truth is that there is not one right way to do it, so this adds to the threat of the task. When your head is full of worries, doubts and negative thoughts, this is going to encourage avoidance and procrastination.

In the first instance, it is helpful to identify your own thoughts and feelings about completing a KSA portfolio. Table 7.1 lists some common reactions and the potential impact this can have on your behaviour.

Table 7.1 – Common reactions before starting the KSA portfolio

Thoughts	Emotions	Behaviours
It's too much. I don't have time and don't know how to do it.	Anxious Overwhelmed	Ask lots of people how they did theirs and still avoid it.
Why should I have to do this?	Angry Resentful	Moan about it and don't do it.
I can't do it. There's no point.	Sad and hopeless	Don't do it.

We can see clearly how these thoughts ultimately interfere with getting started. If you view the KSA as a task, it is going to present as a demand, and demands are always threatening. However, if you change the way you view it, then you can immediately reduce this sense of threat. Instead of viewing it as a task, view it as *your story* because this is what the KSA is. It is a narrative about your personal clinical experiences and learning in the mental health field that makes you equivalent to a core professional. Instead of seeing the KSA as 'a thing', see it as part of your identity. It is an opportunity to tell your story and you do know how to do this. In other words, you are the best person to bring the KSA to life.

Figure 7.1 – Conceptualising the KSA portfolio

Once you view the KSA as your story, you should be able to view it as a friend rather than as an enemy. Of course, this does not remove the demand of having to write your story, or the doubts about how to present it, but hopefully you will feel less daunted.

Tolerating uncertainty

Worry is normal and causes little emotional distress. Dugas and Robichaud (2007) and Robichaud *et al* (2019) identify two types of worry – worry about actual problems and worry about *hypothetical* problems (what if…?). They suggest that excessive worry is maintained by an **intolerance of uncertainty.** Not having answers for every 'what if…?' causes worry to escalate, which reduces your sense of control. This leads to strategies to try to gain more certainty. Some of the most common safety and avoidance behaviours are listed in Table 7.2. This is not a full representation of the behaviours outlined in the model. For further details, see the guide to using the intolerance of uncertainty model on the Resources page.

Table 7.2 – Behaviours associated with intolerance of uncertainty

Safety behaviours	Avoidance behaviours
Needing lots of information before proceeding with a task.	Procrastination – delaying starting the taks or avoiding it completely.
Seeking excessive reassurance from others.	Making excuses rather than decisions.
Checking and re-checking details before starting.	Avoiding thinking about it (out of sight out of mind).
Overpreparing.	Having difficulty committing.

Clearly, all these behaviours are normal to some degree, but when used excessively they keep the threat of uncertainty alive. You may be gathering too much information or seeking reassurance from others to increase a sense of certainty before getting started. This leads to procrastination and reinforces doubt, which maintains the cycle of avoidance. When seeking control over uncertainty, the worry makes our thinking more threat-focused and black and white. It will be harder to approach tasks due to this heightened arousal caused by the worry. This will make you view the task as a problem which has a negative connotation. In the case of the KSA portfolio, it is easy to see how it can become defined as a problem through excessive worry, safety-seeking behaviours and avoidance.

One of the techniques for approaching tasks that feel uncertain in the Dugas and Robichaud (2007) model is the threat-opportunity continuum. Instead of viewing threat as an all-or-nothing phenomenon, it is placed on a continuum with opportunity being at the opposite end. Threat is normally manifested in a stream of 'what ifs…?'. Just recognizing these as hypothetical worries rather than actual predictions is helpful. By considering the potential opportunities that starting the KSA portfolio will afford, the perceived sense of threat is reduced, which in turn should reduce the worry and anxiety associated with it. Even a small reduction will help reduce avoidance.

Figure 7.2 – Using the threat-opportunity continuum to approach the KSA

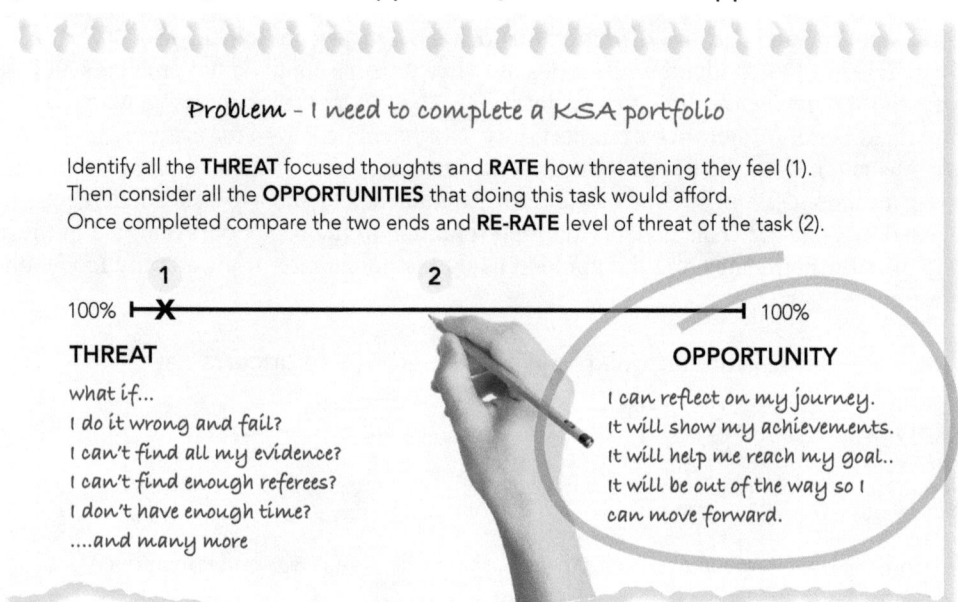

Getting started

If applying for course entry as a KSA applicant, then you need to have your portfolio completed *before* the interview. If you haven't, then you risk being rejected for a place on the course. It is always going to cause more stress the longer you leave it. Make sure you complete it in good time, as leaving yourself little time and having to complete it under pressure will ramp up the sense of threat.

Clearly, there are many ways to approach the portfolio. The advice here is intended to provide suggestions and covers a range of approaches. To reiterate one of the most important messages of this chapter, there is no one right way to do this. Getting started is normally the biggest hurdle, so once you get over this you will hopefully feel more motivated to continue.

Understanding the requirements

The appropriate place to start is with the guidelines written by the BABCP. These can be downloaded directly from their website. The first thing to note is that the documentation is coded in terms of what function it performs. They are labelled with the prefix 'KSA' followed by a number, as follows:

KSA1 – Criterion checklist

KSA2 – Self-statement

KSA3 – Countersigned self-statement

KSA4 – Reference

KSA5 – Self-directed study record

KSA6 – Biography

KSA7 – Documents list

It is easy to confuse these codes with specific KSA criteria. For example, you may refer to each criterion by the number – KSA 1 for life stages and human development, KSA 2 for health and social care approaches and so on – so just be aware of this from the start to reduce confusion.

The guidelines are comprehensive but, with a complex task like the KSA, it is hard to provide a guide that will be easily understood by everyone. Even the BABCP acknowledge this difficulty when making the following statement on page 8 of the guidelines:

> *"Applicants/Candidates, Accreditors and Assessors should use the following information as guidance only, exercising professional judgement as to how information and examples are interpreted"*
> *(BABCP, 2014).*

This adds to the sense of uncertainty described above, but try to see it as an opportunity to apply your professional judgement and reinforce your belief in yourself. The aim of the portfolio is to demonstrate equivalence of a core profession in mental health so there are some basic assumptions you can take as given. It will be expected that you have:

- A first degree (preferably related to psychology, but this is not essential)
- Evidence of study at postgraduate level
- This combined study should evidence the base foundation knowledge and skills that underpin all psychotherapeutic work
- The equivalent of three or four years of full-time clinical experience (see Chapter 6)

It is useful to read through the entire document first without homing in on any specific area, to get a complete overview. This will give you an idea of the shape of the portfolio and provide the framework to start building your story. You will need to read certain parts again, possibly several times, to fully understand what is expected, but try to do this first before asking others to explain it. If stuck on certain points, write them down so that you can seek further guidance.

Shape of the portfolio

The BABCP guidelines provide templates for each section. For course entry, the provider (normally the university) may have their own documentation. In some cases, the course documentation will provide further guidance and examples. Your course may also host KSA workshops for shortlisted candidates before the interview and portfolio submission. The main components of the portfolio are listed in Table 7.3 with reference to the specific documents to use for each component.

Table 7.3 – Components of the KSA

Component	Document to use
Overview of the whole document provided as a checklist	**KSA1** Note: it is normally best to complete this at the end when you have finished the portfolio and gathered all supporting materials.
Self-statements	**KSA2** for self-statements and **KSA3** for countersigned self-statements Note: if in doubt, then use KSA3 for all as this will ensure you can evidence each criterion.
Supporting evidence	**KSA7** – Documents list. **KSA5** for any additional self-directed study. One of these will need to be provided for each specific criterion you used for the self-directed study as part of the evidence. Note: if the criterion is met by other forms of evidence, it is unnecessary to add a KSA5.
References	**KSA4**
Biography	**KSA6** Note: this forms criterion 14. For course entry, it will be a record of clinical experience, whereas for practitioner accreditation application it will be more of a narrative of experience and how this meets the specific criteria.

Full or condensed portfolio?

Since first introducing the KSA route at the start of the IAPT programme in 2008, the BABCP have acknowledged the variety of experiences and professional backgrounds of a KSA applicant. When auditing non-core professional training more closely, KSA requirements for certain applicants have been reduced depending on course content and skills learned in that role. This has led to several condensed versions of the KSA which are explained below. If you do not meet the criteria for any of these then assume that you need to complete a full KSA.

Low-intensity practitioner registration

Possibly one of the most common pathways to enter a CBT training programme via the KSA route is for psychological wellbeing practitioners (PWP) and other trained low-intensity practitioners including child and young people's wellbeing practitioners (CWP) and education and mental health practitioners (EMHP). Due to the high level of relevant knowledge, skills and attitudes developed through these roles and training, the BABCP introduced a registration process for these practitioners who commit to continued professional standards and development. There is an initial fee and an ongoing renewal of the registration fee is payable annually. The requirements for registration help to 'sign off' certain elements of the KSA. For this, you need to:

- Be a BABCP member (can do this at the point of registration)
- Have graduated from a British Psychological Society (BPS) accredited or Health Education England (HEE) approved training course
- Have at least six months of clinical experience in a specified system of care such as NHS Talking Therapies (formally IAPT) or similar
- Be accountable for your professional practice to a senior member of your service
- Provide evidence of specific knowledge and skills via a supervisor's report
- Adhere to the BABCP standards of conduct, performance and ethics
- Be currently working at least two hours a week in a low-intensity role

This list has been summarized. Always check the BABCP website for the most current and detailed versions of registration requirements.

On becoming registered, the KSA can be condensed to criteria 4, 13 and 14 only if you have a psychology degree which includes knowledge relating to human development and life stages (e.g. a module on developmental psychology). If your psychology degree did not contain such knowledge then you will have to do criterion 1 in addition to 4, 13 and 14.

For non-registered low-intensity practitioners, you will need to complete the full KSA.

Professions eligible for condensed KSA

The BABCP have reduced the requirements of the KSA for the following professions. It is assumed that some of the criteria are met within the training and role of these professions.

Table 7.4 – Professions eligible for condensed KSA

Profession	KSA criteria to be assessed
Clinical Associate in Applied Psychology (CAAP) Scotland with 'MSc in Psychological in Primary Care' qualification	4, 12, 14
Medicine – Foundation Doctors – General Medical Council (GMC) full registration	2, 3, 4, 13
Nursing & Midwifery Council (NMC) Registered Nurse – Adult Nursing	3, 4, 14
Nursing & Midwifery Council (NMC) Registered Nurse – Children's Nursing	3, 4, 14
NMC Registered Nurse – Midwifery (Midwives with level 1 Registered Adult Nursing only need to complete 3, 4 & 14)	1, 2, 3, 4, 8 & 13
NMC Registered Nurse – Health Visiting / Specialist community public health nursing (SCPHN)	3, 4, 14
Physiotherapy – Health & Care Professions Council (HCPC) registered	1, 2, 3, 4, 8, 14
Play therapists – British Association of Play Therapists (BAPT) registered	2, 3, 4, 8, 14
Speech & Language Therapist – Health & Care Professions Council (HCPC) registered	1, 3, 4, 8, 14

Professions required to complete a full portfolio

If your professional background is not listed above then it is likely that a full portfolio will be required. Some examples listed on the BABCP website include the following:

- Teachers of special education
- Probation
- Counsellors without full accreditation with a professional body
- Psychology – stage 2 sports and exercise with BPS Chartered Status (cPsychol)
- Psychology – Forensic, Health or Occupational BPS Stage 1 Masters
- Psychology – Occupational BPS Stage 2 (cPsychol)

- Clinical associate in psychology (CAP)
- CAAP Scotland – MSc Applied Psychology Health Care for Children and Young People

This list is not exhaustive. If you have any queries about your professional background, then contact the accreditation team at the BABCP for clarification.

Preparing the portfolio

Once you are familiar with the guidelines and know which criteria you need to include, you are ready to prepare the portfolio. As previously mentioned and illustrated in the examples provided, you may have a preferred approach to written work. For instance, some people like to complete each criterion in order, some like to do the most challenging ones first, and others may prefer to do the ones they find easier to get started.

> **Reflection point**
>
> What is your preferred style? Consider the pros and cons of this approach. Are you prepared to be flexible and try a different approach?

Writing the self-statements

Remember that these statements are personal and unique to your experience. There is no right or wrong way to do them, so comparing with others is not always helpful and can often cause more confusion. Keep focused on your story. The BABCP provide this summary of what to include in a self-statement (BABCP document v2-0611):

A SELF-STATEMENT provides the opportunity to make a full summary of the following information:

- **How** the knowledge, skill and/or attitude was learned and acquired, *for example where the training and/or experience was undertaken, through what trainings, in what work settings etc.*
- Briefly, **what** knowledge and/or skill was learned or acquired
- A **critical appraisal** of how this knowledge and/or skill applies to psychotherapeutic roles
- **Illustrative example/s** of the application of the knowledge and/or skill which demonstrate some critical learning from the outcome

Many people ask how much to write in each self-statement. There is not a definitive word count but an average of two or three pages of the template should be provided. With less than this, it would be challenging to demonstrate how you meet the criterion. For some criteria, you may need more. This is the case for the **knowledge** criteria (1-4), as there is likely to be a lot of material to include.

Treat the statement like an answer to an essay question. This encourages critical thinking that will make the statement more powerful and authoritative. You need to convince the assessor that you have met the requirement, so avoid a passive style of writing and adopt an active voice. Reframing the title of each criterion can help to promote this type of thinking and writing as you are stating your position on that issue. Some examples of possible reframing are presented in Table 7.5 below.

Table 7.5 – Reframing each statement into an essay question

Criterion	Reframing into an essay-type question
Knowledge criteria	
1. Life stages and human development	Describe the theoretical knowledge, from your studies, that guides your understanding of life stages and human development.
2. Health and social care approaches	Describe the origins of your knowledge regarding health and social care systems and how this informs your clinical practice in the mental health field.
3. Psychopathology and diagnostic skills	Critically discuss your understanding of the term 'psychopathology' and how this relates to diagnostic skills in your clinical practice.
4. Models of therapy	Provide a detailed account of four models of therapy, including theoretical knowledge from your studies, and how this has influenced your clinical practice.
Skills criteria	
5. Competency in key relationship skills	Demonstrate your understanding of key relationship skills from evidence to practice.
6. Maintain and manage records and reports	Describe the important factors that guide your competency in maintaining and managing records and reports.
7. Communication with services and colleagues	How do you manage communication within and outside of your service?
8. Awareness of risk	What has informed your knowledge of risk and how do you apply this in practice?
9. Comprehension of research	What skills help you to understand and critically evaluate research?
10. Commitment to ethical principles	How can you demonstrate your commitment to ethical principles?

Attitudes criteria	
11. Fitness to practice and suitability at a personal level	Describe the qualities that make you suitable to be a mental health professional, and how you monitor and maintain your fitness to practice.
12. Self-evaluation and reflection	Critically discuss the use of self-evaluation and reflection in your professional role.
13. Has a enquiring mind and is receptive to the scientist-practitioner approach	What is your understanding of the scientist-practitioner model and how does this relate to having an inquiring mind?

Criterion 14 is the biography. This is presented on the document template KSA6. The biography can be written first to help organize your plan for each criterion. You can use this as a storyboard to unpack your career story to date, linking to the specific criteria you need to complete.

If citing theories in your statements, you can provide a brief reference list, but this is not stated as a requirement in the BABCP guidelines, so it is not expected. I believe it shows diligence and you will not fail for providing something extra.

When assessing KSA portfolios, for course entry to a level 2 course, I would notice some common issues relating to each criterion. I have summarized the feedback used to raise awareness and avoid falling into any potential traps.

The content of Table 7.6 does not tell you explicitly what to include in each criterion, but it should focus your thinking and help you avoid some common errors. If you are still feeling stuck, we will now consider sources of support.

Table 7.6 – Tips for avoiding common traps

Criterion	Common traps
Knowledge criteria	
1. Life stages and human development	■ **Content can be too descriptive.** Theories are often provided as a list, rather than demonstrating a sound understanding of them. So instead of saying "I learned about different theories of child development such as Piaget, Freud and Eriksson" you could say "My understanding of Piaget's theory is …. and this has helped me to adapt my approach when working with young children who may have difficulty understanding an abstract concept such as a vicious cycle".
	■ **Cover the whole lifespan** not just childhood and early adulthood. Most people focus heavily on child development and make loose connections to adulthood. However, you can break this down further to early childhood and adolescence as this is a time of rapid change that can impact mental health.
	■ **Many people omit older adulthood.** What theories and knowledge guide your understanding of this life stage and how you might adapt your clinical practice?
2. Health and social care approaches	■ **Focus on approaches not just legislation.** This is a knowledge statement so state your understanding of the different systems and where you learned about them. Be critical of these approaches by stating any shortfalls. People often focus more on healthcare and forget about the social care side. How do they interact?
	■ **Cite the origin of any act or legislation.** These are often listed without a date or source. Again, state your understanding of the act and how it is used to inform your clinical practice.
3. Psychopathology and diagnostic skills	■ **Define what psychopathology means to you.** There is more than one position. Many people assume that this only refers to the medical model. Back up your position and cite some theories. There is scope to provide a good critical examination of this vital issue. State how your position guides you in clinical practice.
	■ **Diagnosis skills can go beyond matching symptoms to a manual.** Consider other skills to make sense of a person's presenting problem.

4.	Models of therapy	■ **Each model of therapy needs to be covered in detail.** This should be the longest criterion due to the amount of material you have to cover. Each model requires at least three days of study. This can be part of a module during a degree or professional training or workshops and CPD events. If using a supervisor from another modality, you can count this towards your learning but it is not sufficient as the sole source of knowledge on that model. Likewise, self-directed study alone is not sufficient. ■ **Show a good understanding of the model.** Some people provide a basic definition of the model that could have been copied from a search engine. You need to demonstrate that you have studied the model and can provide a more detailed explanation based on your learning. For example, it is not sufficient to state that "person-centred therapy encourages personal growth. It was introduced by Carl Rogers who stated that therapists need to be genuine, and show unconditional positive regard and empathy." Say more about the theory in terms of philosophy and the mechanism of change, and provide a critique. ■ **Be explicit about how you apply knowledge of the model to practice.** It is not enough to just say "I apply these interpersonal skills to all my clients to build a therapeutic bond". Provide an illustrative example for each of the approaches.
	Skills criteria	
5.	Competency in key relationship skills	■ **Provide some theory.** Although this is a skills criterion, good practice is always informed by research evidence. Provide details of the theories that guide your therapeutic relationship skills. ■ **Include evidence of competency.** If providing a countersigned statement then there will be a senior person to verify your statement, but this is not sufficient evidence of competency. How do you monitor your relationship skills and how do you develop them? ■ **Provide examples of any difficulties in the therapeutic relationship and how you overcame them.** Competency is not only demonstrated through smooth practice where everything goes well, but also through how you problem-solve or repair ruptures and end therapy effectively.
6.	Maintain and manage records and reports	■ **Include the bigger-picture perspective.** It is hard to fall into many traps with this one as it is so clear and is a fundamental skill that you should be able to describe easily. However, many people focus solely on records at an individual level, describing how they maintain and manage records in line with guidance and legislation. Include any research on writing records and compare systems to provide some analysis beyond mere description.

7.	Communication with services and colleagues	■ **This is not about communicating with clients.** This is a common trap. When you see the word 'communication' people tend to think immediately about communicating with clients. Remember that those skills are covered in criterion 5. This is about communication at the team and inter-agency levels with other professionals. Situations such as referrals, multi-disciplinary meetings and liaisons are types of communication that fit this criterion.
8.	Awareness of risk	■ **Include some theories on risk, not just policies.** Policies are important, but they will be informed by research and a philosophical position. Demonstrate your understanding of this. ■ **Risk is not always to be avoided.** We live in a risk-averse society. This is reflected in the policies and procedures in healthcare settings. Healthcare professionals are encouraged to assess and manage risk, but is this always best for the person? In this criterion, you can explore positive risk-taking to show a more balanced understanding. ■ **Consider all parties regarding therapeutic risk.** Most people discuss risk presenting to or from the client. Don't forget the risk to you as the therapist in the session. ■ **Risk is not just about suicide or violence.** These are serious matters and require risk assessment and management. However, think more broadly about risk. What other situations could you use as illustrative examples?
9.	Comprehension of research	■ **Demonstrate your critical thinking skills.** Understanding research requires sophisticated skills. When describing research findings, you need to go beyond a summary of the paper to provide a critical evaluation of the quality of the research. This criterion allows you to show yourself as a critical thinker.
10.	Commitment to ethical principles	■ **Go beyond a list of ethical principles to include theory.** We can all identify common ethical principles as outlined in professional codes of conduct. However, try to include some theory behind these principles. How do you apply these principles? Do you use any frameworks to guide practice? ■ **Ethical** dilemmas make good illustrative examples. When describing situations in practice that presented an ethical dilemma, try to demonstrate why it was a dilemma for you, the ethical principles that were potentially compromised, and how you resolved it. Go beyond saying you took it to supervision. Although appropriate to work through with a supervisor, you need to show your thinking processes in this criterion. Remember dilemmas do not have one right answer – it is how you process and respond to them that counts here.

	Attitudes criteria
11. Fitness to practice and suitability at a personal level	■ **Consider factors over and above qualifications and CRB checks.** Of course, fitness to practice does include meeting requirements and demonstrating competence and these are essential. However, how do you monitor your fitness to practice and what would alert you to question it? ■ **How does this relate to your professional attitude?** This is an attitudes criterion so consider your professional values regarding fitness to practice. ■ **What is the connection between suitability and fitness to practice?** Think about your qualities that help you to maintain fitness to practice. Are there any qualities that may interfere with professional judgement? Note, refer to Chapter 2: Building a CBT therapist and your personal reflection exercises.
12. Self-evaluation and reflection	■ **Include some reflective models.** Self-reflection is an important part of any healthcare professional's clinical practice. Discuss some models you use. How does this inform your professional attitude? ■ **What is the difference between self-evaluation and reflection?** They overlap, but is there a difference?
13. Has an enquiring mind and is receptive to the scientist-practitioner approach	■ **State your understanding of the scientist-practitioner model.** Define it and describe its origin. What are the limitations of this approach? ■ **Is this the only approach that encourages curiosity and collaboration?** Be critical to show your professional position.

Seeking support

With a large piece of work like this, we have already established that it will place a heavy demand on you that will feel threatening. It can also feel like a lonely journey interfering with other parts of your life. Even when you understand the requirements and have an idea of what you want to write, motivation plays a big part in terms of moving the process forward. There are different ways you might benefit from some support, and, fortunately, there are different types of help and support available.

Peer support

Being connected to others in the same situation can alleviate the sense of isolation and uncertainty relating to the portfolio. You may be in a service where others are applying for a high-intensity CBT trainee role so can support each other. Alternatively, senior staff may have been through the process and can answer any questions or queries to help guide you. Some groups of people set up chat forums, for example on WhatsApp, so they can support and motivate each other.

If you do not have any colleagues in the same position or you are compiling a KSA portfolio as part of practitioner accreditation, then consider some online groups. One group I set up on Facebook is called the 'KSA Portfolio Support Group'. This provides a forum to ask questions, share experiences and feel connected to a community. One of the aims of the group is to motivate people to complete the portfolio. Materials, videos and suggested reading are shared. When members share that they have submitted the portfolio or passed it, this can instil hope in others.

Be cautious when joining a peer support network as there may be a lot of expressed anxiety which could trigger your worries and anxiety. This is likely to increase uncertainty and make it harder to focus on what you need to do. It is always useful to be clear about what your motivation is for joining a network. Some people are seeking specific answers regarding content for the portfolio which, as already discussed, is inappropriate as the KSA should be unique to everyone.

> **Reflection point**
>
> Identify your support needs. Formulate them as goals. Is there another type of support that will better meet your needs?

University course support

If you have applied for a level 2 accredited course in the UK, ask if they offer any support with the KSA. Some universities provide workshops or materials to guide you through the process. In some cases, you may have the opportunity to submit a draft of the portfolio to obtain feedback, although this is a big undertaking for course staff. Remember that courses want to recruit to capacity, so they want all candidates to succeed. This means that they have a vested interest in you passing the portfolio. Contact the course staff or check the university websites for any KSA support.

BABCP accreditation team

The accreditation team at the BABCP are specialists in the assessment of KSA portfolios. If you have attempted to complete your portfolio and sought support from other sources and you still have specific questions, then you can contact the BABCP. Just be aware that they are extremely busy, as they deal with all aspects of accreditation, so they may take time to reply. They are very helpful, however, and can give you specific suggestions for your situation.

Online support

In this era of social media, you can find videos and self-help advice on practically any topic including how to complete a KSA portfolio. As mentioned throughout this chapter, be careful not to fall into the trap of thinking there is one right way to complete the portfolio.

At the time of writing, there is a series of videos on YouTube by Sid the Therapist (https://www.youtube.com/c/SidtheTherapist). This is a channel produced by Sidrah Altaf who has documented the stages of her psychology career, including compiling a KSA portfolio before entering CBT training. There are fourteen videos for each of the criteria.

I offer KSA portfolio support as part of my CBT career consultation service. Details are provided on the Resources page.

What if I do not pass the KSA?

This is probably the biggest fear for most people. The truth is that you can make amendments and submit them again. There is no limit as to how many times you can have a portfolio assessed. In some cases, not passing a KSA portfolio might mean not being able to start a course at that time, but you can apply again or to another course once your KSA has been amended to the required standard.

Most people who assess portfolios will provide detailed feedback as to why any criterion did not pass. Use this information to guide you when making amendments. Once it does reach the standard, you should feel proud of your work as it represents your professional journey as a mental health practitioner deemed equivalent to a core professional.

Remember, if you meet the requirements for the KSA route then you *can* pass the portfolio. So, the message here is to *keep trying and not give up*. Chapter 10 provides more details on managing failure and rejection.

Summary

This chapter has provided an overview of the requirements for the KSA portfolio and how to approach it. View the portfolio as your story to reduce the threat associated with it. You are not alone. If you need further help, then support is available. A summary of this chapter is available to download from the Resources page.

Chapter 8
Preparing for CBT training

Regardless of your background, there are some general steps you need to take to increase your chances of being accepted onto a CBT training course. This includes making sure you have read and researched sufficiently to demonstrate a good understanding of CBT, the role of the CBT therapist and the expectations of a trainee CBT therapist. You also need to understand the requirements of the course you are applying to. You will need to make decisions regarding funding and how this may impact your quality of life during training.

In this chapter, we discuss how you can prepare yourself for training. We will consider different types of training courses in the UK, funding options, preparing your application and tips for interview preparation. In addition to general advice, there are some sections that apply to specific pathways.

A good understanding of CBT

Before even applying for a CBT training course, make sure you have a good understanding of what CBT is. This sounds basic but is surprisingly one of the fundamental parts of the recruitment process that tends to be weak. There are some common reasons for this. One is that you take it for granted that your passion for CBT will be enough to get you onto a course. Another is the assumption that you will learn everything on the course. Neither of these assumptions is true. Passion is good, but demonstrating a good understanding of the CBT model in your personal statement and during the interview is more important. The course will teach you about CBT theory and the core skills to practice it, but learning will go beyond the course content. There will be an expectation that you have a broad understanding before training on which to build your knowledge. The stronger the foundation, the easier it will be to assimilate and consolidate the content taught on the course as you will have a framework to hang this on.

> **Reflection point**
>
> How would you describe CBT to someone who knows nothing about it? What theories relating to CBT do you currently know of? How much reading have you done about CBT? Are there any gaps in your knowledge? If so, how could you address these?

One of the most important activities you can do is read. During interviews, it is surprising how little reference is made by candidates to books and articles relating to CBT. It is through your own research and reading that you will develop a clearer understanding of what CBT is. You do not need to know everything, or have a deep understanding, but you need to be able to discuss it over and above a brief definition. Remember, CBT incorporates a broad spectrum of approaches informed by different theoretical positions. Reading will help you to develop your thoughts and your position, which will change as you learn more on the course and beyond.

Some courses may expect you to have more than a basic understanding of CBT. It may be expected that you will know some of the protocols used to treat specific anxiety disorders and depression. So, the more you read, the better positioned you will be to state your understanding of the CBT approach and answer questions about it in an interview. It will also strengthen your rationale for choosing a CBT career.

Some activities to develop your understanding of CBT:
- Read a broad range of books and articles.
- Speak to practicing CBT therapists to gain a clear understanding of the role.
- Look at the NICE guidelines for treating depression and anxiety disorders.
- Learn about some of the challenges and weaknesses of CBT to be able to show a balanced understanding of the approach.
- Access webinars or other online videos about CBT, but make sure they are from credible sources such as professional organizations or higher education institutions.

Types of CBT courses in the UK

There are many different types of CBT courses available, so it is essential that you research courses carefully before applying or committing. If you want to become an accredited therapist with the BABCP, you will need to consider the content of the course. The BABCP set two principal standards regarding training in CBT. One is the **minimum training standards** (MTS), which outline all the requirements necessary to become an accredited practitioner. Within the MTS, the BABCP include details of **core curriculum** content. This refers to the content taught on the course. See the BABCP website for more details, but the main requirements are summarized in the following discussion.

CBT training is at postgraduate level which can be offered as a postgraduate certificate (PGCert), postgraduate diploma (PGDip) or master's (MSc) in CBT. The difference between these levels is briefly outlined in Table 8.1. To fulfil the MTS, the course needs to offer a minimum of a postgraduate diploma, which is usually completed over at least one academic year. Some courses are offered on a part-time basis so can be completed over a longer period. It is not necessary to have a full master's degree in CBT to become accredited, but it allows a deeper understanding of CBT theory through the completion of a dissertation. The same applies regardless of whether you complete an adult or CYP-focused training course. It is also possible to do CBT training for people with more severe and enduring mental health problems. These courses are referred to as CBT for psychosis (sometimes abbreviated to CBT-P), and often appeal to mental health professionals such as mental health nurses or clinical psychologists who already work with this client group but want to specialize in CBT.

Table 8.1 – Postgraduate courses in CBT

Degree level	Description	Accreditation
Postgraduate certificate	This is the shortest postgraduate level of study as it provides the least number of credits. They are normally completed within 6-9 months on a part-time basis. Some courses require practice placements, but others are solely academic. They can be used as a springboard into CBT training by showing additional study.	A PGCert in CBT is not sufficient to meet the MTS, but can be combined with other PGCert courses to gain more credits. If choosing a PGCert, make sure you opt for a practice-based course that includes clinical skills not just theory. This level of study is great for continued professional development (CPD) after completing CBT training.
Postgraduate diploma	This level carries more credits, meaning it has more content, includes more assessed work across theory and practice, and is normally run over a full academic year if offered as a funded place. These courses are very intense as they combine theory and skills training which is supervised closely at university and in clinical practice.	This is the minimum level of postgraduate course required to meet the MTS. It is the most common qualification offered to funded CBT trainees in the UK. Accreditation following training will depend on what proportion of the MTS have been met.
Master's degree	Some universities offer a full master's degree in CBT. This is often split into a PGDip, which needs to be completed and passed first. The additional credits that make up a master's degree usually come from a dissertation based on a research project of your choice. A master's usually adds a year of study on a part-time basis and can be completed alongside work.	Although a full master's degree in CBT is not necessary to become accredited, it does allow consolidation of the theory and clinical skills taught during the PGDip component. Arguably, it should allow more opportunities in your career, but there is no evidence that this is currently the case in the UK.

Level of accreditation

The level of accreditation allocated to a specific course relates to how much of the MTS and core curriculum are satisfied by the end of training and not the overall quality of the course. There are some excellent training courses that are not accredited, so it depends on what your career goal is. If you want to become an accredited CBT practitioner, then the university course will need to meet the requirements of the BABCP course accreditation at either level 2 (meets all requirements) or level 1 (meets some of the requirements).

Some university courses do not seek accreditation status. This can be for several reasons, but it is important to recognize that completing these courses will require varying degrees of additional academic and clinical work. In some cases, this can take a few years to meet the MTS. If you are not concerned about becoming an accredited practitioner, then this will not be an issue for you. However, as stated earlier, accreditation provides a standard by which many employers measure competence, so career opportunities will be very limited in the UK public service sector. This is also true for many private healthcare companies who will only allow accredited practitioners to provide CBT to their members.

You do not need to complete the MTS within your principal CBT training as you can make up any outstanding requirements following the course. However, the core curriculum elements should be met on the course. This means that the training needs to be at postgraduate level and include an equal split between theory and practice. So fully academic courses are not satisfactory. If you want to seek accreditation, then you will need to be working in a suitable setting to practice skills taught on the course and have an experienced clinical supervisor who is BABCP accredited, as this is part of the MTS.

If you choose a non-accredited course, it will be more difficult to meet the MTS later. Gaining adequate clinical experience during training is critical, so if a course does not allow this you are unlikely to be able to meet the core curriculum standard. Likewise, if the course does not include sufficient assessment of your academic and clinical performance, you will not be able to apply for accreditation. In some instances, you may have had enough teaching hours and supervision, and had some forms of assessment of your clinical and academic work. In these cases, it is possible to make up the shortfalls as described above for a level 1 course.

Table 8.2 – course accreditation levels

Accreditation level of course	Minimum training standards and core curriculum	Becoming an accredited practitioner
Level 2	Meets *all* MTS and core curriculum requirements. Currently, there are 40 courses with level 2 status in the UK. This comprises a mixture of adult and CYP programmes, IAPT (NHS Talking Therapies) and non-IAPT curricula and some clinical psychology doctoral courses.	You can become accredited on successful completion of the course. This includes KSA candidates as you will have had your portfolio assessed before starting the course so do not need to submit it again. If you fail a level 2 course, it is still possible to apply for accreditation in some cases if you can demonstrate that you have met the failed elements (but seek advice from the BABCP accreditation team).
Level 1	Meets *some* of the MTS and core curriculum. Currently, there are 11 courses with level 1 status comprising of a mixture of adult, CYP and doctoral courses.	You will need to demonstrate completion of the outstanding requirements before applying for accreditation. This may include a KSA portfolio if not submitted before starting training. As above, if you fail a level 1 course, it is sometimes possible to make up the failed elements but this is more complex as there will already be some MTS uncovered on the course.
Non-accredited	This will be variable as there are so many non-accredited courses. Some will be mindful of the requirements, but most will have their own curriculum. You should check this before applying.	This will depend on the content of the course and whether it meets the main requirements of the core curriculum and MTS. Courses that are predominantly theoretical in content will not lead to accreditation. It will likely take significantly longer to become accredited with a non-accredited course as you will need to provide a detailed mapping document to show where each requirement has been met.

Funding

The Five Year Forward View for Mental Health (2016) outlines the workforce planning necessary to adequately meet the demands for psychological therapies in the UK. Since the introduction of the IAPT initiative (now called NHS Talking Therapies) in 2008, NHS England has funded training in line with workforce requirements. Due to an increase in demand for CBT and the attrition of trained CBT therapists to the private sector or independent practice, the deficit remains. This means that there will continue to be funded places on CBT courses for those wanting to train and deliver CBT within the NHS.

Some courses are aimed solely at NHS psychological therapy services. These adhere to an NHS Talking Therapies-inspired curriculum, although arguably the shape of the services and how they are delivered has changed considerably during the past decade since the early days of IAPT. Each locality will be allocated funding depending on a statistical analysis of the need for that geographical area. Services compete for these funded places, resulting in trainee CBT positions for their service. The service will team up with a university course to provide the necessary training in partnership. It is important to state that allocation of these places varies each year, so it is hard to predict which course or service will have trainee positions at any one time.

To meet the requirements for funding, you will need to be a UK resident or have lived and worked in the UK for three years. You can only apply for educational funding for one course at a time, so if you have already had funding for low-intensity training then you are required to wait two years before applying for further training. This is also true for people who have been funded for CBT training and who subsequently want to do a psychology doctorate programme. You will need to wait two years from completion of the CBT course.

Another option is to fund training yourself. One of the biggest challenges when self-funding is finding a suitable placement to complete the clinical component of the course (see Chapter 6 for more details). You still need to meet the requirements for the level of course you are applying for and there will be additional expenses. This often includes clinical supervision in practice. Some of the hidden costs are listed below:

- Administration fee for the application process
- Registration fee if accepted on the course
- Resits for any failed work
- Clinical supervision in the practice setting (this can be a significant expense)
- Loss of earnings if working on a voluntary or low-paid basis

Despite these costs, it provides an option that can lead to becoming an accredited CBT therapist.

> **Tips for choosing a course**
> - Go for the highest level of accreditation possible.
> - If self-funding, don't go for the cheapest course based on price only because, in the long run, it will cost you much more time and money to meet the outstanding requirements for accreditation.
> - It is worth waiting an extra year to strengthen your application for an accredited course.
> - If choosing a non-accredited course, speak to course staff about pathways to becoming accredited on completion of the course.

Applying for CBT training

If you meet the requirements for training and you are in a position to apply, then you need to be prepared for the recruitment process. In addition to having a good understanding of CBT, you also need to know about the course you are applying to. Each university will have course documentation outlining the details of its programmes. Read through this and contact course staff with any questions. It is easy to overlook important details or make assumptions about courses without doing your research. Check the following:

- Level of accreditation of the course.
- Entry requirements.
- Curriculum content to match against BABCP core curriculum.
- Assessment details to match against MTS.
- If self-funding, the cost of the course and, more importantly, what this fee covers.

If you are applying for a funded place then you may not have a choice regarding university, but funded places will normally be at level 2, so all MTS for accreditation will be met. In some cases, training will be at level 1 but the service and university will have processes in place to help you to make up any requirements for accreditation following the course. It is still worth checking out the university course details to have a good understanding of what will be expected during training. It can help you prepare for interviews, too.

Funded places will be advertised on NHS job sites. Timings of these posts will vary so being prepared at short notice is often required – do your research beforehand to optimize your chance of getting a well-prepared application form submitted without excessive stress.

> **Tips for preparing for the application process**
> - Study the person specification for a trainee CBT role. You can download this from previous job adverts or ask any NHS Talking Therapy services to give you a copy.
> - Familiarize yourself with the main course requirements and content of the CBT courses in your area.
> - Speak to current trainees and qualified CBT therapists to learn from their experiences.
> - Gather your documentation needed for evidence of academic attainment.
> - Have details of suitable referees prepared.
> - Prepare your timeline of current and previous employment (use your CV for this).

These items are easier to prepare but can take time due to chasing people and paperwork, so get these in place first. It also allows you to make a start on the application form which will build your confidence.

Preparing a personal statement on the application form

One of the most important elements of the application form is the personal statement. It will be assumed that you meet the requirements of the role, and if any are not met then your application will be rejected immediately. So the personal statement is what will set you apart from other candidates. First, make sure it is written clearly and legibly. This sounds like common sense, but it is surprising how many people submit their statements without proofreading or asking someone else to read them. Remember that the person screening your application will be reading many personal statements so making it easy to read is essential. There is no one right way to present your personal statement, but there are some dos and don'ts that should help you.

The recruiters will be reading many statements so making it clear, comprehensive and succinct is essential. Your statement should not be too long or too short. Although this sounds vague, it is important that you put what is necessary to show you meet the criteria and to introduce yourself succinctly and engagingly. The statement should also be well structured in terms of a clear flow from one point to the next. One of the subtle problems that can occur is the writing style. Using the active voice presents confidence in what you are writing and comes across as more persuasive. It is common for healthcare professionals to feel uncomfortable speaking positively about themselves. Due to high standards and a tendency to put others first, selling yourself can be a challenge. However, presenting skills and experiences in an active voice is not being arrogant. You may have to challenge this before writing the statement.

Table 8.3 – dos and don'ts of personal statements

Do	Don't
Express your personality including your passion for CBT.	Just relay the person specification. Your personality won't come through.
Have a clear structure to the statement. Plan it before writing.	Jump from one point to another in a non-coherent manner. This is easy to do when writing straight from your thoughts without a plan.
Write using the active voice to show confidence in what you are saying.	Use tentative language such as "*I think* I am a good communicator". This can come across as passive and lacking confidence. Instead, state your skills and qualities clearly to sell yourself and what you can bring to the role – say "*I am* a good communicator".
Demonstrate a good understanding of the trainee CBT role and how you can fulfil it.	Assume that it is obvious that you know the role.
Acknowledge any challenges you have faced or that you predict may present during the training.	Avoid stating any difficulties you have faced or fear facing during training. Stating these shows self-awareness and a willingness to move out of your comfort zone.

There is a psychological phenomenon called the 'primacy' and 'recency' effect in terms of our memory, which means that the recruiter is likely to remember the start and the end of the statement most clearly, so make sure these two points make an impact. Introduce yourself confidently and interestingly to bring your statement to life. Start with something personal, such as your specific qualities and experiences that draw you to a CBT career, rather than a generic statement about how you meet the requirements. This will follow in your statement, but make it a story with a hook at the start to grab the reader.

State clearly why you want to be a CBT therapist. What is it about CBT that interests you? Show that you understand what CBT is and how you gained this knowledge. Give some examples from your practice where you have either used CBT approaches or can see how CBT could be applied.

Demonstrate your understanding of the trainee role and the NHS Talking Therapies services in general. Express an understanding of the demands of training and how you can manage them. This might include examples of how you have dealt with stressful situations in the past.

KSA candidates will need the portfolio ready for assessment by the interview date. If this applies to you, then state that it is prepared. This will add weight to your application as it is an essential requirement for non-core professional candidates. Some people do not prepare the portfolio, thinking they will do it if they are selected. However, this is a risky strategy, so you will always be in a much stronger position if the KSA is complete before applying for a trainee post. For more details on preparing your portfolio see Chapter 7.

If you must fund part of your course, such as supervision, state clearly that you are aware of this and are able to source the funding. This also applies to posts where the candidate needs to secure a suitable practice placement. State that you have organized this or else it may be a deal breaker, as you will need to be in clinical practice by the start of the course. Do not underestimate how long it takes to set up a position with a service.

Finish the statement with a strong and personal expression as to why you should be selected. As with the start of the statement, this will provide a narrative account which is more relatable and memorable.

There is a downloadable guide to preparing your personal statement on the Resources page.

Preparing for interview

Remember, if you have been shortlisted, you meet the requirements, so this is your opportunity to demonstrate this 'live'. No one is trying to catch you out or wants you to fail. The course director and the service managers will want to recruit you, so try not to overestimate the level of threat.

The main stages of interview preparation are:

- KSA candidates need to prepare a portfolio first.
- Read about CBT, the course and the service you are applying to.
- Prepare notes for some of the broad questions (see list below).
- Practice saying these answers out loud.
- Practice some potential role-play exercises.
- *Do not over prepare* – leave space to allow for some flexible thinking.

Make sure you are clear about the interview process in terms of any specific preparation they want you to do such as a case study, or role-play. If you need a KSA portfolio, this should be completed before the interview. If it isn't, then state this clearly and have a realistic time scale by which you can confidently complete it to an acceptable standard. Your place will be conditional on the portfolio passing. If you have completed your portfolio recently, then this is good preparation for an interview as many relevant issues will be fresh in your mind. If not completed recently, then look through it again to bring your knowledge, skills and attitudes to the forefront of your mind. This will remind you of your strengths and career story to date.

The list below is not exhaustive and may not be covered in all interviews. Each course will have its own specific approach, but there will be some general issues covered.

You should be able to do the following:

- State clearly why you want to be a CBT therapist. What is it about CBT that interests you?
- Describe the role of the CBT therapist. List the features of CBT.
- Reflect on some CBT literature you have read recently. Be able to name an article or book and describe what you learned from it.
- Give some examples from your own practice where you have either used CBT approaches or can see how CBT could be applied.
- List the NICE guidelines for each anxiety disorder and depression. See Roth and Pilling (2007) for the competences required to deliver effective CBT for people with depression and anxiety disorders (www.ucl.ac.uk/pals/research/clinical-educational-and-health-psychology/research-groups/core/competence-frameworks-2).
- Describe the course overview. Read some details of the course you are applying for. Be able to state some of the content or modules and how it is taught.
- Express a position on your own professional values, the ethical framework you follow and examples of any ethical dilemmas you have reconciled in your clinical practice.
- Answer a question on risk in clinical practice.
- Have some questions prepared that you can ask the interview panel.

A common error that many people make is to prepare answers for questions that may not come up. This includes a range of specific CBT protocols and scenario questions. Having a broad knowledge of these will be sufficient, but spending excessive time preparing notes on these can make you overlook some of the general questions. This can lead to poor answers to seemingly easy questions like "Why do you want to be a CBT therapist?" This question is always asked and often the answer is very vague or not convincing. Make sure you give it some thought. You may see it as a mere icebreaker, but the panel will be assessing your motivation for doing CBT training. This may be to filter out people who are using it as a stepping-stone to a doctoral programme, or for promotion in their current service. So, the key element of this question is *why CBT* and not another therapy modality. Giving a clear and confident answer to this question will set the scene for the interview.

It is important to remember that the answers you prepare for the interview are *unique to your experiences*. A common preparation strategy is to ask lots of people what they have prepared for certain questions, which is not only unhelpful, but it can cause unnecessary confusion. Your answers will be much more fluid and accessible if based on your *actual* experiences rather than what you consider to be an expected answer. Seeking answers to interview questions can be questioned from an ethical point of view. Some would view this as cheating and a sign of low professional integrity. The panel can sense when an answer is generalized or contrived, and will be looking for your specific experiences and opinions. It also makes it easier for you to expand on your answer rather than giving a soundbite that doesn't map onto your autobiographical memory. This will make you stand out more, so be confident in what you know.

Practice answering your questions out loud, even with people who have no experience of the interview process, as this will give you a chance to articulate your answers without any of the anxiety associated with being judged on the content. Once you feel more confident, you can practice with people who do have knowledge of CBT and the interview process. Still, keep in mind that each interview experience is unique, so just because a person has been through it on one occasion does not necessarily mean you can generalize this to all interviews.

Role-play practice will help prepare you for any live exercises in the interview. You may not know the subject of the role-play, but exposure through repeated practice with colleagues or in supervision will help reduce performance anxiety. Recording yourself is also a good way to reduce your self-consciousness.

On the day of the interview, try to keep your focus on the present moment rather than getting stuck in a cycle of worry and rumination or looping through potential answers. Use grounding techniques to bring your attentional focus back during the interview so that you can clearly hear each question before formulating your answer. There is a downloadable guide to preparing for high-intensity CBT interviews on the Resources page.

Due to the highly competitive nature of applying for funded CBT training places, it is extremely common to experience at least one rejection from a course or training place. As hard as this is, try not to let it impact your confidence too heavily and see it as an opportunity to be resilient and try again. Rejection can occur at different stages, so we will consider these in turn.

The overall message is to minimize self-critical thinking as much as possible, as this will maintain worry and rumination and increase feelings of hopelessness. The situation is disappointing and challenging, but not hopeless. Planning for the next time will help to maintain your hope and motivation. It is also important that, during the period before re-applying for training, you remain focused on your job role and see it as an opportunity to hone your skills further before the next application. Chapter 10 focuses on managing failure and rejection in more detail.

Table 8.4 – Tips for moving beyond rejection

Point of rejection	How to move on
At application stage Not shortlisted for interview	■ Remember how many applications are received for each training place (normalize). ■ Ask for feedback from the organization. ■ Revisit your personal statement and see if it can be improved (refer to the list above). ■ Speak to others who have experienced this for peer support. ■ Resist falling into excessively self-critical thinking. This will lower your confidence and self-esteem. ■ Be compassionate to yourself. Acknowledge the disappointment and build yourself up to try again. ■ Do something nice for yourself to reinforce self-compassion. ■ Give yourself time to process this disappointment then make a plan to apply again.
At interview stage Not offered a place following an interview	■ Acknowledge your disappointment and view it as a temporary loss of hope (to get on the training at this time). ■ Give yourself time to process this. ■ Resist excessive worry, rumination and self-critical thinking. ■ Be kind to yourself. ■ Seek support from family and friends. ■ Reflect honestly on your performance, including strengths, rather than just focusing on what you believe lost you points. ■ Ask for feedback from the panel. ■ Map this feedback with your own reflections to maximize learning from the experience.
General	■ Normalize how many people experience rejection during this process. ■ Resist punishing or berating yourself with self-critical thoughts. ■ Practice self-compassion. ■ Show your resilience by trying again.

Pre-course preparation

Due to the intensive nature of CBT training, it is wise to do some preliminary preparation. The checklist below outlines some of the tasks that will help to prepare you before the course begins.

Pre-course checklist

- Most funded places will start before the course to allow you to learn about the service and mandatory policies and procedures. Ideally, you will have some suitable trainee cases lined up and ready for the start of the course.
- Some services will provide a detailed induction process and mentor to prepare you for training.
- If organizing your own placement, make sure you have a contract in place at least one month before the course starts. Ideally, it should be in place three months before the course so that you can have all the checks done and references approved. Even voluntary positions will need to be processed through HR.
- If self-funding, organize a supervisor and start working together before the course starts. Give them all the course details so that they can tailor supervision to the requirements of the course. Give your supervisor details of a contact person at the university so that they can liaise regularly.
- You will need to be seeing patients or clients before the course starts, which is why starting at least a month before will allow you to apply the taught content immediately.
- If there is a delay in starting a placement or trainee position, this can cause problems from the start of the course that will add significant stress.
- Do a broad range of reading to get a head start. Get a copy of the course handbook and reading list to guide you.
- If you have learning needs, then organize support through the university Disability Advisory Service (DAS). They will provide questionnaires to assess your support needs.

Learning support needs

Try to put this in place before the course starts, but if this is not possible then do it as soon as you can once you have started the course. If you are unaware of any learning issues such as dyslexia, you can still approach the university DAS. It might be that you have an undiagnosed problem, or just require some tips for approaching academic study skills. Do not struggle unnecessarily or suffer in silence. These services are in place to provide help for all students.

Summary

This chapter has considered the different types and levels of CBT courses, funding issues, the stages of recruitment and how to prepare for each part. The main message is to focus on your background and experience rather than trying to prepare what you believe to be perfect answers. The process is highly competitive and demanding, so failing to secure a place on your first attempt is common. This will not necessarily reflect your suitability for training, so seek feedback and support and remain hopeful that you will succeed.

Chapter 9
Getting the most from training

Training to become a CBT therapist is incredibly intensive. Some people view a postgraduate diploma in CBT as more demanding than a higher-level degree due to the fast pace, packed curriculum and assessed work. In this chapter, we consider some of the challenges facing trainees on a CBT training course and how to overcome them. It is not just about troubleshooting, we will also discuss the ways you can maximize your learning experience and enjoyment of this fantastic career opportunity.

Training is a massive endeavour, so this chapter provides an overview only. The previous chapter ended with some tips for preparing for training so that you are fully ready, practically and mentally, as you will need to hit the ground running. In this chapter, the process of training will be considered in sequence from acclimatising to the course to managing practice learning and academic assessments. The chapter on getting the most out of supervision provides detailed advice on the supervision element, so this will only be addressed in terms of specific supervision issues relating to training.

Acclimatising to the course

Due to the intense nature of CBT training, you may feel forced into survival mode by the threat of trying to keep up with the demands of the course. Although perfectly normal, this can hinder your learning experience by remaining in the fight, flight or freeze response. In other courses, you may have embraced learning and had a sense of achievement and pleasure that seems more challenging on a CBT course. However, it is possible to have this same experience by approaching the course as you would any other.

CBT training is unique in terms of the variety of backgrounds that trainees bring. Each cohort can have a different blend of trainees which brings a specific group dynamic. This makes comparisons to your contemporaries unhelpful, as each person will have their own personal strengths and experiences. It is common to focus on what you consider to be your weaknesses and compare yourself to someone else who appears stronger in that area. For example, a mental health nurse who has little experience of applying CBT may feel inferior to a PWP with more clinical experience of CBT, but the PWP will not have the breadth of knowledge and skills in a range of mental health problems that a mental health nurse has. Likewise, a trainee who hasn't done an academic course for many years might feel inferior to those who have recently completed other postgraduate training, but may have years of intensive clinical experience directly relevant to CBT practice.

The course staff are tasked with creating a level playing field so that the learning is pitched at a level suitable for this diverse range of backgrounds. It is common for PWPs to work at a fast pace due to their experience using low-intensity interventions in limited time frames, so effort needs to be directed at slowing them down to a high-intensity approach, whereas people from a counselling or mental health nursing background may be accustomed to a less structured and slower pace, so this requires speeding up their approach. This levelling is an ongoing process, so expect the first term or two to feel a bit confusing, as the teaching needs to be assimilated and adapted to your needs. The content is the same but how you apply it will differ. It is important to recognize that this is normal so *don't compare yourself too closely to others*.

There will be a range of methods used on the course. Some of these will complement your learning style, while others may not. You will need to experiment with ways of capturing lecture material that work for you. This may be recording sessions (if permitted) or taking notes on handouts. Some tips are presented in Table 9.1.

Table 9.1 – Methods for recording course content

Learning activity	Methods of recording information	Comments
Lectures	■ Course staff may record all sessions so you can attend to the lecture without the distraction of writing too many detailed notes and re-watch it later. ■ You may be permitted to record lectures, although often they will be beyond the storage of a smartphone. ■ Writing notes during lectures. ■ Using handouts to highlight certain messages. ■ Asking for materials before the session to help process the content.	■ You will have your own style of taking notes. Make them concise as it will be demanding to read later. ■ Try to focus on the live lecture by being present rather than thinking you can watch it later. This will be extra time that you may not have. ■ If watching a recording, take notes like you would a live lecture. ■ If you have specific learning needs, make sure each lecturer is aware of this so they can make any adaptations necessary like producing handouts on coloured paper or larger print.

Clinical skills workshop	■ These will be live and often delivered in groups. ■ The trainer should model any new skills so be present and observe closely. ■ Ask questions before practicing the skill if you are unclear. ■ You can prepare with fellow students and share ideas. ■ Make sure you take notes to remember key learning points. ■ Practice between sessions as the more you expose yourself to role-plays the less anxiety-provoking it will be.	■ Clinical skills practice tends to be very anxiety-provoking but remember that you are all feeling anxious. ■ See it as an opportunity to learn rather than a threat of showing any perceived weakness.
Group tasks	■ If tasked with doing a presentation in groups, it is useful to assign someone to guide the process. ■ Everyone should be given space to express their opinions and perspectives on the task. ■ Assign roles to each person. ■ Set specific deadlines for contributions to be collated. ■ Be clear about outcomes if someone does not fulfil their commitment. ■ Agree how the different elements will be put together. ■ Have a contingency plan in place in case the task is not completed as intended. ■ Avoid conflict by remembering it is a group task so focus on collaboration.	■ Working in groups can be stressful, often due to different ways of working and perceived levels of standards. ■ If you have unrelenting standards or perfectionism, group work will be even more stressful, but this is a good opportunity to make your rule more flexible. See it as an experiment to test your predictions. ■ Dividing work up should actually be less stressful so, while preparing your contribution, try not to focus on the others in the group. ■ Once the deadline has been met, work as a group again to reinforce the collaborative nature of the task.
Supervision	■ You should have supervision logs prepared by the university in line with the requirements of the course, so familiarize yourself with this documentation. ■ Take notes in your own style during the supervision session which can be summarized in the log later. ■ Be prepared for the session by having a relevant supervision question. ■ Listen to other trainees' contributions and take notes on their cases to maximize learning.	■ Like group work and clinical skills, supervision will be anxiety-provoking. Use the tips above for remaining focused, not comparing yourself too much to others and having realistic expectations of your knowledge and skills at each point during training.

Presenting case information	<ul><li>This is required in many contexts including supervision, group work and presentations.</li><li>Always anonymize personal details by using initials or a pseudonym.</li><li>Include age, gender, ethnicity and brief family details of the person as these allow a broader cultural and systemic analysis of the case.</li><li>Provide a brief summary of the presenting problem.</li><li>Always include a formulation of sorts, even an initial maintenance cycle to provide a case conceptualization based on the CBT model.</li><li>This may be enough for some purposes, but if expected to relay treatment then include your diagnosis (and what guided your decision) and rationale for the treatment plan and outcome of therapy.</li><li>In completed cases, you will also need to provide reflections on the process. Make these critical by including relevant literature.</li></ul>	<ul><li>The methods for presenting case information can vary. Your course may have a specific template, so for assessed work you will need to adhere to that.</li><li>If the case presentation is informal then be creative in how you present the information. You can make a poster or PowerPoint presentation to make it more engaging and bring the case to life.</li></ul>

Role-plays

It is worth having a specific section on role-plays as they tend to cause so much anxiety in trainees. Role-plays are part of a broader category of simulation techniques used to learn skills in a safe environment before practicing in a real-life setting. They are used across a variety of disciplines and contexts including research, education, corporate organizational settings and healthcare. Role-plays have always been used in healthcare professional training because academic study alone is not sufficient to learn the clinical skills required to become a competent clinician. In terms of theory, we can relate back to the classic works of Piaget and Vygotsky who both emphasize the importance of role-play in children's development as an active method of learning.

In CBT, we have been influenced by Kolb's (1984) learning cycle, which provides a framework for understanding the role of interactive learning in developing skills and overcoming problems. In this sense, we need to practice what we preach as this is what we encourage in therapy to help the person break a vicious cycle by testing beliefs through experiential learning. We need to take the threat out of role-plays as a learning tool and recognize their value.

Like any threatening situation, we are likely to respond with heightened arousal in the limbic system leading to the fight, flight or freeze response. This will be fuelled by excessive worry and possibly rumination on past role-play experiences that you viewed as negative. If you fear role-plays, then the flight response is likely to be an instinct leading to avoidance. If the fear is very intense, then you could go into the freeze response, not pay any attention to the task at all and just hope it will be over as quickly as possible. However, bringing the arousal down first will help you to approach the task more easily as the level of perceived threat will be reduced. Using a grounding technique to help you focus and bring your attention back to the present moment will help to quieten the worry and rumination and see them as thoughts only.

Thinking of learning theory, we can apply exposure and habituation to the practice of role-plays. We know that the more we repeat something we fear, without using any safety or avoidance behaviours, the more our body will habituate to the distress caused by excessive adrenaline. We may never enjoy role-plays, but if we are less anxious then the learning opportunities are significantly increased. In fact, recording role-plays and watching them back repeatedly also results in habituation.

Another technique from CBT, in the treatment of GAD, is the threat-opportunity continuum. We have used this in other chapters as it is such a useful concept. At the threat end are all the worries and negative automatic thoughts associated with role-plays. By also considering the opportunities, we can gain a more balanced view. It is worth remembering that role-plays are not designed to make you look or feel stupid. On the contrary, they are practiced outside of the clinical setting to provide a safe environment to learn.

Not only are role-plays a means for learning clinical skills, but they are also an intervention that can be used in therapy. For example, when working with someone with social anxiety, you can use role-plays to practice speaking or interacting in different social situations. Changing roles is a useful way of maximizing the learning potential of role-plays both in the training environment and in the clinical setting.

Course work

The coursework requirements for a level 2 accredited course are presented here. This is a course that meets all the minimum training standards (MTS) set by the BABCP to become an accredited practitioner upon completion (see Appendices for a summary). If you are not on a level 2 course, then some of the coursework may not apply to you at this time. However, if you want to go on and become accredited later, then you will have to demonstrate equivalence of this. The details here are a generic summary and assume you that meet the entrance requirements of having a core profession or KSA route. Each course will have its own documentation, so refer to course and module handbooks for specific details of coursework for your course.

Portfolio

All the hours required for clinical practice, supervision and the taught component are recorded in a portfolio. The course will have templates for this. Most courses now have electronic versions of the portfolio, so you can input data directly onto this as you progress through the course. Alternatively, you may prefer to create files and folders on your computer to keep information which can be transferred to the portfolio. The important thing is to keep track of all the details required, as by the end of the course as you will have to hunt through many sources of information to select what you need, and a lack of organization can make completion of the portfolio significantly more challenging.

Typical components of a portfolio include:

- **Case flow chart** which keeps track of all patients or clients seen, session by session, and includes initials, presenting problem, dates, brief content of each session, and whether they completed therapy or not. Most courses will state that you need to have a minimum of five treatment sessions for the case to be considered adequate for case studies or as a closely supervised case in supervision. This document helps to calculate all your clinical hours, the number of completed cases and the number of different presentations treated.

- **Supervision log** documents each supervision session, stating which case(s) were discussed, the supervision question and a summary of the discussion, methods used and if any live material was played. It allows you to calculate the total number of supervision hours and how many cases met the criteria for being closely supervised. This requires bringing the same case at least five times and showing at least two live extracts from that case in supervision. This can be through formative feedback from your supervisor between sessions as most courses allow you to have recordings (referred to colloquially as 'tapes') assessed informally by your supervisor for development purposes before handing in a separate tape for summative assessment.

- **Case summaries** provide evidence of closely supervised cases or examples of the eight completed cases needed to meet the MTS. Courses may vary with regards to this.

- **Reflective learning log** details examples of your self-directed study throughout the course. It will often consist of examples of material you have read with reflections on what you learned and how this has been integrated into your clinical practice.

- **Learning log** includes details of each lecture and clinical skills session taught on the course to log attendance. If any sessions are missed most courses will have a policy for how you can make up these hours. It might be watching a recording of the session and writing a reflective account of learning or attending a BABCP-recommended external session pertaining to the same subject matter.

Assessing CBT knowledge

In line with the core curriculum set by the BABCP for accredited courses, evidence of knowledge learned on the course is assessed as coursework. This is often in the form of an essay, and there may be one or two essays set across the course. In some cases, you may be required to do a presentation on a chosen subject, and in rare cases, some courses may set an exam to assess acquired CBT knowledge. Regardless of the method of assessment of CBT knowledge, there are some common tips for maximizing your performance.

Table 9.2 – Maximizing your essay performance

Tip	Details
Read *before* you start planning and preparing the coursework.	This sounds like common sense but most trainees, and students in general, can launch into a piece of work without adequately reading the literature associated with the topic of the essay or presentation. This tendency will limit your plans and preparation as the reading needs to guide your work. You may have some ideas about the subject matter, but the coursework needs to show a cogent understanding of the evidence base surrounding the topic. Reading will help you to build a position on the subject, which will give you a much clearer idea of the direction you want to take the essay or presentation.
Plan and prepare adequately, but not too much.	It is important to plan your essay or presentation, but if you spend too much time on planning and preparing then procrastination can set in. As above, reading is essential, but printing out several journal articles that go on a pile without reading is likely to result in further avoidance. When doing a literature search, download a few articles at a time so you can read them straight away and take some brief notes. This will start to add up and will guide your ideas for the coursework. It will also minimize the risk of procrastination.
Provide a critical review of the literature.	Avoid just tagging literature in a piece of work without stating its relevance. It is very clear when someone has just glanced through an article or looked at the title and assumed it supports the specific point being made. This is not adequate as the account you are providing will remain descriptive rather than critical. You need to go beyond listing a reference to state the findings and how credible the source is. So, instead of stating "This is supported by Smith and Jones (2009)" (description) you could say, "This is supported by Smith and Jones (2009) but their research presents a single case study of one woman with depression. While case studies provide a valuable qualitative insight into individual lived experiences, caution is needed not to generalize to all women with depression". Remember, you are trying to convince the reader (the course staff) that you have read widely and have the critical thinking skills to highlight any weaknesses of the evidence presented. This will help in the overall task of crafting a personal position on the subject.

Demonstrate a position on the subject.	As above, being critical in your writing is essential. However, you can be critical and not make your own position very clear. This will only demonstrate that you have done the reading and critiqued the studies used in your account. You need to draw the discussion to a close with a concluding statement of where you stand on the subject. This provides your 'answer' to the presenting question in the essay or presentation title. Remember, you are tasked with persuading the reader that your position is backed up with evidence and critical thinking. Using a two-sided argument is always more effective than presenting one side, no matter how much evidence you cite. By presenting both sides of an argument, you can navigate the reader to your conclusion.
Stick to the word limit.	Most students tend to go over word limits in their initial drafts. This is often because the first draft may be more conversational rather than critical. This is more likely the case for people who have read less and plan to add references later. As above, this method will weaken the critical value of the piece of work. Use your words wisely. Remember that you earn many more points for critical analysis and synthesis of literature with your own clinical practice than for merely describing an idea or study.
Proofread your work.	It is surprising how many minor spelling and grammatical errors end up in final versions of essays. This is referring to all students and not just those with identified learning issues like dyslexia. Multiple minor errors can be distracting and disrupt the flow of the work. Although they may be minor, they can be sufficiently distracting to lose marks if the reader needs to re-read sentences or recode an error to make sense of it in the context of the writing. These errors can be avoided through close proofreading by yourself, or by someone not associated with the course who may be able to spot them more easily if not so heavily invested in the material. You can also run spelling and grammar checks to reduce any errors remaining in the final version of your work.

The same applies to presentations. Although you will be verbalizing your ideas, you still need to be critical and form a position. In addition to the above, Table 9.3 outlines further tips relating to presentation skills.

Table 9.3 – Maximizing presentation performance

Tip	Details
Do not read from a script or slides.	Look at the audience and avoid reading from a script or slides. Bring your ideas to life with a case example and diagrams to break up large portions of text. It is good to have some notes to guide your presentation, but make these brief, like bullet points, so you can glance up and down more frequently than locking into the notes more of the time. Reading from a script also encourages a monotone voice, so add emphasis and vary your tone to make it more natural. The audience will lose interest quickly if the presentation is not engaging.
Develop a position.	As with essays, a presentation will gain more marks if you provide evidence of wide reading and critical analysis of the literature, and you guide the audience and assessor to a clear position by the end of the presentation.
Rehearse several times before the live performance.	It is very easy to over or underestimate how long a presentation will take when spoken out loud as opposed to writing down the content and saying it in your head. Rehearsing will also help you iron out any parts of the presentation that you find challenging to explain clearly. This avoids the risk of you getting tangled up on the day trying to explain something clearly and concisely, which could disrupt your flow.
Be interactive.	Presentations come to life when you include the audience. Ask questions, or request an example that you can use to apply the theory or interventions discussed in the presentation. For example, instead of just describing a technique like imagery rescripting, you could ask the audience if anyone has used it. It will make the discussion more interesting and engaging. It also shows that you can think on the spot rather than be tied to a script.
Save enough time for questions at the end.	For assessed presentations, you will be required to include time for questions. This is partly to see how you handle questions, but it is also an opportunity to demonstrate passion and enthusiasm for the subject of your presentation. You can achieve this by quoting literature related to the topic or giving examples beyond the content of the presentation. The assessors are not trying to catch you out; often their questions spring from genuine interest in your case. Often there is *not* one right answer so try not to second guess what the assessor is looking for. If there is evidence of critical thinking and curiosity, this will be sufficient.
If you don't know an answer, be honest.	If you are asked a question and you don't immediately have an answer, take a brief pause. We sometimes panic and freeze without allowing time to think about the question. It is okay to say something like, "That's an interesting question" or "I haven't thought about it in that way" and then formulate an answer. If you don't know, then just say so. This is much better than trying to get away with it by improvising on the spot. You can even put the question back to the person and ask them how they would answer it. This shows a level of confidence and competence necessary for live presentations.

Case studies

Case studies are often included as a piece of academic work on a CBT course, but they provide evidence of both CBT knowledge and skills. For a level 2 accredited course, you are required to submit four. Mostly these will be in written form, but some courses allow one or more to be assessed live as a presentation. The four case studies will be selected from your eight completed cases and should cover at least three different clinical presentations. One is normally expected to be a depression case.

Follow the guidelines set by the course as these may vary slightly, so refer to the course handbook. However, Table 9.4 details some broad requirements for presenting a case study. The BABCP also provide guidance which can be found on their website. The table provides a general structure for the case study with notes on each section. Use headings to maximize the organization of your case study.

Table 9.4 – General guidelines for CBT case study

Element	Notes
Brief description of the case	This is a very brief introduction to the case, normally including demographic information, the presenting problem and length of therapy.
	You can use initials or a pseudonym for the person and state details of consent and confidentiality.
Literature review	This provides evidence of reading around the subject of the case and the context for how you approached the case.
Assessment	Sometimes this is combined with other sections such as the brief description of the case or within the case conceptualization.
	Details of the assessment include the route of referral, previous history of therapy, medication, risk and suitability for CBT.
	You may assign a diagnosis here based on the assessment information, any measures and reference to a diagnostic manual such as the DSM-5 or ICD-11.
Case conceptualization	This is one of the most important sections as it provides your understanding of the presenting problem from a CBT perspective.
	Case conceptualization refers to formulation. This can be done at different levels starting with a cross-sectional model such as a five areas or other maintenance cycle. This is normally part of the assessment, but you may do multiple maintenance formulations throughout therapy.
	A full case conceptualization will include historical information to provide a longitudinal perspective. This allows us to theorize about the onset and development of the presenting problems in the context of the individual's life experiences and belief system.

Treatment rationale	This should be influenced by the evidence base and national guidelines. This includes NICE guidelines and the Roth & Pilling (2007) CBT competency framework.
The treatment should also match the designated diagnosis (if applicable) or case conceptualization.
Make sure you do a problem statement and set goals that are SMART (specific, measurable, achievable, realistic and time managed) and appropriate to the presenting problem and treatment approach.
Course of therapy	Describe what you did in therapy, session by session. You can cluster sessions together if you are working on the same goal for more than one session. Summarize what you did, why you did it and how it went. Also include what homework was set after each session.
Outcomes	This will include a combination of quantitative data such as the psychometric measures and qualitative outcomes in terms of reduction of impact of the problem statement and achievement of therapy goals.
Discussion	Identify issues for your discussion and research these to provide a *critical* reflection of your case. Use a framework for your discussion such as a reflective model, helicopter view or systems model. The systems process model allows you to reflect on the case from three perspectives: the client's, the therapist's and the therapy process's.
References	Make sure you include all material cited in the main text. It is normally expected that you use the Harvard referencing system, but check the course handbook.
Appendices	Only include appendices if necessary. Do not use excessive appendices. Only include them if they add to the presentation. For example, it is not necessary to include the diagnostic criteria of a disorder as an appendix if you have described it and cited the source (e.g. DSM-5) in the main body.
Examples of completed worksheets and extra formulation diagrams not included in the main text make useful appendices.

Tips for approaching your case study

- Stick to the word count as you will be penalized and lose marks if you're significantly under or over the expected word count.
- Use tables and diagrams to make information clear.
- The strength of the case study is not determined solely by how successful the treatment was. You are being assessed on what you learned from treating the person. You can sometimes provide a much more thorough critique and learn more from a case that didn't produce significant clinical gains, so don't dismiss these cases as options for your case studies.
- Often there is no single right or wrong way to approach a case. What is more important is providing your *clinical rationale* for each decision made. This demonstrates your thinking processes and how you are using your knowledge and experience to guide treatment.
- Do a lot of reading around the subject of your case study before writing it. This will help you to contextualize your therapy experience.

Assessing clinical competence

This often causes the most stress for trainees. It involves a combination of formal assessment of live material in the form of a recorded session and supervision reports across the length of the course. Like role-plays, recorded sessions can feel very exposing. However, they are an excellent method of learning and building competence (Muse *et al*, 2022).

Recordings of live material

The minimum training standards for a level 2 accredited course require three assessed recordings. These will be of closely supervised cases. They should be of three different presentations and need to include at least one depression case. On training courses, you are advised to record as many sessions as you can to maximize your learning opportunities. This means asking for consent from every patient. Your university will provide you with a consent form as it is necessary to declare that you are a trainee and permitted to use the recorded material. You are likely to be nervous about asking people, but don't make assumptions as most people agree. They always have the choice to withdraw their consent at any time. If they are anxious about being recorded, then you can suggest the camera face you only. Although not as good as a recording of both of you, it will provide sufficient information to assess your skills.

Previously, audio recordings were deemed satisfactory for assessment, but this has been discouraged by the BABCP for several years in favour of video feedback. No one likes seeing or hearing themselves on video, especially when being assessed and rated for clinical performance. However, the more you expose yourself to this practice the easier it becomes.

Rating yourself using a credible rating scale of CBT competence is a very complex task and takes time to master. There are many elements you are being assessed on, so first familiarize yourself with the relevant manual. The most frequently used scale is the Cognitive Therapy Skills (Revised) (shortened to CTS-R), which was developed in the 1980s and revised by Blackburn *et al* (2001). A more recently developed scale is the ACCS (Assessment of Core CBT Skills) by Muse *et al* (2017). Links to both manuals are presented in the references section and on the Resources page. The competency scales cover skills relating to CBT structure, style, and content. Examples of each of these are provided in Table 9.5.

Table 9.5 – Skills relating to CBT structure, style & content

CBT element	Examples	Skills
Structure	This refers to the mechanics of a CBT session and includes: ■ Agenda setting ■ Reviewing homework ■ Pacing ■ Focus on an intervention ■ Setting appropriate homework	This requires good time management but also an ability to be flexible. This includes the ability to zoom in and out during the session, focusing on a specific issue while holding the bigger picture in mind. Flexibility can also mean agreeing to change direction if necessary and adapting the agenda. Pacing helps to maximize the gains from each session and provides flow. This includes saving sufficient time to set a meaningful piece of homework that follows on from the content of the session.
Style	Although the structure and content are essential to maintain fidelity to the CBT model, how you approach therapy includes your personal style. This can be seen as the art and science of CBT. It allows you to be authentic and creative rather than purely mechanical. Style aspects include: ■ interpersonal effectiveness ■ collaborative ■ checking understanding ■ flexibility in approach ■ creativity	The therapeutic bond requires us to be authentic, so we need to show some personality and identity. We are all unique so our style will vary also. The techniques take us so far, but the bond allows a deeper understanding. Skills include active listening, checking understanding from both sides and helping to understand from a CBT perspective. This requires skillful use of formulation and any CBT model appropriate for the person and presenting problem. Style can change over time, with confidence. For example, as a trainee, you are likely to rely heavily on printed handouts – but with more experience and understanding you can be creative, adapt to the individual's needs and think on the spot more.
Content	This refers to the application of the CBT model within each session. It should be evident that it is a CBT session by the content. This is a mixture of using a formulation as an explanatory framework and interventions that target therapy goals.	Formulation is a critical skill that provides the roadmap for understanding a presenting problem and how to address it using a CBT approach. Referring to the problem statement and goals in the session is another way of making the content relevant. The interventions will be based on the chosen model, and this will take time to learn. As a trainee, you won't be expected to do everything perfectly. Your tape (recording) will be marked according to the stage of training.

Figure 9.1 – Preparing live material for assessment

Tips for preparing recordings

- Ask for consent from every person
- Make sure you have suitable recording apparatus
- Be mindful of safe storage – encrypt videos securely
- Label each recording clearly – date, initials of client, session number
- Record as many sessions as possible
- Exposure – watch them!
- Practice self-rating
- It's okay to focus on particular skills instead of all the criteria each time
- Develop a habit of selecting extracts for supervision
- Try not to compare yourself to others

For assessment you need to provide:
- Brief description of the case
- Context of the recording: session number and overview of the contents
- A self-rating for the taped session

There are some very useful online resources to help you prepare tapes for CTS-R rating. See the Resources section. Figure 9.1 above provides some tips for preparing recordings.

Clinical supervision

This is the other means by which your CBT skills are assessed during training. Chapter 13 provides a comprehensive overview of how to get the most from supervision at all stages of your CBT career and should be read in conjunction with this chapter. In this section, we focus on specific aspects of supervision that apply during CBT training.

Clinical supervision provides the evidence of clinical skill development across the course. This is partly through receiving the required number of hours of closely supervised cases (logged in the portfolio) and through your supervision log. This is a reflective account of the learning from each supervision session. During training, you receive supervision in groups with fellow trainees. This allows further learning through the sharing of cases. There is a formula for calculating how much supervision time you can log which takes account of the shared learning.

> Group supervision formula = number of minutes divided by number of trainees times two
>
> So, in a two-hour group supervision session with three trainees it would be as follows:
>
> 120/3 x 2 = 80 minutes

Through regular supervision sessions you can practice skills, ask questions and share case conceptualizations in a safe space. Your course supervisor will have specific skills for working with trainees and maximizing learning for your stage of training. This is the zone of Proximal Development (ZPD), where you are being nudged out of your comfort Zone but not so far that it is beyond your capability. This is expanded in Chapter 13.

You will also receive clinical supervision in your service setting. This may be individual or group supervision, depending on the service. They will also have a different focus in terms of case management, so learning may not be as theoretical. There may also be differences of opinion or perspectives between your course and practice supervisor. You should not take the same case to two supervisors, so this should minimize any confusion caused by supervisor position.

Tips for getting the most from supervision during training include:

- Prepare a supervision question to help you stay focused during the session.
- Use the case that you need the most support with rather than the one you think is doing best.
- Try to select a video extract for each session relating to your case as this will bring it to life.
- Don't avoid bringing recordings for fear of judgement.
- Your question can be skills related such as practicing imagery rescripting or introducing a worry diary.
- Don't interpret feedback as criticism. Your supervisor just wants you to learn and progress.
- Try to avoid comparing yourself to other trainees in supervision. All experiences will be unique.
- Take notes on all contributions as these will be part of your reflective log.
- If you have any issues with your supervisor, try to address these with them directly one-on-one before they escalate. If you continue to find supervision problematic, then see the course lead.
- Avoid discussing personal grievances openly with other students. This is not professional or appropriate.

Summary

This chapter has provided an overview of CBT course contents and expectations. Consideration has also been given to how you can acclimatise yourself to the trainee role. The next chapter looks specifically at how to manage failing an assessment or a whole course. This does not need to mark the end of your CBT journey. The same message applies to other challenges highlighted throughout this guide. In many ways, the most essential resource required for a CBT career is resilience.

Chapter 10
Managing rejection and failure

We have stressed the fact that becoming a CBT therapist takes many years and involves multiple challenges. It is common to experience rejection from trainee places or job interviews due to the competitive nature of the funding within psychological therapy services and universities. During training, it is also common to fail a piece of coursework on the first attempt. Even the most competent and experienced practitioners can experience rejection or fail a piece of coursework. You must learn to manage this from an early stage in your career journey to minimize the long-term effects.

This chapter considers some broad themes in relation to rejection and failure before and during CBT training. This includes what may seem like a worst-case scenario, which is failing the whole course. Even in this distressing situation, however, there is hope that you can continue your CBT career journey. Formulation is a useful framework to help us understand why some of us are more fearful of rejection and failure. Resilience is a theme running through the chapter, with Padesky and Mooney's (2012) personal model of resilience (PMR) suggested as a practical approach. This sits alongside other techniques and theories from CBT that can help to manage rejection and failure, which supports the CBT from the inside-out, self-reflective model espoused by Bennett-Levy *et al* (2014).

A storied account of Zack's (a pseudonym) CBT career journey is threaded through the chapter. His is a remarkable story of resilience after a series of rejections at interview stage, then, once on a CBT course, failing several assignments. Adverse life experiences led to delays and pauses in his journey, but several years on he is a successful CBT therapist who is openly proud of his unrelenting determination to reach his goal.

Nobody sets out to fail

Most people set goals because they want to achieve them. You may lack confidence or you may fear failure, but it is unlikely that failure begins as a goal. Normally, the goal is an aspiration. Below is the first part of Zack's story, which we have called 'The Dream'.

> ### Part 1: The dream
> I always wanted to work with people, and during my careers talk at college, 'criminologist' came up and I thought "that sounds good". I completed my degree and was surprised with a 2:1, which gave me the push to apply for an MSc in forensic psychology. The 90s TV show 'Cracker' had become a hit, and everyone wanted to be a criminal profiler, including me.

Having a dream and a goal is great. Some people drift for years not knowing what they want, and some people never find a satisfying job or career. There is a feature in Zack's dream statement that most people in the healthcare professions will recognize – wanting to work with people and make a difference. It is important to hold onto the dream no matter what. The next part of the story outlines the reality, which is that life can get in the way of our dreams. For Zack, this was the case.

> ### Part 2: Reality and dream adjustment
> After aiming to work for the Post Office for a few weeks while I completed my MSc, I stayed for three and a half years, dealing with customer complaints and refunding lost parcels. I was lucky; I'd gained a placement at a prison while on my MSc and I was able to secure a role there as a trainee forensic psychologist. After a year of commuting, at the age of twenty-six, I was able to leave home, and I thought I would never return. However, my dreams of qualifying were not panning out.
>
> After eight years, I left, slightly deflated, and joined a local community criminal justice drug team. A different environment to what I'd been used to, but I found that I was still working with the same client group. I wanted to work therapeutically and had heard about the IAPT programme and wanted to train as a CBT therapist.

For Zack, this started a long journey of trying to get accepted onto a high-intensity training (HIT) course.

> ### Part 3: The long road to acceptance
> Over eighteen months, I had six or seven interviews, but just couldn't seem to land a role. I'd completed a PGCert in cognitive behavioural therapy but was still struggling. I felt like I was in a position to get my CV accepted, but I flunked every interview I was given.
>
> Finally, in 2011, I was accepted onto a course. This was the good news. The bad news was that I had to relocate and leave my wife and children for the course duration. So, in my mid-thirties I moved back in with my folks, and the twelve-month course turned into eighteen months.

Getting onto a course was not the end of the struggles for Zack. Not only had moved away from his family, and back in with his parents, to devote his time to a course that was miles away from home, but the demands of the training, failing assessments, and stresses within his family, meant that the process took longer for him.

> **Part 4: CBT training and life events**
> The IAPT training was hard, and I failed quite a few tapes. I had pressure at work and at home. But the hard work paid off: I passed the course, and I was able to get a job closer to home.

This is not the end of Zack's story. We can already see his determination and resilience in these extracts. Later in the chapter, we learn what helped him overcome these setbacks in his journey to what was to become an extremely successful CBT career.

Separating the situation from the person

When we fail something, it is easy to start thinking that we are a failure as a person, but this is not true. We can relate this to CBT theory as, in this case, our thinking is affected by the emotional reaction to the situation (failing). Our brain is highly aroused at these times, making thinking more threat-focused. This leads to some common thinking habits:

- Overgeneralization
- Catastrophising
- All-or-nothing (black-and-white) thinking
- Emotional reasoning
- Critical thinking
- Negative comparisons
- Mind reading

Negative core beliefs become activated when a rule is broken. This may be related to very high standards or expectations. You may have some negative core beliefs about yourself that are more easily activated when you do not perform as well as you expect. These include:

"I am a failure."

"I am not good enough."

"I am stupid."

When these beliefs are activated, they will seem very convincing, like facts. We will be reminded of times in the past when these beliefs have been activated and it can be very painful. We are likely to ruminate on failing an assignment or interview, which maintains the distress and reinforces the belief. This is through a combination of the content thoughts and the thinking processes, such as the thinking habits, attentional focus on threat and excessive worry and rumination.

We need to break the cycle of rumination as it leads to hopelessness and is demotivating, preventing us from trying again. There are various ways in which we can do this by using the tools of CBT. Before we consider some techniques, it will be useful to reflect on how you normally respond to failure.

> ### Reflection point
>
> Think of a time when you have failed at something in the past. Consider the following questions:
> - How distressed did you feel on a scale of 1-10?
> - How long did the distress last?
> - How did this impact your behaviour?
> - Did you manage to move on from it? If so, how?

If you have managed to overcome situations in which you have not performed as well as you had hoped, then this demonstrates your resilience. We keep returning to this as it has been identified as an essential quality for CBT therapists – the ability to pick yourself up after a set back without engaging in excessive self-critical thinking.

Using CBT from the inside out

We have already established how useful it is to apply the theory and practice the techniques used in CBT to gain perspective on our beliefs and reduce the distress caused by them. The following sections cover a range of techniques and practices to help overcome the disappointment of rejection and failure.

Building resilience

In Chapter 2, we discussed the qualities necessary for becoming a CBT therapist, and resilience was identified as a key quality. Padesky and Mooney (2012) published their four-step model for building a personal model of resilience (PMR) using a strengths-based approach to help the person recognize and build on current strengths. This fits nicely into the inside-out framework of CBT as we can apply it to ourselves.

The PMR encourages reflection on when we have overcome a challenge in the past. We need to ask ourselves how we overcame it and apply this same approach to other challenges and problems. The four steps are presented in Table 10.1 alongside an example of how to apply them.

Table 10.1 – Outline of Padesky and Mooney's (2012) PMR and example

Steps to the personal model of resilience (PMR)	Example of how to apply the PMR
1. Identify strengths in relation to overcoming problems in the past.	I had to travel to a new place and my navigation system wasn't working in my car. I found an app on my phone, had a paper map and asked my dad how to get there. I was able to find more than one solution.
2. Develop a personal model of resilience based on these strengths.	I can think creatively and problem-solve. I can use my initiative and I can also ask for help.
3. Plan how to apply these strategies in current and future problem areas.	When I fail at something, I can think of different ways to approach the problem next time, and I can ask for help if I need to.
4. Test them out using behavioural experiments focusing on resilience rather than the outcome.	I can test this out by setting some experiments: ■ Read the guidelines again to make sure I understand them. ■ Process the feedback from the failed activity. ■ Be creative in how I approach it next time. ■ Ask for help if I am still unsure.

Look back at your answers to the questions in the 'Reflection point' box above. Now try to expand on this by applying the PMR. Test it out in other areas of your life to strengthen your belief and confidence in your resilience. Padesky and Mooney (2012) suggest the use of imagery and metaphors to reinforce the development of the PMR.

Threat-opportunity continuum

Failure and rejection put us on threat alert and our thought processes very black and white, leading to all-or-nothing thinking and behaviours. It also means that the object of the threat (the CBT course, in this instance) is viewed in negative terms, characterizing it as a *problem*. This is likely to affect your confidence. To break the all-or-nothing thinking we need to approach the 'problem' with a different mindset. Rather than viewing the threat as all or nothing, we use a continuum with threat at one end and opportunity at the other end, and we want to consider all the potential opportunities that approaching the feared activity could afford. This also applies to failing an assignment and having to re-write it.

The threat is associated with failing again and what this would mean. This is likely to be a stream of 'what ifs' relating to uncertainty which makes you question your ability to be successful. Even confident trainees will have self-doubt at some points. The threat-opportunity continuum will allow you to focus on the opportunity end, which will include recognizing the benefits of re-doing each piece of work or clinical skills practice to achieve your goal of becoming a CBT therapist.

Imagery techniques

The opportunity end of the continuum can be approached by using imagery techniques. This can be through meditation, by closing your eyes and imagining overcoming any challenges you are worried about, or fast forwarding to the future and imagining yourself as a competent and confident CBT therapist. By doing this, you are activating the right-side of the brain, which allows more creative thinking. This reduces the arousal of the threat system and helps you to feel more relaxed.

You can also achieve this by using art or other creative media to draw a picture or mind map of where you see yourself in the future. By practicing imagery techniques, you are providing an opportunity to experience the effects of this well-established CBT approach to treating anxiety and depression. Relating back to the PMR, you can use imagery to enhance the strengths identified in the model. For example, after hearing you have failed an assignment, imagine yourself at an easel exploring creative ways to produce the re-submission.

Another way to use imagery is to help distance you from the failed interview or piece of work. In other words, separating self from situation. Close your eyes and visualize yourself holding a piece of paper with the word 'failed' on it. Begin by seeing the piece of paper held on your forehead as if a label. Now imagine gradually lifting it away from the body and holding it out in front of you. See the words and the piece of paper getting smaller and eventually let go of the paper completely and see it fly away into the distance. This will allow you to view the failure as part of the past and not something stuck to you as a label.

Mindfulness

We discuss this in much more detail in Chapter 14 on managing stress, but mindfulness should be an everyday practice to experience optimum effects. It encourages present-focused thinking which reduces the tendency to engage in excessive worry and rumination about the demands of life, including those of your course. Bringing your attention back to the here-and-now will also help you to focus on what needs doing in that moment and reduce procrastination.

Some common mindfulness techniques include:

- Meditation
- Paying more focused attention to the five senses when doing any task or activity
- Going for a mindful walk to break the freeze mode when worrying and ruminating
- Breathing exercises to calm the brain's arousal

A guide to mindfulness is presented on the Resources page.

Self-compassion

Another repeated message throughout this guide is the importance of practicing self-compassion, which can help us to soothe the distress we might feel at failing or being rejected at interview. It is easy to fall into self-critical thinking which becomes ruminative and has a negative impact on mood. When mood is low, it is harder to approach tasks and motivation is reduced.

In the first instance, we need to recognize the distress caused by failing. Rather than immediately engaging in self-critical talk we can take a step back and try to soothe or nurture ourselves. Try this reframing of typical self-critical thoughts relating to failure.

Table 10.2 – Reframing self-critical thoughts

Self-critical thought	Reframing
I'm rubbish at interviews	I tried my best at the interview, but I found this one very hard and anxiety-provoking.
No wonder they didn't give me a place	This performance isn't a reflection of my potential. They could only decide based on what they saw.
I didn't deserve to get a place	Not getting a place this time has upset me. I don't deserve to suffer for being disappointed.
I don't have what it takes	This is a learning opportunity. I can try again, and I can succeed.
Everyone thinks I'm a failure	People who care about me don't think this and won't want me to think it either.
I'm not good enough	This is not a reflection of me as a person. There are many examples where I have achieved things.

This can be combined with the other techniques above. Imagery can be used to develop a self-compassionate image to protect the wounded self, and mindfulness encourages refocusing on the present moment to reduce the distress of self-critical thoughts.

Reflection point

To use a CBT from the inside-out approach, try out the techniques listed above. Which one(s) did you find the most helpful? What did you notice about the emotions you felt before and after using the techniques? And how can you build on this learning experience? Make a plan.

Remaining hopeful

The message throughout this chapter is one of hope. Zack's story is inspiring as it details a journey of twists and turns and multiple setbacks, but he remained on the path that led to his dream and ultimately to a very successful career.

> ### Part 5: Reflecting on my journey
> My path to becoming a cognitive behavioural therapist hasn't always been fun, but I have learned a lot about myself along the way. My career has been varied; I've joined and resigned from IAPT twice, both while working in private practice on the side. I've taught at university on a PG Dip CBT course for eighteen months, had a twelve-month stint at a personality disorder service, and now have a therapist role in an early intervention team. I'm forty-six. In my twenties, I thought I had my path laid out. Finding this career I'm so passionate about in my mid-thirties seemed inconceivable to me. But I wouldn't have had it any other way.

Summary

This chapter has addressed the difficult subject of failure and rejection at interview. Zack's experience is used to inspire you to move past these challenges. Practical suggestions are provided using a CBT from the inside-out approach, which encourages the use of theory and interventions that inform CBT practice. They are designed to allow you to take a step back and gain perspective, recognize your strengths and separate the situation from you as a person. The take-home message from this chapter is to maintain hope and not to let go of your dream. As upsetting as it is to fail, you are not alone and there is help available to nudge you forward in your journey.

Chapter 11
Accreditation

We discussed accreditation briefly in Chapter 1. This was within the current UK context, with the British Association for Behavioural and Cognitive Psychotherapies (BABCP) being the leading professional organization and accrediting body. They set a standard of practice and training based on the minimum training standards (MTS) required to become an accredited practitioner. Once accredited, you will appear on the CBT register for UK and Ireland, which can be accessed by the public and potential employers.

If you have completed a level 2 accredited course, then you will meet these standards on successful completion of the training course. The process of accreditation is straightforward as the university will verify your award. If you have not completed a level 2 accredited course, there will be some additional requirements you will need to meet before you can apply for accreditation. If you do not have a core profession, then you will need to complete a KSA portfolio as part of the application process. Chapter 7 provides a detailed account of preparing a portfolio for entrance to a level 2 accredited course. The KSA process is the same for all applicants without a core profession, so refer to the information in Chapter 7 and the KSA guide on the webpage.

The accreditation process can be confusing, time consuming and stressful. This chapter discusses the different types of accreditations that form the CBT register, the requirements for each, and suggestions for completing the application process. Information is accurate at the time of writing, but it is always advisable to check directly on the BABCP website at the time of application in case any of the guidelines have changed.

Why accreditation?

You do not have to become accredited with the BABCP. The title of CBT therapist is still unprotected, which means that there is no legal requirement to be part of a professional register. However, as discussed earlier, this leaves the public at risk of poor-quality and potentially harmful therapy. The BABCP have set standards of practice and training to protect people seeking cognitive behavioural therapy by way of the CBT register. The register covers five types of professional, each with a specific set of standards. These are:

- Cognitive behavioural psychotherapists (referred to as 'CBT practitioners' on the drop-down menu of the register) including those trained in rational emotive behaviour therapy (REBT).
- CBT trainers
- CBT supervisors

- AEidence-based parent trainers
- Wellbeing practitioners, including:
    - Psychological wellbeing practitioners (PWP)
    - Children's wellbeing practitioners (CWP)
    - Education mental health practitioners (EMHT)

Accredited evidence-based parent trainers (EBPT) are practitioners with specific core skills and knowledge within this specialism. They work with children and their families and are highly skilled. Wellbeing practitioners are not the same as accredited therapists but are included on the register if they have met the standards set for wellbeing practitioner registration with the BABCP.

In 2023, the BABCP CBT UK and Ireland register was approved by the Professional Standards Authority (PSA). According to the BABCP website (CBT register page), "This means that BABCP and AREBT have satisfied the PSA's high standards in our governance, managing of the register, providing information, complaints handling, as well as the standards we expect of our registrants".

Within UK psychological therapy services, employers are increasingly expecting CBT therapists to be accredited. For newly qualified therapists, there may be a reasonable time scale given in terms of working towards accreditation, for example if the trainee completed a level 1 accredited course and is required to make up some additional elements of the minimum training standards.

Although accreditation aims to provide a level playing field in terms of quality standards for CBT clinical practice, it could be argued that it also potentially causes a divide within the CBT community. The process is expensive, and some practitioners may be highly skilled and experienced but fall short of the MTS or do not have adequate time or money to complete the requirements for accreditation. There is a risk, then, that it could become divisive and exclusionary, only accessed by the most privileged therapists. The cost of remaining accredited and maintaining membership is significant, so means testing could be a way to encourage inclusion.

It should be said that the BABCP have widened their scope from England to include the rest of the UK and Ireland as having equivalent standards.

Another issue is the lack of widespread availability of the minimum training standards and core curriculum requirements *before* CBT training. One of the reasons for writing this book is to help people make informed choices about pathways to becoming an accredited CBT therapist. Unfortunately, without this information, it can add years to the process, which can limit your career opportunities.

Remember that, in addition to meeting the MTS, you need a core profession or to complete a KSA portfolio.

Criteria for accreditation

To become accredited as a cognitive behavioural psychotherapist, you must:

- Be a BABCP member
- Be a resident of the UK, its territories or Ireland
- Have a relevant mental health core professional training to degree level or provide evidence of equivalence by completing a KSA portfolio
- Show how your CBT training meets the BABCP's minimum training standards (MTS) and adhere to their Standards of Conduct, Performance and Ethics for the Practice of Cognitive and Behavioural Psychotherapies
- Use cognitive and/or behavioural therapies as your main (or one of your main) therapeutic models in clinical practice
- Show at least two episodes of live supervision in the twelve months practice before application

Accreditation pathways

The minimum training standards can be met via course accreditation. Level 2 meets all the requirements, and level 1 accredited courses meet most of them. Some clinical psychology doctorate programmes have course accreditation status (check the course accreditation page on the BABCP website). There are different application forms for each pathway or circumstance.

Practitioners who were previously accredited but have been out of practice for a period will need to complete a 'Return to Practice' pathway to become re-accredited.

If you completed a non-accredited course in the UK or Ireland, or completed professional training abroad, then you will need to check you meet the main criteria above and provide evidence of how you met the MTS. In some circumstances, the BABCP will also consider practitioner accreditation for people who have not completed or who have failed a CBT course. These would be treated as special cases and need to be explored via direct contact with the accreditation liaison team before completing any documentation.

> ### Reflection point
>
> Do you want to become accredited? What is your current status regarding MTS?
>
> Use Table 11.1 to see where there are any shortfalls and how you can address them.

Mapping the accreditation and criteria minimum training standards

If you have not completed a level 2 accredited course, then you will need to provide evidence of meeting the accreditation criteria above. You need to demonstrate how you meet the MTS. Table 11.1 provides the MTS and can be used as a checklist. Suggestions for meeting any gaps are included. A blank copy of this table is available for download on the Resources page.

Only a few suggestions have been included on the table as some elements of the core curriculum are required during the specific training programme. If you fall short of some of the hours, then these may need to be topped up by further training. There are some postgraduate certificate level courses that build on basic CBT training, but make sure they target any identified missing elements of the MTS.

Once you know you have met the criteria, then you are ready to apply for accreditation.

Table 11.1 – Mapping requirements for practitioner accreditation

Criterion	Do I currently meet it?	YES What is my evidence?	NO How can I meet this criterion?
General			
Member of the BABCP.			Join and maintain membership.
Resident of the UK, its territories or Ireland.			
Have a core profession.			KSA portfolio (see Chapter 7).
Use CBT as main therapeutic model.			Increase usage and get a CBT supervisor.
Show at least two examples of live practice in supervision during the 12 months before application.			Start bringing live material regularly.

Minimum training standards and core curriculum			
450 hours of study at postgraduate level, with at least 200 hours of direct structured training by BABCP-accredited practitioners.			Attend BABCP workshops or do some top-up training (as long as provided by BABCP-accredited practitioners).
Of the 200 hours of structured teaching, at least 100 hours need to have been completed by graduation from a postgraduate course and validated by the Higher Education Institution (HEI).			
The remaining 250 hours need to be logged with evidence and can include self-directed study.			Use the portfolio from your course or create a log of self-directed learning. Include certificates of attendance at workshops and CPD training events.
200 hours of supervised clinical practice.			Make up any remaining hours with a supervisor who is a BABCP-accredited practitioner.
40 hours of clinical supervision, as this needs to be at a ratio of one hour of supervision for every 5 hours of clinical practice during training.			
There must be a 50:50 split between theory and clinical skills teaching.			
Assessment of theory and knowledge of the fundamentals of CBT can be through essays, exams or research projects.			
Completion of at least 8 training cases including assessment and treatment under supervision using evidence-based protocols or formulation-driven approaches.			

Across the eight cases, there must be at least two anxiety disorders, one anxiety disorder and a trauma or stressor-related disorder as well as a mood disorder presentation.		
At least four of the eight training cases need to be presented as case studies, covering at least three different presentations, and formally assessed.		If you do not cover four during primary training, then you can have case studies assessed independently by a suitably qualified assessor.
Three cases need to be closely supervised with live material formally assessed either in vivo or through the marking of recorded sessions.		Any outstanding tapes can also be assessed independently.
Of these three cases, at least two should be anxiety disorders, or one anxiety disorder and a trauma or stressor-related disorder, as well as a mood disorder presentation.		
A closely supervised case needs to be taken to supervision at least five times with at least two examples of live practice shared during supervision of these cases.		

Preparing your application

Guidance for applying for accreditation can be found on the 'Accreditation' section of the BABCP website. I advise printing out a copy of the practitioner accreditation application form, which will help you to familiarize yourself with the information required. Remember to choose the right form for your circumstances. The outline of the form below is a general application form (non-level 2 accredited courses):

- Applicant details
- Document submission checklist
- Reports:
    - Supervisor report
    - Professional reference
- Criterion 1 – Core professional requirements and background needed to train in CBT
- Criterion 2 – Professional accountability and practice
- Criterion 3 – Specialist behavioural and/or cognitive training

- Criterion 4 – CBT clinical supervision
- Criterion 5 – Practitioner accreditation declarations
- Submission

Before you start, it is useful to gather all the information you are likely to need, such as training certificates and transcripts and your portfolio from your course (as this often has logs of hours for teaching, supervision and clinical practice during your training). Approach your current supervisor with a copy of the supervisor's report and select a suitable professional referee – it needs to be someone who can vouch for your clinical practice, but it does not have to be a current manager or colleague.

The form may appear daunting at first sight, but make a start at the easiest place by filling in your personal details. Once you have input these details you are more likely to continue. Core professional details require membership and registration of professional bodies and evidence of training. If you follow the KSA route, be aware that this carries an additional cost due to the time needed by the accreditation team to assess the portfolio.

Criterion 3 is the most detailed section. It comprises a series of boxes for you to input evidence of how you met the MTS during your specialist CBT training.

Summary

This chapter has provided an outline of the accreditation process and the different routes you can take. No matter what your circumstances, there are many options to make up for any shortfalls relating to the minimum training standards. If there are too many gaps, then you can consider top-up training. If accreditation is your career goal, then it will be worth it. Although not necessary to practice as a CBT therapist in the UK, accreditation affords more opportunities in the long run and provides a good basis for your personal career development.

Chapter 12
Maintaining skills and knowledge

Qualifying as a CBT therapist demonstrates that you have met the expected standards to complete a training course. Depending on the accreditation level of the course, your next step may be to apply for individual accreditation as discussed in Chapter 11. If you are an accredited practitioner with the BABCP, then you have met the minimum training standards, which means you are considered competent to work as a CBT therapist.

Developing as a CBT therapist requires continued professional and personal development. On completing training, it can feel very daunting to work alone without the intensive support of course staff and service mentors. We have established that it is common among all therapists to have self-doubt and negative therapist schemas. At the point of completing a course, this is likely to be at its highest level. It is important to recognize that *this is normal*. Regardless of background before qualifying as a CBT therapist, everyone will feel a level of anxiety as there is so much uncertainty. This is due to the lack of opportunity to work with every presenting problem during training, or possibly having a breadth but not depth of knowledge due to the length and intensity of the training course.

Now you are qualified, it is time to take a breath and ground yourself. Part of this is accepting that you do not yet have all the skills and knowledge to enable you to work with every type of presenting problem, but this will come with time and patience. It is often stated by course staff and experienced CBT therapists that it can take on average three to five years after training to fully develop your confidence and competence. Resist the urge to identify with the term 'imposter syndrome'. This is purely driven by beliefs, so try not to indulge this thought.

This chapter considers how to retain the skills and knowledge already learned through continued professional development (CPD), self-directed study and self-monitoring. There are certain core skills and knowledge requirements that must be maintained if you are to remain accredited, and this chapter will outline what they are.

Transition from trainee to CBT therapist

Transitioning from a trainee to a qualified post can be challenging, but remember that you meet the standard to practice as a CBT therapist. It will feel like a period of flux after such an intense training course, and this is normal and expected by employers. It is a recognized period of consolidation. All newly qualified healthcare professionals experience this, and some core professions incorporate a transition period during which more support is provided. This is the case in nursing, where a preceptorship model is used to allow time to grow into the role and adjust to the expected level of responsibility.

The level of support you receive as a newly qualified CBT therapist will vary. For this reason, it is important to recognize your own needs and develop strategies to meet these needs. It is common to confuse a lack of confidence with a lack of competence. They are *not* the same. A lack of competence requires action, such as learning new skills, whereas a lack of confidence is driven by worry and requires no action.
It requires tolerance and strategies to help manage the worry. Remember not to label yourself negatively with terms like 'imposter', as this will maintain your anxiety.
Try to use the **positive data log** CBT technique.

Write down all the positive observations you make each day to reinforce your beliefs about your competence. You can also use the Theory A versus Theory B technique here to recognize how worry affects confidence levels.

Theory A	Theory B
I am not competent enough to be a CBT therapist.	I *worry* that I am not competent enough to be a CBT therapist.

To gain a realistic perspective on your current level of competence versus confidence, try the reflection exercise below.

Reflection point

Write a list of all your concerns about working as a qualified CBT therapist. How many of these are specific areas you can work on, and how many are hypothetical worries about not being good enough? Try to let go of the excessive worries and write an action plan for any skills or knowledge areas you believe are lacking.

Low-intensity to high-intensity CBT therapist

The transition from PWP to CBT therapist is a common pathway, so it is useful to consider how to consolidate your knowledge and skills at both levels of CBT delivery. The low-intensity role gives you a broad foundation that is rooted in CBT, so as a high-intensity CBT therapist, you will have a full range of evidence-based approaches to draw on. See this as an asset to celebrate. You made the transition from PWP to high-intensity trainee, so this transition is just a continuation. You already have the following skills, and they will simply be developed further as a high-intensity therapist:

- Caseload management – including time management and organization
- Using CBT-focused supervision
- Formulating a problem within a CBT framework
- Using evidence-based CBT treatment models
- Self-reflection and monitoring skills
- Use of peer support

Later, you may decide to return to a senior low-intensity role or combine low- and high-intensity roles. Chapter 16 addresses this as one of the many options available to you now that you are a qualified CBT therapist.

Working ethically

It may seem strange to address ethical practice at this stage, but this is in relation to ongoing clinical work. It is likely that a code of professional conduct and ethical principles have threaded through your journey to date, as this is essential for entering CBT training. Now that you are qualified, it is important to maintain these standards during the transition to becoming an accountable CBT practitioner.

'Accountability' refers to the legal and moral obligations of healthcare professionals to work within national guidelines and the best evidence to uphold their duty of care to members of the public. As a newly qualified CBT therapist, you are accountable to follow your employer's contract of duty and that of the professional regulatory bodies to which you belong. If you have a core professional background and maintain registration, then you already adhere to their professional code of conduct. Regardless of background, all CBT therapists who are members of the BABCP will be accountable to their standards of conduct performance and ethics. These state the following:

1. You must act in the best interests of service users.
2. You must maintain high standards of assessment and practice.
3. You must respect the confidentiality of service users.
4. You must keep high standards of personal conduct.
5. You must provide (to us [the BABCP] and relevant regulators and/or professional bodies) any important information about your conduct and competence.
6. You must keep your knowledge and skills up to date.
7. You must act within the limits of your knowledge, skills and experience and, if necessary, refer the matter to another practitioner.
8. You must communicate properly and effectively with service users and other practitioners. As part of this process, you must tell people who use your service how they can complain about you and your practice to BABCP and any other regulatory bodies you are accountable to.
9. You must effectively supervise tasks that you have asked other people to carry out.

10. You must get informed consent to give treatment (except in an emergency).
11. You must keep accurate records.
12. You must deal fairly and safely with the risks of infection.
13. You must limit your work or stop practicing if your performance or judgement is affected by your health.
14. You must behave with honesty and integrity and make sure that your behaviour does not damage the public's confidence in you or your practice. In addition, you have a professional responsibility to be open, honest and transparent with clients, patients or service users when something goes wrong. This responsibility is the professional 'Duty of Candour'.
15. You must make sure that any advertising you do is accurate.

Core skills and knowledge

First, it is important to really acknowledge the skills and knowledge you already have. We often need to jump straight into a new role and have little time to focus on or celebrate our CBT learning achievements. The focus will tend to be on the perceived deficits in skills and knowledge, which will maintain your doubts, feelings of threat and self-critical thinking.

Developing a position on CBT

Now that you are qualified, you can take a step back and reflect on what you learned during your training. Your course and lecturers may have had a particular position on CBT that influenced their teaching. This is normal, as CBT has such a broad spectrum of theoretical positions. We introduced this in Chapter 1 as the CBT continuum. From now on, your clinical experience and professional development will begin to shape your personal position. This will build on your critical thinking skills. Every piece of research you read will be part of this process, so make sure you approach reading with a critical mind.

We often know that a piece of academic writing is good or bad but cannot say quite why. We need to be able to substantiate these views and opinions. Most of the criticism will concern the actual style of writing of the author and whether they managed to impart the aims and findings of their research to the reader effectively. When you approach any research paper, book or academic writing, it is useful to have a set of questions to bring to the task. This will enable you to critically analyse the writing in a relevant and appropriate manner.

Ask yourself these questions:

- Does the **title** give you sufficient information about the topic or theme of the article?
- Is the **abstract** clear and easy to understand? Do you get a sense of what the article is about? Does the title match the summary presented in the abstract?

- Does the **introduction** make a good argument for examining the issues under investigation? Are there sufficient references to previous literature to give context to the current investigation? Does the introduction end by clearly stating what is going to be examined- i.e., are there any research questions explicitly stated?
- Is the **design/approach** adopted appropriate for the purpose of the study?
- Are the **methods** appropriate for this kind of approach and study? Do you get a clear enough sense of *how* the research was conducted to be able to replicate it?
- Is the **analysis** clear and appropriate for this research? Is any of the raw data available for scrutiny or is it all 'cleaned up' and reduced to numerical values in tables? Have statistical tests been used, and if so, are they appropriate and clearly explained, or do you get lost in the figures?
- Does the **discussion** explain the analysis in terms of the arguments set up in the Introduction? Is the discussion backed up by relevant and contemporary literature? Are the limitations of the study identified? Are ideas for improvements to the design offered? Is a clear conclusion presented at the end of the article?
- **Overall**, do you understand this paper?

With practice, this process will become internalized and you will be able to critically review articles automatically. A copy of this **critical reading exercise** is available on the Resources page.

Meta-competencies

When considering key knowledge and skills, it is useful to refer to Roth and Pilling's (2007) CBT competency framework, which outlines generic CBT skills and skills necessary to work with specific presenting problems. There are also **meta-competencies** that are deemed necessary to work at a level of proficiency across time and circumstances. This refers to our capacity to use clinical judgement effectively to be flexible while maintaining fidelity to evidence-based practice (Whittington & Grey, 2014). It requires self-efficacy and ongoing reflective practice and learning (Bennett-Levy *et al*, 2014). Castonguay and Hill (2017) noted some additional characteristics of effective therapists as being responsiveness, creativity, a sense of humour and the ability to adapt communication style.

Methods for developing meta-competencies include:

- Self-monitoring competence through the regular recording and rating of practice sessions
- Using supervision effectively to explore new and creative methods in clinical practice
- Developing formulation skills to work more idiosyncratically
- Continuing regular self-reflective practice
- Challenging yourself to explore areas of practice you have avoided

- Basing clinical decisions on the best available evidence, but when this is lacking, thinking laterally to justify your clinical judgement – this may include previous experiences of working with similar presentations or combining approaches based on discussions with other therapists and self-directed study
- Adopting a more flexible approach to practice to maximize opportunities for guided discovery
- Using humour to strengthen relationships with clients by showing your humanness

Developing your formulation skills

Formulation is a critical part of CBT as it enables a shared understanding of the presenting problem from a CBT perspective. It should be at the centre of CBT practice as it facilitates the process of guided discovery inherent in the scientist-practitioner model. When done well, a formulation can change lives. During training, there is so much to learn at a very fast rate and not enough opportunities to apply all formulation frameworks or develop confidence. There is a guide to CBT formulation on the Resources page, but we will consider how to develop some of the fundamental skills relating to formulation.

Formulations can be developed at different levels, starting with a vicious cycle in the here-and-now to understand what is maintaining the emotional difficulty. We can also develop a longitudinal formulation that provides a theory about the onset and development of the person's beliefs and how they become activated and cause distress. Building a formulation is a collaborative process. You are developing an understanding based on the person's lived experience and your skills in using CBT theory and practice to provide an explanatory framework that can make sense of their distress. Resist the temptation to control the process and take the time necessary to do it well. It is a complex skill and will develop with experience. As a trainee you may have worked at a faster pace, so now is the time to slow down and develop your formulation skills.

Formulation begins at assessment and involves more than identifying a vicious cycle. You are observing and listening and starting to make sense of the bigger picture. Although you will normally start with the here-and-now, you will often hear things that begin the process of theorizing about the current problem in its broader context. I use the metaphor of a house with a porch. At assessment, you are on the porch focusing on what is in front of you, but sometimes you can peep through a window and see a bit more. Formulation allows you to zoom in and out when building an understanding between the past and present.

Figure 12.1 – The house metaphor for formulation

Maintenance cycles

When developing a maintenance formulation (also commonly referred to as a vicious cycle), it is important that it be done collaboratively. This means that the pacing needs to be slow enough for the person to assimilate the information. The cycle is an abstract concept, so not everyone is going to understand it easily. It is useful to introduce the brain first, via either a picture or model, and describe the cycle in a concrete way as shown in Figure 12.2. You can download this diagram from the Resources page.

Figure 12.2 – Explaining the vicious cycle effectively

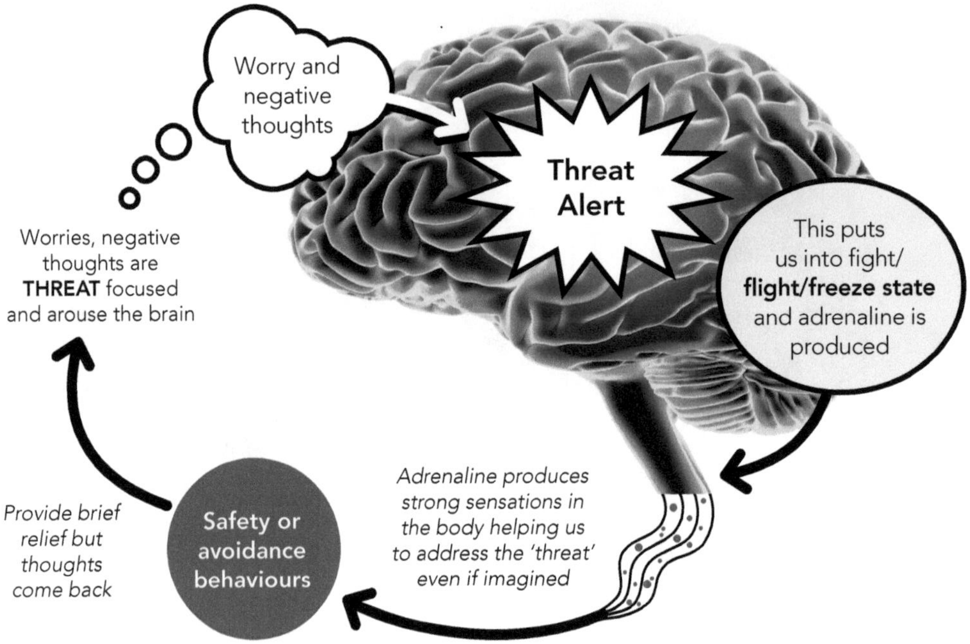

Worry and negative thoughts

Threat Alert

This puts us into fight/**flight/freeze state** and adrenaline is produced

Worries, negative thoughts are **THREAT** focused and arouse the brain

Provide brief relief but thoughts come back

Safety or avoidance behaviours

Adrenaline produces strong sensations in the body helping us to address the 'threat' even if imagined

To encourage conceptualization of the CBT model, we can use this initial maintenance cycle to start the psychoeducation regarding cognitive processes. This includes **attentional focus**, which we know is more threat-focused when we are anxious. By highlighting this to the client, we can also map out the effects of this attentional focus on the formulation – explaining that the physical sensations are a result of **adrenaline** and that their behaviours will fall into the **fight**, **flight** or **freeze** responses. Exploring the pervasive nature of worry and rumination as cognitive processes also helps the client to see how the cycle continues. By adding these features, learning and understanding is increased.

Figure 12.3 – Enhancing the vicious cycle

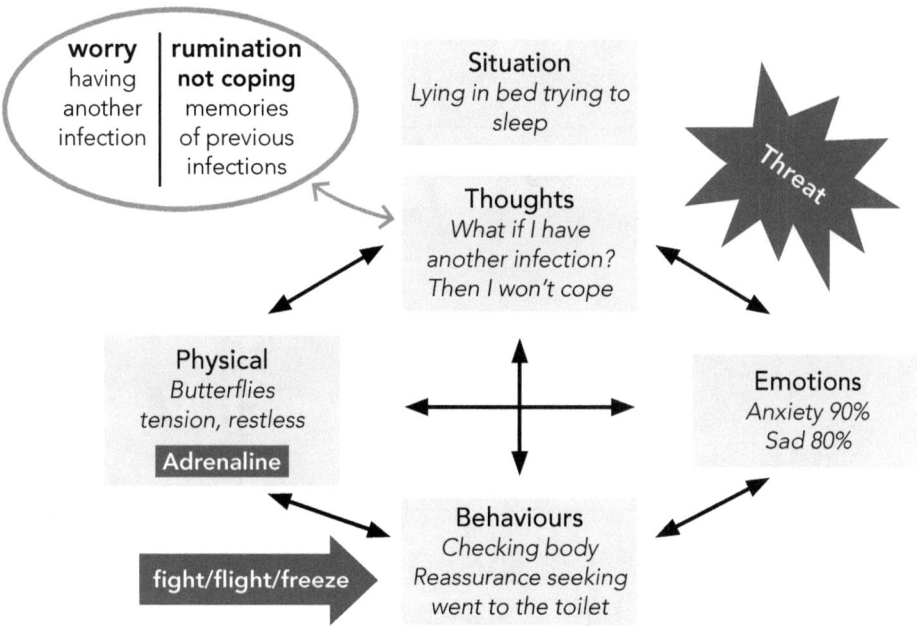

You can also include different levels of cognition to point out a rule or identify a potential core belief. This can be done with good Socratic questioning to explore whether a particular thought is a Negative Automatic Thought (NAT) specific to that situation, or if it resonates at a deeper level and is triggered often and in many situations. Philip Kinsella developed a template that combines cognitive content and processes. Philip and I used it when we worked together, and I have named it the 'maxi formulation' as it provides a link between maintenance and longitudinal formulations. A template and an example of how to use it are available on the Resources page.

Figure 12.4 – The maxi formulation (developed by Kinsella)

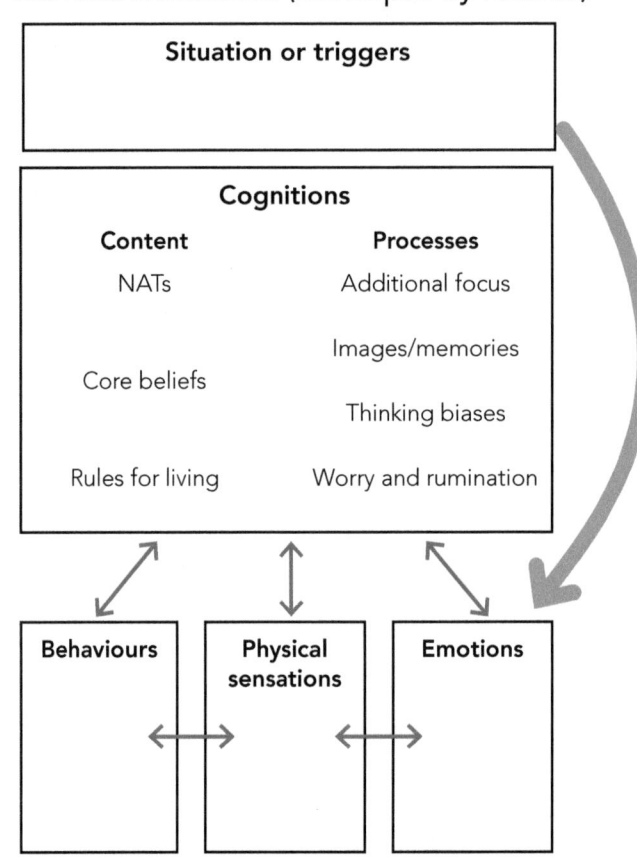

Longitudinal formulation

Longitudinal formulation is part of the cognitive therapy approach introduced by Aaron Beck. It provides an explanatory framework that describes the onset and development of a person's belief system. This helps to understand what might make them vulnerable to developing depression or anxiety. The basic structure starts by exploring the client's early experiences which make them vulnerable to developing negative core beliefs about themselves, others, and the future (this is called the 'cognitive triad'). These key early experiences are often referred to as **predisposing factors**. The resulting **core beliefs** then give rise to **rules for living**, which help us to either negate or minimize the activation of the core beliefs.

Training courses vary in terms of how much they focus on longitudinal formulation, so you may have very little experience once you qualify. It is a sophisticated skill, but is worth taking the time to develop. I view it as a gift of the CBT approach. There is little training specifically on formulation, which is why I chose to develop some sessions in my private practice. You can develop your formulation skills with your supervisor and in peer groups in your service, or through personal self-directed study if you do not work in a team.

Here are some tips for developing a longitudinal formulation:

- Go through a hypothetical example with the client first to explain the principles.
- Go at a pace that suits them.
- Be creative when gathering information about past experiences. Try doing a timeline or ask the person to create a mind map or collage of important events and people from their past.
- Include positive core beliefs and strengths.
- Formulating rules in the negative form can make it easier to test them out. For example: "If I do not put others before myself, then I will be rejected", rather than "I must put others before myself". Seeing what is at stake if the rule breaks will help you to work on them through behavioural experiments.
- Be creative in how you produce the formulation. A typed copy can make it seem rigid and final, whereas using Post-it notes or erasable pens will emphasize how beliefs can become more flexible.

When working with children and young people, CBT therapists tend to avoid creating longitudinal formulations as they can be confusing and difficult to understand. However, even younger children can benefit from understanding the bigger picture surrounding their current difficulties. Dummett's highly recommended article (2010) developed the **systemic CBT formulation**. This is an excellent framework for building a longitudinal formulation that takes account of systemic and developmental factors, including information about the parents or other caregivers, the child's position in the family, developmental issues, school, and other cultural factors. It may be too complex to share with the child, but it provides a sophisticated formulation for the therapist to understand the child's problems and for them to plan an appropriate treatment. It can also be broken down and shared in stages. There is a blank formulation template and an example of a completed one on the Resources page. A simpler formulation for children and young people has been developed by Triste (2023) in her excellent workbook for children of all ages.

Maintaining accreditation

The previous chapter identified the requirements for getting accredited with the BABCP. Whether you are accredited or not, they serve as a useful starting point to guide your personal development.

If you applied for practitioner accreditation, then after the first twelve months you will be required to submit your **first accreditation audit application**. It is important that you follow this procedure, otherwise you will no longer be accredited and will be removed from the CBT register. You need to use the specific application form on the BABCP website. Accompanying the form is the list of criteria you need to meet:

- Hold current practitioner accreditation.
- Adhere to our [BABCP's] Standards of Conduct, Performance and Ethics.
- Be a resident of the UK, its territories or Ireland.
- Be accountable for your CBT clinical practice.
- Show twelve months of supervised CBT practice since being awarded practitioner accreditation, as described in CBT Practice Guidance.
- Provide evidence of and Reflective Statements on five pieces of CBT Continuing Professional Development including at least six hours of CBT skills workshops, as described in CPD Guidance. You can count CPD completed between applying for and receiving your practitioner accreditation award. Include a note with the application explaining this.
- Be receiving adequate CBT supervision, including at least two episodes of live supervision. You can find more details in Supervision Guidance.
- Be supervised by an appropriate supervisor – please see Supervisor's Credentials.
- Provide a Supervisor's Report from your current supervisor.
- Pay the correct fee within **one month** of submitting your application. Please check our Accreditation Fees page.
- Sign all the Declarations.

If you take time off or are out of the country in your provisional year, the first accreditation audit due date can be extended by up to two years so that you can meet the criteria. You must submit an extension request form which can be found on the BABCP website.

Ongoing annual reaccreditation

Subsequent reaccreditation is a similar process, although you won't be asked to show evidence each year. However, you may be selected at random as part of their audit process, so it is important to keep a log of the requirements for reaccreditation each year. This is done via a declaration form where you agree to the following (taken from the BABCP's website):

- You must either be in current CBT practice when you make your Declaration or returning return to CBT practice within twelve months of your Declaration.
- Your practice must be in the UK, its territories or the Republic of Ireland.
- You must make the Declaration even if you have had time out of practice in the preceding year.
- You must have paid your annual Reaccreditation fee. This is due on the same date each year. Please check our Accreditation Fees page.
- You must have adequate, current and ongoing professional indemnity insurance for your practice.

Life-long learner model

The importance of life-long learning in healthcare professions is well recognized (Teunissen & Dornan, 2008). Continuing professional development (CPD) is necessary to maintain skills and knowledge in line with ongoing changes in evidence-based practice and policies. In a systematic review of life-long learning strategies in nursing, Qalehsari *et al* (2017) identified some common strategies used by professionals to maintain learning once qualified. This includes a mixture of independent and collaborative learning methods, recognition of one's own needs and a positive attitude to learning. All these qualities are important to consider within a clinical supervision context.

No matter how long we have been qualified or how many qualifications we have, we are all following the same journey of life-long learning. If you are not currently a trainee, it is useful to think back to when you were, and recall the structure and emphasis placed on supervision as a space to be vulnerable, with the belief that this will lead to improved skills and clinical practice. It is easy to forget how powerful this is as a motivator. We cannot assume that, over time, we reach a level of skill and knowledge that requires no further development. On the contrary, this attitude will prevent learning and growth.

Learning isn't always linear. You may revisit old messages and update your understanding based on discussions with your supervisor that provide a new position or perspective. It is important to be open-minded and humble in your approach to learning. Supervisors need to model this and foster curiosity in their supervisees. Not everyone has had positive experiences of learning in the past, so supervision may feel threatening due to negative memories and the beliefs they activate.

> **Reflection point**
>
> What is your attitude to learning? What experiences have influenced this? What learning style do you have? What are your barriers to learning?

Monitoring your continued professional development (CPD)

Whatever learning you engage in, it is important to log it. This will keep you on track with the CPD requirements for reaccreditation, or evidence of mandatory training required for organizations. Over and above these administrative purposes, monitoring your learning should involve reflective practice. This continues the self-reflective style adopted during CBT training.

Summary

Maintaining skills and knowledge as a CBT therapist is an ongoing process. On completing training, your learning will continue and it may take years before you feel confident. It is important to recognize that **you are competent now**, so maintaining the skills and knowledge learned to date will reinforce this belief. This includes working ethically and maintaining accreditation standards. Formulation is a fundamental skill that will enhance your clinical practice.

Chapter 13
Maximizing clinical supervision

Clinical supervision is a fundamental requirement for all models of psychotherapy and health care professions. It provides the opportunity to develop skills, reflect on practice, problem-solve, and grow as a therapist. During CBT training, clinical supervision is more frequent and intensive as this is a period of rapid learning and skill development. Once qualified, regular supervision will be ongoing. If accredited by a professional body, then frequency and duration will be determined by their requirements. On average, it is expected that you receive a minimum of one to one and a half hours monthly depending on the number of hours worked and your caseload.

Like therapy, supervision can become repetitive and personal goals can slip off the radar. Drift can occur and the sessions may lose focus (Grey *et al*, 2014; Roscoe, 2021b). In a recent review of discussing the effects of supervision on clinical outcomes in CBT therapists, Alfonsson *et al* (2018) found little evidence of a direct impact on therapist competence at all levels of experience. Novice learners appear to apply supervision learning more cogently to clinical practice, but this may be due to several factors. This implies that more experienced therapists may not use supervision to its full potential.

This chapter is aimed at both supervisors and supervisees and includes issues relating to clinical supervision during training. An illustrative overview of this chapter is presented as a guide on the Resources page.

Therapy and supervision as processes

Applying the principles of CBT treatment to supervision practice has been termed the 'reflexive approach' (Milne, 2008). This has been criticized for being too general and broad and does not ensure effectiveness. Milne (2017) went on to describe the three functions of supervision as restorative (by understanding a difficulty and overcoming it we build confidence), normative (guiding supervisees using appropriate methods for their level of experience), and formative (helping them to develop through self-reflection). The model presented here moves on from a purely reflexive approach by viewing therapy and supervision as processes with overlapping elements. A diagrammatic representation of the model is presented in Appendix 4.

The therapy process model considers the interaction between the therapist, the client, and the therapy approach as being interrelated. Success depends on the overlap of these elements. There are also the broader systems around this interaction, which include the culture, relationships, and organizations outside the therapy room. We can apply the same process model to supervision, viewing the supervisor, the supervisee and the supervision approach and methods as being interrelated. Successful supervision requires attention to all three elements. Once we think of supervision as a process, it should reduce the pressure and responsibility we put on ourselves as supervisors or supervisees and help us to navigate the best route to maximizing outcomes.

Zone of proximal development

The zone of proximal development (ZPD) is a concept introduced by Vygotsky (1978) in relation to the development of thinking through language and learning. He described zones of learning as being like stages, and explained that, to develop, we need to be pushing ourselves beyond our current level of understanding to build on our knowledge in that area. Staying at one level impedes learning by being too comfortable, which risks boredom or apathy, but pushing too far beyond our current understanding will also compromise learning as there may not be adequate scaffolding in place to make sense of new information. This can lead to frustration and confusion and cause anxiety (Murray & Arroyo, 2002). The ZPD is the space just ahead of a person's current knowledge, which allows their development through the assimilation and synthesis of new information with existing understanding.

Figure 13.1 – Zone of proximal development

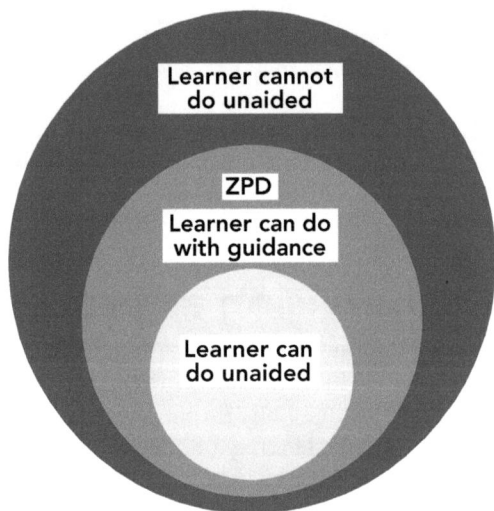

The ZPD has been an influential concept within educational settings. Educators guide the learner to the next stage by focusing on the following three factors:

- The presence of someone with knowledge and skills beyond that of the learner (a more knowledgeable other).
- Social interactions with a skillful tutor that allow the learner to observe and practice their skills.

- Scaffolding, or supportive activities, provided by the educator, or a more competent peer, to support the student as they are led through the ZPD.

Shabani *et al* (2010) provide a comprehensive critique of Vygotsky's ZPD, citing consistent support across time and educational settings. However, the concept of scaffolding is less robust when examined in practice. There is an implication that the teacher provides the scaffold for the learner which contradicts the collaborative essence of the ZPD, risking the teacher becoming didactic in style (Verenikina, 2008).

it is important that the responsibility for learning is still shared between the supervisor and supervisee, so collaboration and a good working relationship are important.

Finding a good fit

In some situations, we do not have a choice of supervisor. This is the case during training and in many large organizations like NHS Talking Therapy services. However, in some organizations and in independent practice, we can choose our supervisor. As with therapy, the bond between supervisor and supervisee is a critical part of supervision, but not the only determiner of success. For example, you may have a very nurturing supervisor who makes you feel safe and secure but who may not nudge you into the ZPD. Arguably, this is impeding personal growth on the part of both the supervisee and the supervisor. Likewise, you may want a supervisor who challenges you, but if their style is overly didactic and critical then this can cause anxiety through threat-system activation making it harder to focus and learn. Getting the balance right can be challenging, but thinking of it as a process like therapy helps us to accept that it will take time to build a bond to an optimum level for learning to be effective and safe.

Regardless of circumstances, it is important to remember that the aim of clinical supervision is to facilitate learning and development and focus on personal goals. In their qualitative study of CBT supervisors' and supervisees' expectations of supervision, Roscoe *et al* (2022) identified some unhelpful assumptions that can contribute to supervision drift. With regards to the relationship, a fear of judgement by the other can interfere with the learning process and can lead to the avoidance of important aspects of supervision, such as reviewing live material together.

Reflection point

Do you make assumptions that your supervisor or supervisee knows more than you? If so, how does this impact your supervision experience? What can you do to address this? Can you see the connection between your beliefs and the therapist's schema?

Setting goals

Having realistic and aspirational goals will help you to get the most out of supervision. Due to the busy and intense nature of the job itself, we may not allow ourselves time to reflect on supervision goals. We may be relying on past goals that are no longer relevant or that are too limited. Setting goals makes you proactive in the process, and supervision should be based on these goals and nothing else. Once we slip into a rut, we may use supervision more like case management, merely updating our supervisor on the progress of cases previously discussed.

If we use the ZPD as an initial marker, then supervision needs to be a vehicle to both consolidate and extend CBT knowledge and skills in order to build competence and confidence. Your supervision goals need to reflect the level you are at and appeal to your interests. This will make supervision more engaging and help with your broader career development. For example, if you have an interest in applying CBT to a particular client group or clinical problem, then developing some goals around this will help you build skills and knowledge in this area.

Examples of supervision goals

I have been supervising CBT therapists at all levels for many years. When I was the course director of a CBT programme, I provided supervision to trainees based on the core curriculum. I have a special interest in long-term conditions and working with ADHD, and I am passionate about formulation and the use of creative methods in CBT. I am trained in working with adults, children and young people, so my experience covers the life span.

I now provide private supervision as part of my independent practice. Some supervisees are attracted by my educational background and some by my special interests. This will guide their specific supervision goals, which I always ask before we start working together. Some examples are given in Table 13.1.

Table 13.1 – Examples of supervision goals

Stage of CBT career	Goals	Comments
Consultant psychiatrist who is a self-funded trainee on a master's course in CBT.	1. To monitor my work with clients. 2. To develop CBT skills to enhance professional growth. 3. To address challenges in the therapeutic relationship. 4. To reflect on the interface between personal and professional issues. 5. To address complex cases within the CBT model.	This course requires trainees to source private supervision. The trainee has a wealth of experience in general psychiatry but wanted to focus on developing knowledge and skills within a CBT model. His goals make sense within this context. As a psychiatrist, the therapeutic relationship is different to that of a CBT therapist and client, and complex cases would be treated with medication rather than psychological therapy. Trainees without this background may have a different focus.
Qualified for five years, moving from an NHS role to private practice.	1. To revisit the evidence-based protocols. 2. To improve my formulation skills. 3. To use more creative methods in practice.	This therapist is very experienced but has been practicing CBT in a very time-limited manner for the past five years leading to a repetitive approach. They wanted to use supervision to reconnect to the fundamentals of CBT they learned in training. This included formulation beyond a generic maintenance cycle, revision of the evidence-based protocols and the use of creative methods to increase engagement.
Working in private practice with little experience of using CBT for ADHD.	1. To understand the signs and symptoms of ADHD. 2. To manage these in the session to maximize engagement. 3. To learn how to adapt CBT for treating ADHD.	This is a highly skilled therapist who had avoided working with people with ADHD until recently after an increase in referrals. She had attended my training and approached me to provide supervision before accepting some referrals from people with ADHD. We used supervision to follow these cases through as you would do with training cases on a CBT course.
Working in NHS role. Has a special interest in using CBT for people with long-term conditions (LTC).	1. To develop a formulation that addresses LTC. 2. To adapt CBT interventions when working with health-related anxiety and depression. 3. To address barriers in therapy.	This therapist has good supervision in her service. Both the supervisor and this therapist have attended training on LTC but have little experience of applying the theory to practice, so she wanted to have this additional supervision to focus solely on these goals.

| Therapist with a background working with children and young people moving into an adult service. | 1. To integrate current knowledge and skills from CYP to working with adults.
2. To apply the evidence-based protocols to adults.
3. To develop therapeutic style for adults. | Another experienced and highly skilled CBT therapist who has worked for many years with children and young people. Her goals were focused on reconciling her current approach with CYP to working with adults. In particular, she wanted to revisit the evidence-based protocols as they were designed for adults and apply them under supervision as in training. |

Reflection point

Supervision should be driven by goals. Take time now to make a list of your current supervision goals.

Make sure a supervision contract is agreed upon between the supervisor and supervisee with the goals regularly reviewed and updated, as you would in therapy with a client.

Addressing culture and diversity in supervision

If we focus only on individual cases in supervision, then we can miss broader cultural and systemic issues. Chapter 4 addressed some broad issues relating to diversity in CBT. All therapeutic encounters occur in a cultural context, and there are also the cultural backgrounds of the client and therapist to consider. When it comes to supervision, there is also the cultural background of the supervisor. Figure 13.2 shows the supervision process diagram which has been extended by adding two outer rings. This includes the nuances and individual differences which may not always be visible. It is essential that we see the full scope of supervision in these terms. Equally, we need to address diversity by asking questions and having a curious attitude. Never make assumptions, and be prepared to make yourself vulnerable by admitting that you do not understand aspects of someone's life.

Hays (2008) introduced the acronym ADDRESSING as a framework to embed culture into therapy:

- **A**ge and generational influences
- **D**evelopment disabilities
- **A**cquired Disabilities
- **R**eligion and spiritual orientation
- **E**thnicity (and race)
- **S**ocioeconomic status, which includes education
- **S**exual orientation
- **I**ndigenous heritage

- **N**ational origin (and generational status)
- **G**ender

Graham *et al* (2013) suggest that focusing on these facets of identity allows for a multicultural approach to counselling and psychotherapy based on a recognition of power and privilege. In the supervision context, this framework could be used to compare the backgrounds of the therapist and the client to make such issues more transparent.

Andrew Beck has written extensively about the importance of integrating culture into all CBT practices including supervision. His book *Transcultural CBT* (Beck, 2016) is a great resource and outlines ways in which we can make supervision more culturally informed. Dummett's (2010) systemic formulation accounts for cultural and developmental factors. This model is aimed at children and young people but can be adapted for adults. It makes a good framework for discussion in supervision and as a developmental tool to build culturally orientated formulations in clinical practice. An example of a systemic formulation is presented on the Resources page.

Figure 13.2 – Addressing culture and diversity in supervision

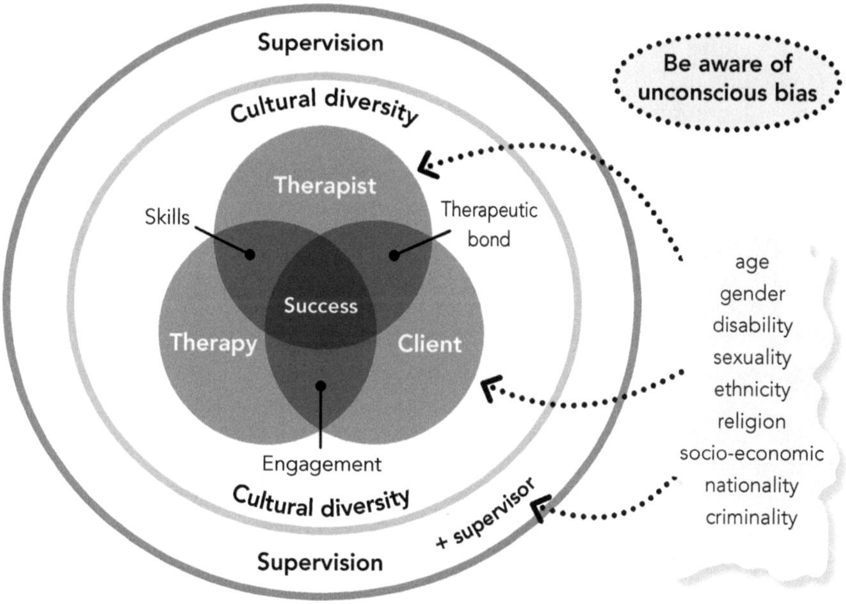

Reflection point

How often do you address issues of culture and diversity in supervision? What specific supervision questions have you used to address these issues? What methods helped you to understand these issues?

Preparing for supervision sessions

Supervision questions encourage examination of specific issues and challenges faced by the supervisee. Without a specific question, there is a risk of drift, and supervision can become case management sessions which serve to update previous case presentations. Christine Padesky's supervision worksheet (also known as the supervision roadmap) provides a series of questions to guide learning before, during and after supervision. It helps to orient to a suitable supervision question. The full worksheet can be accessed on Padesky's website (Padesky.com) and is referenced on the Resources page.

It is vital that we continue to watch **live examples of our clinical practice** beyond training. It is a requirement of the BABCP that live supervision is part of your ongoing professional development. Good practice is to have at least two complete sessions rated by self and supervisor per year, and at least five recorded extracts played in supervision sessions. Supervisors should state this in their supervision contracts.

Presenting cases

Case presentations are the most-used supervision method. Perhaps because of this, they can become repetitive, ill-prepared, and result in case management as opposed to a full critical examination and exploration of a focused supervision question. You should always present a formulation for each case.

To maximize learning potential, *prepare your case presentation in advance*. When training, we are encouraged to prepare cases carefully before supervision. This allows us to focus on the case and start the process of reflection, which will lead to a suitable supervision question. This level of preparation tends to reduce once we are qualified. Often, we are in a rush and do not spend enough time before the session preparing cases. It is common for therapists to access information during the session, forgetting simple details like the age of the client or how many sessions they have had with them.

Be creative when preparing your case for supervision. Make the presentation engaging by using Post-it notes or a mind map to cover all relevant aspects. There is an example of a completed case which was reflected on at the end of therapy on the Resources page. This is a great way to complete a case, and is not often done as we tend to take issues during treatment and then give brief feedback once the person has been discharged. Other creative methods are the use of Canva or PowerPoint, which can be shared easily online.

Critical reflection skills

Reading is the best way to develop a position on your CBT practice. This will enhance your critical thinking skills. You can make the supervision session like a journal club. The supervisor and supervisee can agree on a text to read before the session and have a critical discussion. A critical reading exercise is presented in Chapter 12. Supervision is a space to reflect on practice. So that this process is critical, we need to use a framework or model to maximize learning. We have discussed the therapy process model at the start of the chapter with a diagram presented in Appendix 4. This provides a robust method for critical reflection. An example of how it can be used to explore supervision issues is presented on the Resources page.

Another model that also provides a good explanatory framework to guide reflection is the helicopter view (see Appendix 6. This is a broad systems model used in business. It encourages reflection at three levels – from the **individual** (or micro) level, **local environment** (or meso) level, and **bigger picture** (or macro) level. This refers to the systemic perspective sometimes forgotten in our reflections on specific cases. This model is good for learning from critical incidents, encouraging reflection at the different levels and going beyond 'gut' reactions. It is not the only framework for this and there are many reflective and critical incident analysis models that also allow such examination, but the helicopter view is simple and robust.

> ### Reflection point
>
> What helps you to think critically? Are there any models you use? If not, then try using one in supervision to develop your position on the issues discussed.

Experiential learning

Kolb introduced his experiential learning cycle in 1984 as a way of reflecting on learning in a teaching environment. It outlines the process of learning through the examination of concrete examples which are actively observed and reflected on to inform future practice. It is a simple but eloquent model, and has been used in CBT training and practice as a means for implementing the scientist-practitioner model using behavioural experiments. This has been added to the model in Figure 13.3.

If we keep supervision at an intellectual level, we are limiting the opportunity for active learning. Doing exercises, role-plays and engaging in CBT interventions helps us to empathize with the people we work with by experiencing what we ask them to do. Supervision is an appropriate place to build these skills. CBT from the inside out (Bennett-Levy *et al*, 2016) encourages ongoing active learning and self-reflection. This could be keeping a worry diary or activity schedule between sessions, or doing an imagery rescripting exercise or mindful meditation in supervision.

Figure 13.3 – Kolb's learning cycle as a scientist-practitioner model

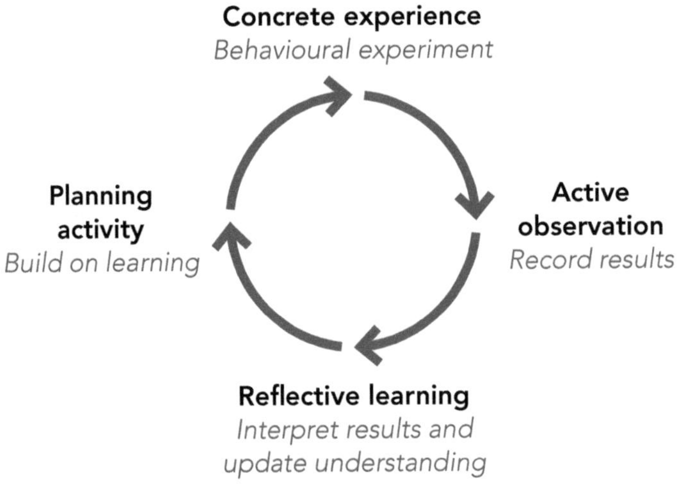

Concrete experience
Behavioural experiment

Active observation
Record results

Reflective learning
Interpret results and update understanding

Planning activity
Build on learning

Modelling in supervision

Supervision is more than troubleshooting. Sometimes things are running smoothly and we cannot identify a specific 'problem' to take to supervision. If this is the case, then you can refer to your supervision goals and see if there is any area of CBT about which you want to enhance your knowledge, for example learning how to apply the cognitive model of PTSD. If you do not have any current patients with PTSD, the supervisor can use some of their case examples to work through. Supervisors can also model rating tapes (recordings) by sharing their own recordings in supervision. The supervisee is likely to be more focused. This is a good opportunity to practice rating recordings when they are feeling less threatened.

By doing experiential exercises in supervision, we are applying Kolb's learning cycle. Here, the supervisor can demonstrate a skill (concrete example), the supervisee observes, both discuss learning and then plan together how the supervisee can apply the skill. This may be immediately in supervision or applied later in practice. This approach is outlined in Milne & Dunkerley's (2010) tandem model of clinical supervision where the front wheel is the supervisor's experience and the rear wheel is Kolb's learning cycle in the session where modelling, observation and collaborative reflection takes place. This moves away from a didactic style of supervision where the supervisor merely tells the supervisee what to do. Modelling in sessions encourages a more academic supervision approach by examining literature to explain clinical decision-making or having a critical debate.

Difficult situations

Supervision should be a safe place to honestly explore all issues relating to clinical practice. This includes difficult situations like ethical dilemmas, disclosures relating to risk or safeguarding, fitness for practice and ruptures in clinical and supervision contexts.

We must always work ethically, adhering to our professional code of conduct. Sometimes situations present that do not have a clear resolution and require a lot of thought and discussion to reconcile. These are ethical dilemmas and should always be brought to supervision. Use an ethical model such as Beauchamp & Childress' (1979; 2013) model of biomedical ethics. This states that as healthcare professionals we need to operate by four principles: autonomy, non-maleficence, beneficence, and justice.

Safety is always the priority. Difficult situations can often be resolved through critical reflection. If a situation can't, then this may mean seeking help or acting outside of the supervision relationship as you would in clinical practice. Supervisors need **supervision of supervision** and should be prepared to discuss issues with professional bodies if necessary.

Peer-supported learning in group supervision

During CBT training, a group supervision model is used. This allows peer-assisted learning (PAL) which is a well-established learning approach within healthcare professional education (Topping, 1996). PAL can take place between practitioners at all levels and provides an opportunity to learn through a process of peer-tutoring. In the 1970s, Bruner (1978) introduced the concept of peer-tutoring as a developmental process whereby newly learned information becomes reinforced by sharing with peers who are at a similar level. It allows the 'scaffolding' of new learning onto existing knowledge and experience required for effective learning within the ZPD. Different models of peer-tutoring have been developed, but the one that is most used in healthcare professional education is reciprocal peer-tutoring. In their systematic review, Gazula *et al* (2017, p65) define reciprocal peer-tutoring as "a form of collaborative learning that involves students of similar academic backgrounds experiencing interchanging roles of tutor and learner".

For group supervision to be effective, Burgess *et al* (2020) suggest that PAL requires two key factors: **agency** on behalf of the learner, which refers to a willingness to engage in the learning process; and **affordance** of the educational setting to provide suitable opportunities for PAL to take place. During CBT training, the educational setting and curriculum requirements provide the affordance for this type of learning. However, the trainee needs to be an active agent in the learning process. This can be challenging due to the demands of the course and lack of confidence. The advice provided throughout this chapter is relevant for both individual and group supervision, but there are some unique features of group supervision, so it is useful to consider these specific tips:

- **Time management** – the supervision time will be shared between the group members, so adjust your supervision question to fit the available time. The time may not be allocated evenly, which requires flexibility and patience – accepting that in one session you may be allowed a long time slot, but at other times it may be shorter.
- **Learn from your peers** – it is tempting to focus all your attention on your own case. PAL allows you to learn from your peers about problems and presentations not yet experienced. Likewise, they may bring something which you can identify with. This allows comparisons and reflections, as required by Kolb's learning cycle.
- **Log everything** – include peer learning on your supervision log.
- **Don't be scared to share** – remember, you are all in a similar position so you should feel safe to share.

Peer supervision is not exclusive to trainees. It is a useful way to check in with colleagues and add variety to your supervision provision. The BABCP accepts peer and group supervision for accredited practitioners. They stipulate that **only time received** in the supervision session will be counted. So, if you have a peer supervision session with one other therapist for an hour, and you split the time evenly, then you can count thirty minutes as supervision time.

Summary

Supervision is a process that goes beyond the roles of supervisor and supervisee. The supervision approach, methods and learning models all contribute to the quality of the experience. To maximize your personal and professional development, you need to be active in this process.

Chapter 14
Managing stress and preventing burnout

We have reiterated throughout this book that the journey to becoming and developing as a cognitive behavioural therapist is extremely demanding. We have also acknowledged some of the common beliefs and thinking styles that can make the job feel even more challenging. These tend to relate to self-doubt and a heightened sense of responsibility for the wellbeing of the people we treat. Over time, we can become stressed both physically and mentally to the point of burnout. This is characterized by fatigue, mood disturbances and reduced functioning. Unrelenting standards and emotional neglect make it hard for us to identify and express our needs.

This chapter aims to help you take a step back and spend some time reflecting on your current state of wellbeing. By using the CBT from the inside-out approach, we will explore a range of exercises and interventions used in CBT practice. This includes mindfulness, worry-management and compassion-focused exercises. Checking in with our work-life balance is also important, so we will include an action plan to commit to some self-care practices. There are some accompanying guides on the Resources page.

Recognizing stress

It is important to distinguish between stress and pressure. We all feel pressure daily, and it can be useful to a point, but when we experience too much pressure without time to recover, it can lead to stress. It is the body's way of alerting you that it is being challenged. Stress is not an illness, but it can affect our wellbeing and make us vulnerable to becoming physically unwell. When we are stressed, the brain chemistry changes and we experience an excess of adrenaline and cortisol which affect the autonomic nervous system. Learning to respond to these signs allows us to develop adaptive coping strategies. The first skill is to recognize when you are stressed and what triggers it. Common symptoms include:

- Tiredness and fatigue
- Poor concentration
- Finding it hard to make decisions
- Being irritable or short tempered
- Tearfulness
- Low mood
- Avoiding social events

Answering the questions below will help you to understand and monitor your stress levels.

> **Reflection point**
>
> How do you know you are stressed?
> - What physical signs and symptoms do you experience?
> - What impact does it have on your emotional wellbeing?
> - Do you recognize what triggered it?
> - How does it affect your behaviour?

Once you become adept at recognizing stress, you need to respond to it in helpful ways. It is easy to fall into patterns of behaviour that maintain the stress, which are usually excessive behaviours such as overeating, increasing your alcohol intake, or spending more time watching TV or on a phone or computer. These are mindless activities and serve to disconnect us. Although you may feel switched off from the stress temporarily, it does not provide physical relief. This requires a proactive approach to allow your mind and body to rest and replenish.

Stress at work

There is a body of evidence that recognizes the impact of work on our physical and emotional wellbeing (Bamber, 2011). The Health and Safety Executive (HSE) is the government body responsible for developing policies and guidelines to maintain safe work environments. They set management standards under UK law, outlining employers' duty of care to ensure the health, safety and welfare of their employees. This includes work-related stress. The HSE definition of stress is "the adverse reaction a person has to excessive pressure or other types of demand placed upon them". The HSE identifies six risk factors for work-related stress:

- The demands of your job
- Your control over your work
- The support you receive from managers and colleagues
- Your relationships at work
- Your role in the organization
- Change and how it's managed

One of the largest independent employment advice services in the UK is the Advisory, Conciliation and Arbitration Service (ACAS). It receives government funding and provides free and impartial advice to employers and employees on any work-related issue. ACAS highlight the importance of recognizing external stresses outside of work that may impact on your work performance. The mental health charity MIND has produced a guide to managing stress at work which includes a wellness action plan. This can be downloaded from their website and a link can be found on the Resources page.

Workplace stress can make you feel powerless. A popular term in occupational stress literature is the 'golden handcuffs' to describe a sense of being trapped at work, and feeling stressed due to the need to earn money. Bamber (2011) introduced a CBT model for overcoming stress in the workplace. He identified three levels of intervention to manage stress. **Primary** interventions are aimed at removing the source of stress in the environment. However, this is not always possible. **Secondary** interventions are measures we can take to protect ourselves from stress such as leading a healthy lifestyle, effective time management, assertiveness and coping skills. **Tertiary** interventions are deemed necessary when stress is at a level where secondary interventions are no longer possible or effective. These include psychological therapy or other internal supports, such as occupational health services or mentoring from a line manager.

Although employers have a duty of care to look after their staff, you may not have an employer and you also need to be accountable for your own wellbeing to ensure you are fit for practice as a mental healthcare professional. You have a duty of care to the people you treat. There are actions you can take to minimize your risk of stress, and strategies that can help you manage the pressure of being a CBT therapist.

Relaxation and downtime

We have established that one of the main symptoms of stress is fatigue. When the brain is highly aroused, we are on constant threat-alert and it is difficult to switch off and rest. Having fatigue affects your physical functioning, which in turn can impact your ability to work and engage fully in meaningful relationships and pleasurable activities, and can make you view yourself negatively. This can lead to burnout. Resting is not just about physically stopping activity – there are different types of rest listed in Table 14.1.

When you are working long hours and feeling continually stressed, you will find it hard to transition between activities and tasks. Pushing yourself too hard leads to an all-or-nothing approach (sometimes referred to as 'boom and bust'), which makes everything feel more demanding. Instead, a strategy of 'little and often' needs to replace all-or-nothing thinking and behaviours. This includes taking frequent breaks in order to pace yourself and allow your brain to decompress.

Table 14.1 – Types of rest

Types of rest	Description
Physical rest	Resting to relieve the body of physical stresses: ■ Sleeping, napping, sitting, or lying down ■ Activities such as yoga, meditation, watching TV, stretching or massage therapy
Sensory rest	Resting to lower the sensory input from the world around you: ■ Closing your eyes ■ Turning off your electronics in the evening
Mental rest	Resting to calm your mind and refocus on things that are important to you: ■ Keeping a notepad around to write down your thoughts ■ Focusing on your breathing
Creative rest	Resting to allow you to sit back and appreciate nature, natural beauty and art to inspire and motivate you: ■ Colouring, painting, crafts ■ Cooking, gardening, decorating
Emotional rest	Resting so you can express genuine feelings: ■ Noting down your feelings on paper ■ Reaching out to a friend, family member or a stranger to talk
Social rest	Resting to reflect on relationships that are positive to you: ■ You may have to turn down plans, to give yourself time to rest ■ It is important to recognize when you need to slow down and take a step back
Spiritual rest	Resting to connect or engage in your religious or spiritual beliefs: ■ This can give you a sense of belonging, purpose and acceptance ■ To engage in prayer, meditation and religious practices ■ Connecting with others who share your beliefs

Progressive muscle relaxation

Progressive muscle relaxation (PMR) is an exercise to reduce stress and tension in your body. It targets the physical sensations part of the CBT vicious cycle. By tensing and then relaxing each muscle group in your body, you will feel an immediate sense of relaxation. When the tension reduces, your mind will tend to settle down too. This can aid sleep if performed at bedtime. It needs to be practiced regularly as it can significantly reduce daily anxiety. There is good research evidence for its effectiveness in several conditions including insomnia and generalized anxiety disorder (GAD). There are links to a script and video to practice this technique in the worry-management guide on the Resources page.

Mindfulness

Mindfulness can help you to focus on your present moment experience, paying attention to what is going on around you, outside your head, rather than focusing on internal worries and negative thoughts. You are not trying to avoid thinking about problems or physical symptoms; rather, you are recognizing that you can choose to direct your attention to something more pleasurable that you value.

The principles of mindfulness date back centuries in the Eastern world, including meditation, which is often associated with Buddhism. More recently, Jon Kabat-Zinn's definition is one of the most highly quoted: "paying attention in a particular way: on purpose, in the present moment, and non-judgementally" (1994, p4). It has long been recognized that worry and rumination focus our attention away from the present moment and prolong the unpleasant feelings associated with unhappiness, fear, anger and other distressing emotions. Pain and physical discomfort cause our attention to focus more on bodily sensations, which we then 'react' to by thinking and behaving in ways intended to reduce the pain. This creates a cycle of worry and rumination which increases emotional distress.

One of the early applications of mindfulness in clinical and other organizational settings was the mindfulness-based stress reduction (MBSR) programme. In his book *The Mindful Workplace*, Chaskalson (2011) provides a detailed description of how to build resilience at work using MBSR.

Mindful meditation

Meditation is a tool used in mindfulness. Some people have misconceptions about meditation, believing we must clear our minds like a 'blank slate'. This is not the aim of mindful meditation. We are trying to increase our present-focused experience by noticing things, sensations and even thoughts, but learning that we can choose to move gently away from them. There are many apps and videos available, and some suggestions and examples are included on the Resources page. A great free app produced by Anxiety Canada is called 'Mindshift'. This has some brief guided meditations on the 'Chill zone' section.

Meditation can feel like an additional demand when you are tired and stressed, but doing short practices more frequently will maximize the benefits. It is not a quick fix, but a preventative and maintenance measure. Experiment with different types of meditation to find one that works for you.

Mindful activities

Mindful activities encourage you to focus on the present moment. If you are finding it difficult to focus, then try a grounding technique first to calm your busy mind. A simple and effective one is called the 5-4-3-2-1. This is related to the five senses. When the brain is overactive, we tend to switch to autopilot which reduces our sensory experience. The 5-4-3-2-1 technique helps us to switch our senses back on and engage with what is happening around us. It is simple to follow. Just take notice of your surroundings and name five things you can **see**, four things you can feel (**touch**), three things you can **hear**, two things you can **smell**, and one thing you can **taste**.

You can extend this grounding technique by going for a walk and using your senses more fully. Notice all the things you can see, hear and smell on your walk. Touch leaves or run your hand along a wall as you walk and pay attention to all these sensations. You can apply this to any activity such as cleaning your teeth or making a hot drink – any activity that focuses your attention on the present moment can be used as a mindful practice. Examples include art and crafts, puzzles and word searches, technical tasks, and purely enjoyable activities that you can become engrossed in. This may be catching up with friends or listening to your favourite music. A mindfulness guide is available on the Resources page.

Maintaining your values

We have emphasized the importance of maintaining your identity through the process of becoming and developing as a CBT therapist. When we are stressed, this may be a sign that we have lost touch with things we value, or are having to compromise our values due to work stress. For example, not keeping in touch with friends because we are too tired.

The values compass is a concept used in Acceptance and Commitment Therapy (ACT). It depicts different domains of our life to reflect on our values in each area. It is a useful way to take stock of where we are right now in terms of maintaining our values. When we focus solely on work, this can overshadow other aspects of our life and we lose balance.

Figure 14.1 – The values compass

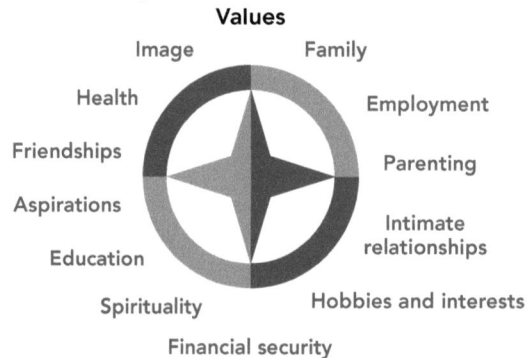

Reflection point

Look at the values compass. Which values are you focusing on most? Which ones are receiving the least attention? What is the impact on your mood and stress level? Can you create a plan to reconnect with at least one of your neglected values over the coming week?

Managing worry

Worrying is a normal thinking process. It focuses your attention on the future, leading you to question or imagine negative things that might happen. If you think of worry as being on a continuum, there is a 'normal' range, where you move up and down depending on what is happening in your life. When you worry excessively, however, it leads to symptoms of anxiety including muscular tension, unpleasant sensations in your stomach such as butterflies or churning, and headaches. When you worry, it is often about things you aren't sure about and want answers to. They typically start with a 'what if...?' and can lead to a worst-case scenario very quickly. At this point, your thinking becomes very threat-focused, which fuels your anxiety. Not all worries will have answers, as they can be hypothetical and may never happen. However, some worries are about problems that do require your attention, such as tasks you have been avoiding. Recognizing the difference between these two types of worry is helpful in identifying what requires action and what does not. The worry tree in Figure 14.2 is a helpful tool.

Figure 14.2 – The worry tree

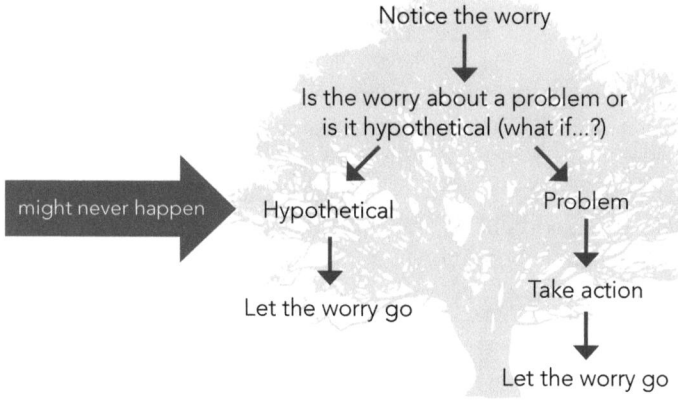

Monitoring worries

Keeping a worry diary is a useful activity as it can help you to get the worries out of your head and onto paper, which can help to diffuse them. It also allows you to identify if they are real problems or hypothetical worries. You can download a worry diary from the Resources page or create your own. Another technique you can use to monitor and manage your worries is 'worry time', which is explained in Figure 14.3.

Figure 14.3 – The worry time technique

The idea with **WORRY TIME** is to provide a designated time when you allow yourself to think about all the worries that have popped into your head throughout the day. It is not designed to **STOP** worry but to **REDUCE** the time we spend thinking about things that are beyond our control.

Step
Set up your worry time
Where? When? How long?

Step
Postpone your worries at all times other than your worry time. Write them down and review at worry time.

Step
At worry time use the worry tree to see if action is needed.

Problem-solving

For worries that are actual problems, applying simple problem-solving strategies will allow you to act and let that worry go. Often our worries relating to work are hypothetical. When we worry excessively, it is harder to identify actual problems that do require our attention. The arousal and anxiety caused by worry can lead to ineffective problem-solving such as rushing to complete a task without adequate planning or considering all options. A basic five-step model for problem-solving provides a structured approach. There is a worksheet for this on the Resources page.

Overcoming procrastination

Procrastination is normal, but when we are stressed and have very rigid beliefs and rules it is likely to occur more frequently. We will avoid things that need doing due to the extra demand it places on us. This will reinforce negative beliefs and self-critical thinking which adds to the stress, making daily functioning even harder.

One technique that helps with approaching tasks and breaking the cycle of procrastination is to have a realistic expectation of how long you can currently focus on each task and identify the factors that may interfere. You can then have a strategy for overcoming these current barriers. Figure 14.4 provides an example of writing clinical notes. You may put this off when feeling stressed at work. Rather than trying to write notes for thirty minutes at a time and finding yourself unable to complete the task, ask yourself what a realistic amount of time is for writing notes in one go. If it is ten minutes, then this becomes a task 'chunk' for this activity, so you will break the notes into 3 x 10-minute chunks. Also, identify any potential distractions and how to overcome them. This will help you to manage your environment, feel more in control of tasks and hopefully reduce stress.

Figure 14.4 – Monitoring task demand and managing your environment

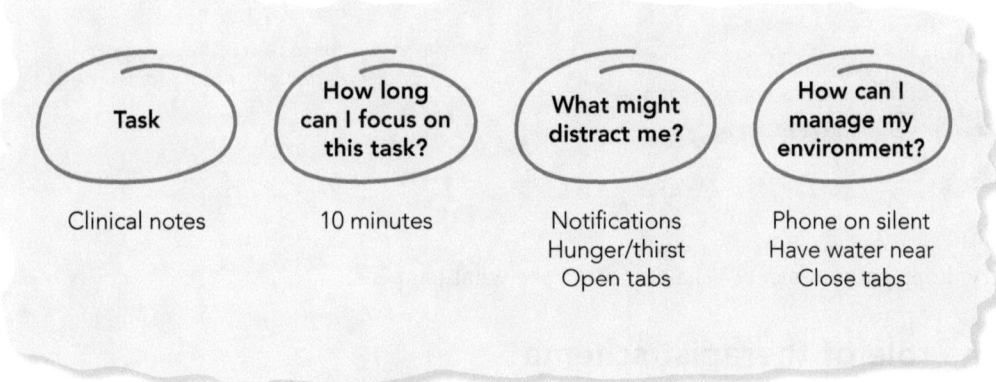

Reflection point

What tasks are you currently avoiding? Is this due to feeling stressed?

Try the task-monitoring technique and see if this helps reduce procrastination.

If stress continues, seek help rather than trying to continue working.

Tolerating uncertainty

If you are a qualified CBT therapist, you may be familiar with the intolerance of uncertainty (IoU) model (Dugas & Robichaud, 2007; Robichaud *et al*, 2019) used for treating GAD. Rather than seeking more certainty (by trying to control situations or prevent harmful outcomes), it is more helpful to **tolerate uncertainty** – recognizing that you cannot control everything. It is useful to recognize what safety and avoidance behaviours you may be using excessively when you are stressed. The list shown in Figure 14.5 is based on Dugas & Robichaud (2007).

Figure 14.5 – Common safety and avoidance behaviours associated with intolerance of uncertainty

Safety Behaviours Things I do MORE of when I feel uncertain	Avoidance Behaviours Things I do LESS of when I feel uncertain
■ A need for lots of information ■ Checking and re-checking ■ Not delegating (doing **everything** yourself) ■ Excessive 'to do' lists ■ Arriving early for things ■ Reassurance seeking ■ Doubting decisions already made ■ Over-protective to others ■ Over preparing	■ Procrastination ■ Not going out (behavioural avoidance) ■ Mental avoidance (thought suppression) ■ Commitments - avoiding or remaining in jobs or relationships ■ Making excuses rather than making decisions (especially when put on the spot)

Try dropping your safety behaviours and see what happens.

The role of therapist schema

We have established that CBT therapists, like all healthcare professionals, tend to have strong beliefs based on the need to help people. The most common ones are unrelenting standards and self-sacrifice, which push us to help others to the point of neglecting our own needs. We discussed the cognitive triad of beliefs about helping in Chapter 2. It is an example of how our beliefs about self, others and the world (the cognitive triad) maintain this drive to push ourselves to help others. Over time, it is unattainable and leads to stress and burnout.

It is important to recognize when these beliefs are active and how you respond. Although difficult, these beliefs can become more flexible through increased awareness and experimentation. Heath and Startup (2020) present innovative and creative approaches to schema therapy. We can use some of these methods to address our therapist schema. As stated in the previous chapter, this should be an integral part of clinical supervision.

> **Reflection point**
>
> Revisit the worksheet on therapist beliefs introduced in Chapter 2. Does the cognitive triad resonate with you? Can you identify which therapist schemas relate to you? What is the impact of these beliefs both at work and in your personal life?

Expressing needs

Before applying any strategies to manage stress, it is necessary to identify your own therapist schemas and the impact they have. One of the most common problems for therapists is the inability to recognize and express their needs. The technique below will help you to identify your needs, consider how you are currently addressing them and evaluate how effective this strategy is. It provides a framework for reflection and to plan experiments using new strategies such as asking for help when you need it rather than pushing on alone.

Need	Strategy	Outcome
To make my avoidant patient engage in therapy.	Try harder. Use lots of different interventions. Ignore the fact that they haven't done homework.	The patient is still not engaging. I am feeling exhausted and resentful and the belief "I am not good enough" is being triggered.

We can see how this strategy of carrying on regardless is not effective in the long term. Asking for help may seem threatening if you have unrelenting standards, but you could see it as an experiment. Making use of the help and support around you is essential not only for your wellbeing but also for developing your skills and knowledge. This may make it more appealing if you recognize how it can benefit you. The example below reframes the need and provides alternative strategies which should lead to a more satisfactory outcome.

Need	Strategy	Outcome
To understand why my patient is avoidant in therapy.	Take to supervision. Apply reflections in practice. Explore avoidance with the patient. Decide if CBT is suitable at this time.	Discussing this with my supervisor helped me to reduce my sense of responsibility.

The reframing in the second example removes the implied responsibility of the therapist to effect a change – "I must make the patient engage" – and recognizes instead that it is a situation that requires understanding from a broader perspective. Avoidance is the issue, and this may or may not be influenced by your clinical approach. By assuming responsibility you will tend the first strategy of pushing harder, which is the drive response to the threat of not getting the patient better. This leads to self-criticism ("I am not good enough") that will keep this threat-driven approach going. By asking for help in supervision, you are engaging with the soothing system which will promote a more self-compassionate response.

Summary

Being a CBT therapist is stressful. We have high standards and beliefs about helping people that often push us very hard. This chapter has highlighted the ways in which stress can impact our physical and emotional wellbeing. By adopting a CBT from the inside-out approach, we can use tools and techniques to manage stress and avoid burnout. This requires constant attention to our own needs and asking for help and support when necessary. This will build your resilience and self-compassion, which are resources required for your long-term CBT career journey.

Accompanying guides and worksheets available on the Resources page:

- Fatigue guide
- Mindfulness guide
- Worry-management guide
- Problem-solving worksheet
- Needs/strategy/outcome sheet
- Cognitive triad example and template
- Task-monitoring form
- Procrastination guide
- Self-compassion exercise

Chapter 15
Your CBT career vision

In Chapter 3, we considered a range of stories from individuals from different backgrounds to illustrate the broad variety of job options available as a CBT therapist. It gave a flavour of what a typical working day could look like in each role. The storied accounts also included details of the journey to get to this point. Returning to these stories will help provide perspective when considering what you would like your CBT career to look like.

The intensity of the journey and the job itself allows little time to step back and view the bigger picture. You may have had an idea of where you wanted to be after training, but perhaps not a clear vision of many years beyond that. It is easy to get stuck in a position that may no longer serve your needs or match your values. This chapter allows a space to reflect on your career to this point and think about what you want moving forward. This involves examining your values.

Although we have not gone into detail about career options for personal and professional development, this chapter allows you to explore your vision and how it may have changed up to the present. You are encouraged to return to this after you have read and considered the information in the following chapters, and indeed as a regular reflective practice to prevent getting stuck in a job that no longer meets your needs or matches your values.

How broad is your vision?

Traditionally in the UK, there have been two clinical pathways for CBT therapists – the NHS (or other public service organization) or private work. This creates a dichotomous way of thinking, and can narrow your vision considerably. Even if this is the basic choice for you at this time, we can expand the possibilities within each pathway as shown in Figure 15.1.

At the basic level of whether you want to work in the NHS or privately, you can get stuck thinking only of the NHS Talking Therapies services formerly (IAPT) or personal private practice. The diagram shows the different settings for each pathway. CBT can be practiced with different client groups within the NHS across a range of services including non-mental health services. There is an increasing recognition that CBT can benefit people with physical health conditions (Kinsella & Moya, 2021) so it is possible to specialize in this area, which may be practiced outside of a mental health service. Some examples include chronic pain clinics, stroke units, coronary care and oncology departments.

Figure 15.1 – Broadening the view of NHS versus private pathways

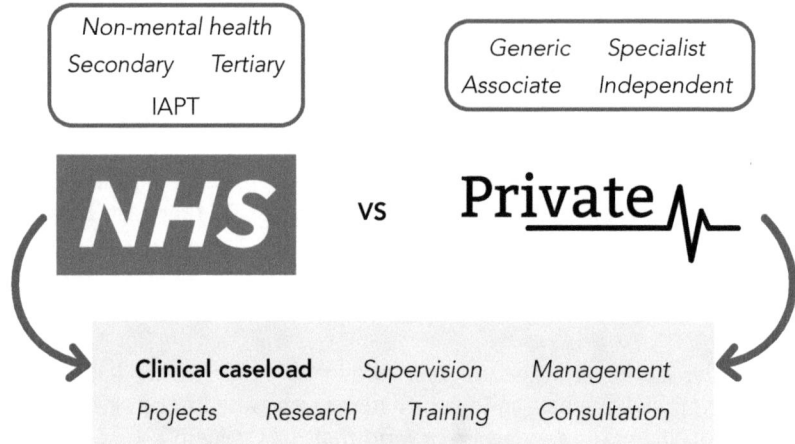

Private practice is not limited to running your own business. Chapter 17 considers independent practice as a CBT therapist in broader terms, but to summarize this can include:

- A full private practice within your own business
- Working independently for a private organization
- Being an associate for someone else's private therapy business
- Consultation work for organizations

Figure 15.1 also shows the range of roles you may have within both pathways. Although a clinical caseload will always be necessary, if you want to remain accredited, you do not have to stick solely to clinical work with patients. Other tasks or roles can be combined to give variety to your work. This includes:

- Clinical supervision
- Consultation
- Training
- Management
- Project work
- Involvement in any local research

The next chapter covers these different roles in more detail within the context of the ARD model, but for now it is sufficient to recognize that other options are available when considering your personal CBT career vision.

Taking stock

No matter where you are in your CBT career, take some time to reflect on your journey to date and consider some of the options you might want to explore in the future. We can do this using the exercises below.

Career timeline

Drawing a timeline of your journey to date is important so you can recognize where you have come from and all the steps you have taken to get to this point. It is easy to get stuck thinking about the problems in the here-and-now relating to work stress, self-doubt and feeling trapped in roles that are no longer fulfilling.

A timeline will show your resilience and development over time. This should help build your confidence and re-ignite or heighten your passion for CBT. With experience comes greater opportunity, so leave space on the timeline to include ideas for the future.

An example of my own career timeline is provided on the Resources page.

Another way to take stock of where you are now is to create a personal annual review, listing what you have done in the previous year and what you would like to explore or achieve in the coming year. An example is presented in Figure 15.2. This is one of mine. My roles are varied as I am currently working independently, so your review may not be as diverse or detailed, but include all the different roles, achievements and your personal goals and aspirations for the coming year.

These reflections will help you gain perspective on where you are and where you would like to be. Speak to colleagues or talk to other CBT therapists working in the areas you are interested in to allow more flexible thinking when approaching this exercise.

Figure 15.2 – Example of personal annual review for Helen Moya

2022/23 Reflections and plans

2022	2023
■ Part-time role in Mental Health Support Team (MHST) delivering CBT in schools all year ■ Clinical trainer role at Trent Psychological Therapies Service (PTS) – finished in August ■ Completed PGCert in Enhanced CBT (child & adolescent pathway) at Oxford ■ Round table discussion on placements for self-funding CBT trainees ■ Developing ADHD specialism ■ New training provision on CBT & ADHD ■ New disorder specific formulation training ■ Article on CBT career model in *CBT Today* ■ Produced **LOTS** of free CBT guides ■ Anxiety in pregnancy project involvement ■ CBT Careers group growth reached 2K ■ Ongoing clinical supervision caseload ■ Helped people to complete their KSA ■ Supported people to enter CBT training ■ Some face to face training events	■ Seek part-time role in NHS ■ Continue current training provision ■ Add to training portfolio: ■ Intolerance of Uncertainty training event ■ Develop ADHD work ■ Produce **MORE** free CBT guides ■ Anxiety in pregnancy training provision ■ Book proposal (*CBT Career Guide*) ■ Continue clinical work in Moya CBT ■ Continue providing clinical supervision ■ Explore outreach work options ■ PLUS...... **A big space for creative activity!**

Working to your values

We have established throughout the book that a strengths-based approach to CBT is a helpful way to maintain emotional wellbeing. The previous chapter covered this in some detail, but it is important to relate it to career vision here.

Your choice of work role may be influenced by factors other than personal goals and aspirations. For example, if you would like to do additional training in a specific area of CBT but do not have the financial resources to support this, then you may feel forced to work full time in a job that has lost its appeal. There is no easy response to this situation, but it is useful to consider how it fits with other domains across your life at any given time. Figure 15.3 highlights the dominant and sometimes opposing values that might be in play.

Figure 15.3 – Values in relation to your CBT career choices

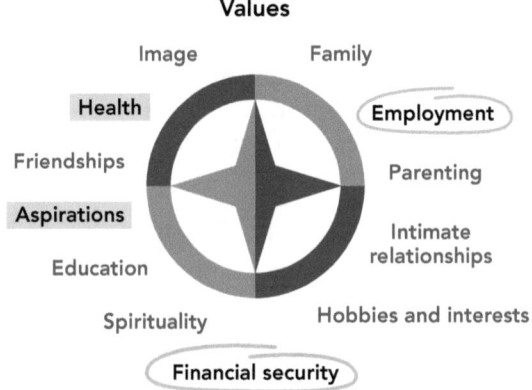

This diagram highlights the importance of looking beyond financial security in terms of full-time employment only. Engaging with your aspirations can lead you to a place of financial security in a new direction that matches your goals. This could potentially have a positive effect on your health and wellbeing.

CBT career bucket list

Because of the need to focus on financial security, you may lose sight of your aspirations. There does not have to be a timeframe on these goals, but if they slip off the radar then it is less likely that you will ever achieve them. You can think of them as your CBT career bucket list.

> **Reflection point**
>
> Draw a timeline of your CBT career to date. Do this in your own style and leave some space for the future. Are there any roles you would like to explore? If you are not sure, then write your **CBT career bucket** list to help you start planning your next steps towards reaching these goals.

Broadening your perspective

We have considered traditional career pathways and how to align your vision and goals with your values and aspirations. The following chapters present different pathways and how you can combine them. Even with the options discussed so far, you do not need to feel trapped in an 'all-or-nothing' position such as either working full time for the NHS or other public service role or having your own business. The messages that follow aim to help you think more flexibly about your CBT career.

The next chapter presents more suggestions for extending your career beyond a purely clinical role based on the 'development' stage of the ARD model (Moya, 2022). Chapter 17, on working independently, emphasizes the options for combining roles and working flexibly as a CBT entrepreneur by adopting a portfolio style of working. You can consider options outside the UK to broaden your career goals and bucket list even further.

Your journey is ongoing, and no matter how long it takes to reach your personal goals, or if they change along the way, the important thing is to keep them in sight and to review them regularly. The choices available to you are wider than you may expect, so do not doubt your capabilities, skills and experience. This is likely to hold you back.

Remember that it is currently a 'buyer's market' in the UK due to the high demand for CBT therapists across services, so you do not have to settle for a role that does not match your experience and interests.

Summary

This chapter has encouraged you to take stock of where you are right now and where you would like to be in the future. You do not need to feel stuck. Even within traditional CBT clinical jobs, there are options to create variety within your working role. The aim has been to broaden your perspective and connect with your values and aspirations for your career. The next chapters provide more details about different career pathways to broaden your perspective further.

Additional supporting online resources available on the Resources page:

- CBT career timeline template
- CBT career vision worksheet
- Copy of the values compass
- Copy of the personal annual review example
- CBT career journey narratives

Chapter 16
CBT career options

The development level of the ARD model (Figure 16.1) provides suggested pathways you might take to develop your CBT career. The clinical pathway is the most common, as we need to work clinically to remain accredited. However, it is easy to become limited in our thinking about this, especially if we have worked in one setting or service for a long time. Most CBT therapists who have followed a funded route will stay in a psychological therapy service on completion of training. Once in this intensive role, it is difficult to consider alternative clinical roles within and outside of the NHS or other large providers.

Figure 16.1 – Stage 3 of the ARD model

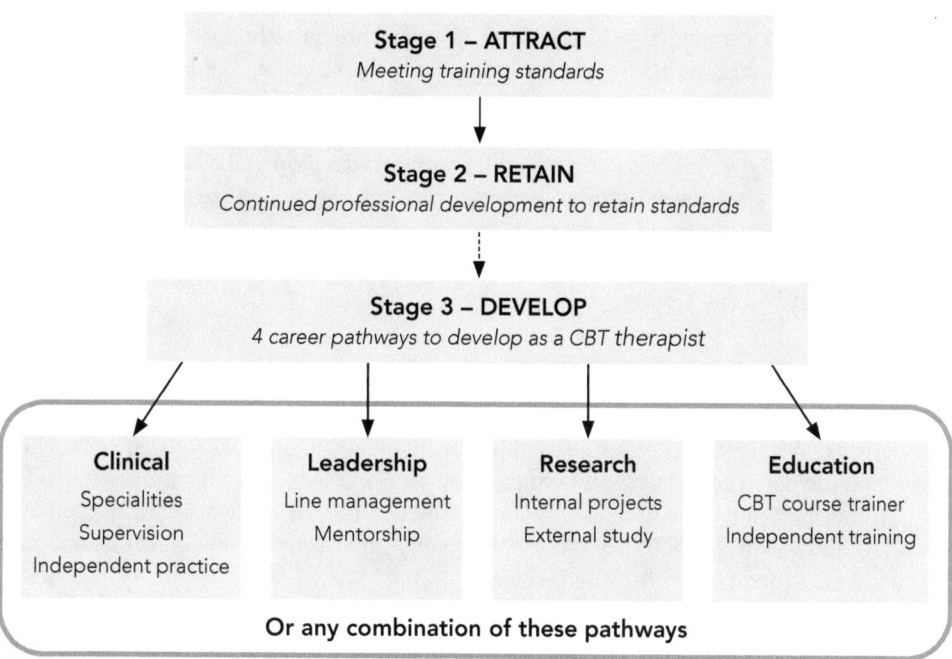

This chapter provides a broader perspective on the clinical options available to you as a CBT therapist, including working with different client groups, specializing in an area of CBT you are passionate about, and developing as a clinical supervisor. The next most popular pathway followed by clinicians in the NHS and other larger organizations is management and leadership. However, not everyone aspires to be a manager, which leads to many CBT therapists feeling trapped in a stressful role with no prospects for promotion. The longer you are in this position, the more skilled you become – but without financial reward, which means you are working beneath your potential.

The ARD model suggests alternative pathways to purely clinical and leadership options. This chapter will discuss developing an academic career in education as a trainer on CBT programmes or moving into a research role. These pathways are not mutually exclusive, and they can be combined.

Clinical pathway

This is the most common starting point following training. We have emphasized the importance of developing knowledge and skills to build confidence and competence. This may be in the service in which you trained, as some funded places will expect a period of post-qualification contracted employment. This is not always the case, but most services will require you to be accredited or able to work towards accreditation within a specified time frame.

Clinical experience can be gained across the stepped-care system in the NHS. It is typical to initially move into a step 3 role in an NHS Talking Therapies service. Some therapists remain in this role for many years, because they enjoy the consistency of the step 3 model. Others become saturated by the repetitive nature of the process, as the tendency to see the same presenting problems leaves little room for specialization.

CBT posts within step 4 services offer an opportunity to develop skills working with more complex presentations. These are often within a broader psychology service, where you would be part of a multi-disciplinary team working alongside practitioners using different therapy models. These are for more experienced practitioners so they represent a career progression point to a more senior role.

Becoming a specialist CBT therapist

Career progression in a purely clinical position at step 3 is rare, but each therapist will develop a special interest in certain presenting problems or using CBT with specific client groups. In some services, it is possible to develop your clinical expertise in these areas. Normally, these are not considered promotion points so do not carry a financial gain. However, it allows you to focus on an area you enjoy and become a specialist as opposed to a general CBT therapist within the service.

With the initial mission of IAPT to increase access to psychological therapies, many care pathways have emerged over time in response to the level of need within the country. We have already discussed inequities relating to people from diverse backgrounds; however, NHS Talking Therapies encourages special interest groups for staff to develop services that promote inclusion of underrepresented groups. Some services use the term 'champion' for the therapists who lead these groups.

Many psychological therapy services will include some specialist care pathways. These will vary across NHS services in the UK, but common ones include:

- **Integrated care pathway for long-term health conditions** – this has been part of government policy since 'No health without mental health' (Department of Health, 2011) where the connection between physical and mental health was emphasized. Previously treated separately, in a dualistic manner, there was a gap in services for people experiencing both. IAPT introduced top-up training for PWPs and CBT therapists in 2011, which has since been rolled out widely across services. The pathway covers people living with a long-term physical condition that is impacting their mood or causing anxiety. Conditions include diabetes, heart conditions, neurological disorders, bowel diseases and cancer. The CBT skills are the same, but you will help the person understand the impact of the LTC on their emotional wellbeing through developing a detailed formulation. There is a large evidence base for CBT for LTC and medically unexplained symptoms (see Kinsella & Moya, 2021).
- **Perinatal care** – there is a growing recognition that pregnancy is a time of increased stress, which can lead to anxiety and low mood. Some women will be more vulnerable if they have a history of anxiety or depression, have had previous complicated pregnancies, have miscarried or have lost a baby. Previously, there were only specialist perinatal services for women with complex mental health problems, leaving a massive gap for those with common but distressing conditions that can be easily treated using CBT.
- **Neurodiversity** – this includes ADHD and autism, which are classed as neurodevelopmental conditions resulting in specific differences in brain functioning, although impact and presentation can vary widely between individuals. CBT can be adapted to allow for differences in information processing, attentional focus and specific symptoms that cause distress to the individual. Some protocols are being developed, but the evidence base is still growing in this area. Due to the proliferation in assessment and diagnosis of people with ADHD or autism across the life span, these specialist CBT roles are essential.
- **Working with Black, Asian and ethnic minorities (BAME)** – as discussed in Chapter 4 on diversity, there is an ongoing need to increase access to services for people from a minority background. The BABCP guidelines support the Equality Act (2010) providing guidelines for CBT therapists to take a transcultural approach to increase awareness of culture and its impact on mental health.
- **Working with LGBTQ+ people** – gender and sexuality are part of identity and are not conditions. However, those who identify as lesbian, gay, bisexual, queer or transgender are more likely to experience mental health problems due to discrimination, prejudice and victimization. This often prevents people from seeking therapy for fear of being misunderstood or mistreated. NHS Talking Therapies continues to explore ways to increase access to services and to use the best available evidence for therapeutic approaches for this community. This includes the recommendations from early research by Pachankis and Goldfried (2004) which have informed guidelines by the British Psychological Society (BPS, 2019) and the development of the LGBTQ+ special interest group within the BABCP. The work of John Pachankis and colleagues has led to the transdiagnostic LGBTQ affirmative cognitive behavioural model (Pachankis *et al*, 2022) discussed in more detail in Chapter 4.

Natalie's story

After completing my psychology degree in 2010, I worked as a support worker in a residential home for people with learning disabilities. I was also an honorary assistant psychologist in a service for adults diagnosed with Asperger's Syndrome.

After two years, I did the PGDip in low-intensity cognitive behavioural therapy interventions and worked as a psychological wellbeing practitioner (PWP) in various IAPT services. Due to both my previous work experience and personal experience of having a sister with Down's syndrome, I chose to begin specializing in working with clients with a learning disability when I started my first PWP job. I was the learning disability 'champion' (key contact and driver for change) for most of the services that I worked for. For three years I worked on a major project alongside the Department of Health (DoH) to improve access to psychological therapy for clients with a learning disability.

I also volunteered to become the long-term health conditions (LTHC) 'champion' during my time as a PWP. I have a chronic pain condition myself and felt that my personal experience would be beneficial to this client group. I was a participant in a pain-management group which used a combination of ACT and CBT – this was the first time I had been introduced to ACT. My passion for ACT developed very quickly from that point, and I began a process of self-learning the principles and applying ACT to myself. I went on to support a CBT therapist to run an ACT-based LTHC group and thoroughly enjoyed this type of work.

After four years of working as a PWP, I did my high-intensity training and became a CBT therapist in the same IAPT service. I continued my work as the LTHC and learning disability 'champion'. I attended a course for adapting high-intensity CBT to LTHC work in 2017 and attended ACT training. I continued to run an ACT-based course for clients with LTHC in this service, and began the process of improving access for clients with a learning disability using information and contacts from the previous DoH project.

In 2018, I became an LTHC CBT therapist in a different IAPT service. I began a role purely seeing clients with LTHC while also becoming the 'champion' for learning disabilities for this new service. My experience in IAPT made me want to be able to spend longer with clients, so I chose to set up my own private practice in 2021 to offer longer-term therapy to those living with chronic pain. My lived experience of chronic pain and the personal benefits of ACT also contributed to my decision to specialize in this area in my private practice.

Natalie's story is an inspirational account of how she followed her passion for helping people with learning disabilities and people living with chronic pain from the start of her CBT career journey. She is highly motivated by her own lived experience in both areas, and she continues this specialist work in her private practice. This clear vision explains how she has achieved so much in a relatively short period.

Clinical roles in non-NHS settings

As the evidence base for CBT applications grows, so does the development of CBT in organizations and services outside of the NHS or traditional health and social care settings. Chapter 3 provided a brief insight into the possibilities of using your CBT qualification. This included Anna's story of working in the prison service. The list below is not exhaustive. It provides a range of organizations or settings that employ CBT therapists:

- Schools
- Prisons
- Armed forces
- Police forces
- Universities and other higher education institutions supporting students in distress
- Employer-based wellbeing services (occupational health services)
- Autism charities
- Domestic abuse charities

You can also become a specialist CBT therapist in third-sector or private healthcare organizations. The next chapter discusses developing as a specialist CBT therapist as an independent practitioner.

> **Reflection point**
>
> What aspects of clinical practice do you enjoy the most? Are there specific conditions or client groups you prefer to treat? How can you develop this interest? Create an action plan.

Developing as a CBT supervisor

Becoming a clinical supervisor is another means for developing as a clinical practitioner. It is a commonly available development pathway within psychological therapy services. Most organizations will require you to have a year in post before offering training in clinical supervision. In that time, you can familiarize yourself with the course details and entry requirements and discuss this with colleagues who have been through the process.

There is often much confusion regarding the requirements to be a CBT clinical supervisor. Of course, this will depend on the context in which you work, but in UK psychological services you just need to be a qualified CBT therapist who is accredited with the BABCP as a practitioner. The accreditation ensures a level of knowledge and skills that meet the minimum training standards (MTS) of the BABCP. In non-NHS settings, accreditation may not be a requirement but a high level of skills and clinical experience will be expected.

As previously discussed, CBT therapists tend to share some negative schemas that can erode their confidence. Becoming a clinical supervisor can escalate these beliefs, making the transition very threatening. By the time you are taking this step, you will have practiced as a qualified CBT therapist for some time. This is when you need to draw on your personal qualities and resources to continue building confidence.

Chapter 13 provided a broad overview of supervision and how to get the most out of it. We now turn to consider the available research and guidelines on CBT supervision practice and some of the shortcomings of this evidence base. The challenges of being a supervisor are addressed, with some suggestions as to how to approach and overcome them. The lack of rigid recommendations can be a potential opportunity to develop your personal supervision style based on your values and theoretical position within the CBT landscape.

Milne (2008) highlighted a lack of research into clinical supervision within the CBT model. Townend *et al* (2007) repeated their survey of CBT supervisors five years after their original study (Townend *et al*, 2002) and found no change in practice or skills. This was attributed to a lack of clear supervision training and development. Milne (2008) suggested that in the absence of a specific model, applying the principles of CBT to the supervision process provides a reflexive approach that is rooted in the evidence base for CBT treatment. Since this time, encouraged by the rollout of the IAPT initiative in England since 2008, supervision has received much more attention, different models have been developed, and training is offered at postgraduate level. This recognizes the level of skills and knowledge required to be an effective clinical supervisor.

More recently, Roscoe *et al* (2022) examined the reflections of supervisors and supervisees and found inconsistency in their approaches, a tendency for autonomy rather than using models, and the importance of the supervisory relationship for maximizing supervision effectiveness. Along with a lack of adherence to models, there was also a lack of standardized reviews of supervision using evidence-based measures such as Milne's (2017) Evidence-Based Clinical Supervision Framework (EBCSF) or the Supervision Adherence and Guidance Evaluation (SAGE) produced by Milne and Reiser (2014) with a shortened version produced by Reiser *et al* (2018).

Considering Roscoe *et al*'s (2022) findings that many supervisors prefer to use the reflexive approach, based on the broad principles of CBT treatment, developing as a supervisor may include studying and experimenting with different supervision models. It also needs to include regular supervision of supervision and CPD events with a clinical supervision focus. Corrie and Lane (2015) introduced their CBT supervision model which provides a clear and robust framework for approaching clinical supervision.

Becoming an accredited supervisor

The BABCP offer additional accreditation options for supervision and training. This is for an accredited practitioner who can demonstrate ongoing professional development in these areas and has been an accredited practitioner for three years or more. This is an attempt to provide a standard. At the time of writing, you do not need these additional levels of accreditation to practice as a clinical supervisor or to teach on a CBT programme. You do need to be an accredited CBT practitioner with the BABCP to support trainees or others seeking accreditation.

> **Reflection point**
>
> Why do you want to be a supervisor? Answering this question is important as it highlights your motivation and expectations of the role. It is useful to identify your values regarding supervision.

Management and leadership pathway

Within traditional NHS psychological therapy services, this is the most common, and often the only, promotion pathway for high-intensity CBT therapists. Services are organized into teams and have a hierarchical management structure. Team leader will be the first point of promotion in terms of moving to a higher pay band.

If you have a PWP background, you have the dual option of becoming a team leader for either a step 2 or step 3 team. You can combine your roles, as some services will still require you to have a small caseload of step 3 clients to maintain your accreditation as a CBT practitioner. This makes it a more flexible role as you are using the full range of your skills and knowledge across low- and high-intensity CBT. Some services will accept CBT therapists in a step 2 leader role, so a good understanding of low-intensity CBT is essential if you do not have a PWP background. Faz's story, first shared in Chapter 5, demonstrates this flexibility.

Faz's story

I worked in low-intensity CBT for about four and a half years as a PWP and was one of our NHS Trust's first senior PWPs. I then went onto high-intensity CBT training, and after about eighteen months I moved into a PWP lead / team leader role (Band 8a) with lots of line management and supervision responsibilities. I then focused on another team leader/senior therapist role supervising qualified and trainee CBT therapists.

The job description of a team leader in an NHS Talking Therapies service is provided below. This is a summary of duties, so always check the specification of the role you are applying for carefully for any differences or additional duties.

Summary of NHS Talking Therapies team leader role:

- Provide strong visible leadership within the area of responsibility.
- Ensure that all staff in the service area are clear about what is expected and are working together in successful teams to achieve the organizational vision.
- Promote a culture where staff feel empowered and accountable for service improvement at the local level.
- Accurately and systematically record and monitor performance against local and national targets and proactively manage any variances.
- Regularly review the service area workforce to ensure it has the right numbers at the right level of knowledge, skill and expertise to deliver services most effectively and efficiently.
- Support the delivery of service in line with the organization's agreed financial plan and implement opportunities for cost improvement.
- Ensure that staff within the service area are providing optimum quality of care in line with national healthcare standards.
- Promote a culture where governance and risk management are seen to be everyone's responsibility.
- Help develop and implement effective systems to record and monitor governance and risk information, and contribute to reports to the relevant forums.
- Support the introduction of new and innovative business management strategies to maximize the organizational efficiency of the service area.
- Lead on trust-wide and national IAPT initiatives and projects as required.
- Represent the service area at local meetings.
- Ensure that staff have been trained in core HR policies such as equality and diversity, discipline, recruitment and change management and are competent in dealing with first-line HR issues.

In her story below, Sue shares her experiences of moving from several long-term CBT roles as a mental health nurse in secondary care, spanning twenty years, to a team leader post in an NHS Talking Therapies service.

Sue's story

Being a team lead has been one of the most influential career decisions of my career so far. I had the chance to fully appreciate and understand the costs of healthcare provision, which was not something in my conscious awareness in secondary services. Most therapists work hard; as leads, you won't always show what you are having to do behind the scenes, and you'll get no medals, but you get a massive sense of satisfaction from building a cohesive team and helping clients get a quality service. I realized when I was in IAPT how much secondary care could learn from working even 10% closer to an IAPT model. One of the keys to survival as a clinical team manager is good relationships with the team and peers.

In relation to staff, communication about what needs to be done and why and a genuine respectful approach are needed. Prioritizing tasks rather than being reactive helps to keep you focused on the team and organizational goals as opposed to firefighting.

Moving up the management ladder can be difficult due to the hierarchical nature of the career structure. There are fewer senior management positions, but you can consider roles outside of a clinical service. For example, management and leadership experience can enable you to enter national-level posts within the NHS or other organizations – such as NHS Talking Therapies advisory roles to drive national service development in line with policy requirements and deadlines. The shift from local service management to a national position will enable you to make a difference at the macro level.

There are different models of management and leadership. The NHS Leadership Academy describes the Healthcare Leadership Model (HLM). This encourages people to develop as leaders by recognizing and identifying a set of values and behaviours that promote the principles of the NHS at all levels of the service. It contains nine dimensions briefly described in Table 16.1.

Table 16.1 – The nine dimensions of the Healthcare Leadership Model (HLM)

Dimension	Description
Inspiring shared purpose	This is at the heart of the model and requires the leader to act in ways that promote the values of the service. It includes an awareness of diversity and factors affecting patient care, which involves actions that show staff they are valued. It is leading by example to inspire others to commit to the shared vision of the organization.
Leading with care	This requires an approach to leadership based on compassion for staff and their emotional wellbeing. This is important at the individual and team levels, recognizing factors that may impact performance at both levels. It involves self-reflection on one's own needs and attention to personal wellbeing to lead by example.
Evaluating information	Services need to be evidence-based, but the sources of this information should extend beyond research. It is essential to be open-minded and consider the perspectives of others to make services as inclusive as possible. Evaluation from service users and staff is part of this, but leaders need to look widely, think creatively and keep up to date with initiatives outside the service.
Connecting our service	This dimension recognizes that the service is part of a bigger system within health and social care. It involves exploring ways to connect with other teams and organizations to encourage collaborative working across services.
Sharing the vision	A shared vision needs to be established within the team and organization before sharing more widely. This helps each staff member to recognize their role within the service vision.

Engaging the team	Leaders need to be visible and listen to the views of staff to maintain a shared vision that values everyone within the organization. It involves fostering an environment that promotes creative thinking while supporting everyone to develop their potential.
Holding to account	An effective team needs clear goals and performance indicators to provide a quality service. Accountability for performance involves modelling this to all staff by maintaining personal and professional standards and acting in an ethical way to set clear expectations.
Developing capability	This is about developing people to reach their potential and increase esteem. It is more than training; it includes recognizing the team's strengths and using them to build capability across the workforce.
Influencing for results	This involves a commitment to best practices through actions that may not be supported by everyone. It requires effective communication, modelling good practice and collaboration across diverse groups to encourage best performance.

The main features of the HLM are collaborative working, modelling good practice and being a caring leader. This aligns with a more recent model of leadership based on the compassionate minds work of Paul Gilbert (2009). Compassionate-focused leadership training has become popular in the NHS, and fits with the philosophy and approach of psychological therapy services to focus on the emotional wellbeing of staff at all levels. The traditional approach of performance management produces results by activation of the 'threat-drive system'. This will increase anxiety and self-critical thinking, and increase the rate of burnout. A compassion-focused leadership style attempts to help staff practice self-care and self-compassion both inside and outside the workplace. More information can be found on the NHS Senior Leadership Onboarding and Support website.

Education pathway

The most common academic role for a CBT therapist is as a tutor or lecturer on a CBT course at a university. There is a saying that as a therapist you may help hundreds of people to gain from CBT, whereas training CBT therapists will mutliply this impact through passing on your knowledge, skills and experience. This is often the motivation for a career move into training. You may have a background in education through working in schools, or in your core profession, or have supervised trainee CBT therapists in practice and want to develop this further. The education pathway allows you to become a **CBT clinical academic**.

To be a CBT trainer or lecturer you will need to be actively engaged in a minimum number of clinical hours to maintain practitioner accreditation, which is a requirement for those contributing to BABCP-accredited courses. Even if working on a non-accredited course, you will be impacting the trainees' chances of becoming accredited in the future, as the MTS require CBT training to be delivered by BABCP-accredited practitioners. To be a lecturer on a course, you may require additional training in teaching in higher education (such as the postgraduate certificate in higher education (PGCHE) or equivalent). Some posts offer the training on appointment.

Summary of a CBT trainer role

- Maintain ongoing professional memberships and accreditation.
- Be a practicing CBT therapist in line with accreditation and university requirements.
- Responsible for the planning and delivery of lectures.
- Adherence to national and professional guidelines and requirements for CBT training and practice (BABCP minimum training standards and core curriculum, Roth and Pilling CBT competency framework and NICE guidelines).
- Developing and marking academic and clinical assignments.
- Generally supporting the trainees in their development.
- Being a professional tutor.
- Providing clinical supervision.
- Involvement in trainee recruitment.
- Service liaison and mid-way review visits.
- For some trainers and lecturers, there could be further leadership opportunities.
- Ongoing personal professional development.

It is useful to gain experience of teaching at this level by contributing to workshops or supervision on a CBT programme. Courses are always looking for active practitioners to provide a realistic and credible perspective on how CBT is delivered in real-life settings. This is a good way to infiltrate a course at your own pace while still in clinical practice.

Polly, who we met in Chapter 3, describes how the transition from full-time clinical practice to a teaching post proved to be an enriching step in her CBT career journey.

Polly's story

After many years as a CBT therapist, for both adults and children, I began working at a university teaching a BABCP-accredited CBT training course. All our trainees are employed by NHS or other healthcare providers. I had completed supervisor training while still within the NHS, and I love that this new teaching role enables me to supervise, deliver teaching and have time to read up on current developments. I link in with different CAMHS and mental health support team (MHST) services around the country, so I very much still feel a part of the NHS and the drive to improve access to mental health services for children and young people.

Tips for gaining an academic role

One of the advantages of this pathway is that you can gradually immerse yourself in an academic role. The following list of suggestions is not exhaustive but should provide some ideas to help plan your journey.

- Reflect on your training and critically appraise what was done well and what could have been improved. This will help you to develop a position on CBT education.

- Familiarize yourself with the key educational requirements for CBT training – the minimum training standards and core curriculum.
- Look through the course handbooks of your local universities offering CBT training.
- Speak to course staff about the role and any opportunities to contribute.
- Offer to co-facilitate a session on a topic you are interested in or have expertise in. Lecturers and trainees value teaching sessions that include the perspective of a CBT therapist currently in clinical practice.
- Look for supervision opportunities on a course. Trainees require weekly group supervision, so this is a good way to integrate yourself into a course and have regular contact with the course team.
- Prepare some session plans and present them to course staff.
- Read up on research into education and teaching models.
- Run training sessions in your clinical service to gain experience of teaching and develop your presentation skills.

Becoming an accredited CBT trainer

As described above, the BABCP offer additional accreditation options for supervision and training. As for supervision accreditation, you will need to be an accredited practitioner for three years or more. For trainer accreditation, you will require significant experience of teaching, supervising, and assessing the coursework of trainee CBT therapists in line with the BABCP MTS and core curriculum. You will also need to demonstrate ongoing professional development relating to education and training. This is an attempt to provide a standard. As with supervision accreditation, at the time of writing, you do not need these additional levels of accreditation to teach on a CBT programme.

> **Reflection point**
>
> What attracts you to an educational role? What skills and experience do you already have? What can you do to develop your skills and experience? Who can advise or support you? Write an action plan.

Research pathway

CBT is recognized for its strong evidence base derived from research. Clearly, research can be practiced at different levels and the teams who engage in the randomized controlled trials (RCTs) are highly qualified and experienced researchers. However, they all started somewhere, so if you have a passion for research then there are different ways you can move forward on this pathway. Careers in research tend to be very hierarchical and include years of study and research output. It appeals to those who have a passion for learning and who love working in an academic environment. Research positions are often combined with an educational role. CBT therapists who have a full-time (or substantive) lecturing post are expected to produce some form of research output. Likewise, university-based researchers are often expected to contribute to teaching or marking coursework. Practicing research as a healthcare professional allows you to combine your CBT practice and research skills to develop as a **clinical academic**.

If you completed a master's degree in CBT, this normally includes a dissertation. Typically, this is an independent piece of research that requires ethical approval and has the potential to be published. You can use this opportunity to make a mark in an area of CBT that you have a special interest in. Your supervisor may have contacts in the CBT research community, so build your own research networks to increase future opportunities. There are stages to research-based career development, normally starting with a research assistant post. After completing a doctorate-level degree such as a PhD or an applied psychology doctorate in clinical psychology, forensic psychology or counselling psychology, you can apply for post-doctoral fellowships.

A research assistant (RA) supports the principal research team to collect and analyse data, present findings and ensure processes and procedures are adhered to. As you become more experienced, you also become more autonomous. Becoming a principal researcher normally requires years of research experience at fellowship level. Most research assistants and fellows move from one job to another, as contracts tend to be on fixed terms according to the specific research project. You need to be resilient to manage frequent transitions and apply for numerous posts. It is based on funding attached to different research projects and they are normally highly competitive. These posts are also very output-driven, and carry a similar level of performance pressure as an NHS Talking Therapies post.

Examples of research output include:

- Scientific research articles in a credible journal that uses an anonymous peer-review process. Academic journals are ranked in terms of impact factor, the higher the better, but these journals have long waiting times so other outputs will be necessary.
- Citation numbers of your work are another way of measuring the impact of your research.
- Books that present research findings aimed at a scientific audience are normally valued more highly. But professional books and guides are also important and arguably have more impact.
- Book chapters and co-authored works.
- Conference papers, presentations and posters.

Being a CBT researcher requires excellent analytical skills, a passion for investigation and advancement of CBT practice, an openness to share ideas and receive constructive criticism, and the ability to communicate findings to a wide and varied audience.

Tips for developing as a CBT researcher

As with training roles, you can build experience at your own pace. You may already have qualifications in research such as a master's degree or doctorate. Or you may have done a dissertation for an undergraduate degree and completed modules on research methods. You can build on this.

- Revisit your academic coursework to review your current research skills and knowledge of research methods.
- Read as many research papers as possible relating to CBT to hone your critical thinking skills (see critical reading exercise on the Resources page).
- Attend seminars in your local service or universities to assess the local research landscape.
- Network with local CBT researchers.
- Look out for requests for research participation and get involved.
- Study the job specification for research assistant posts and note any gaps in your current experience.
- Do a postgraduate research-based degree. This will allow you to undertake a piece of research in an area of interest, and increase your opportunities to apply for a research post.
- Offer to do a piece of research in your service. Identify an area that would benefit the service, and prepare a proposal.

Beyond these individual pathways

The options provided within this chapter may appear mutually exclusive and unilateral. However, you can mix and match them by combining elements within your dominant role. For example, if you work in a clinical role within a large organization, you may seek a part-time position on a CBT training programme one day a week and explore the options for reducing your hours within the clinical role. Zack's story, shared in Chapter 10, detailed the challenges he faced on his journey to becoming a CBT therapist. Below, he describes his experiences of varied roles and combinations of posts during the past fifteen years as a qualified CBT therapist.

My career has been varied; I've joined and resigned from IAPT twice, both while working in private practice on the side. I've taught in university on a PG Dip CBT course for eighteen months, had a twelve-month stint at a personality disorder service, and now have a therapist role in an early intervention team. I'm forty-six, and in my twenties I thought I had my path laid out. But finding this career I'm so passionate about with such a broad range of opportunities has been incredible, and I wouldn't have it any other way.

One of the messages to emphasize here is this: *never be scared to ask your employer about reducing hours*. This can be a barrier to moving forward if you believe you must either remain in a full-time position or leave altogether.

Summary

The development level of the ARD CBT career model has provided the framework for this chapter. It outlines four distinct career pathways for a qualified CBT therapist working in an employed position. It moves beyond clinical and leadership pathways to consider education and research options, but none of these need to be mutually exclusive. Roles can be combined by reducing hours in one post and freeing up time to try another role on a part-time basis. The take-home message is to think laterally, plan where you would like your career to go and facilitate change. This requires you to be proactive and seek out opportunities. If they don't already exist, make them happen. Sometimes an employer will not have thought of your idea, so it is always worth asking. There are more choices for a CBT career than you might think, so there is no need to tolerate a job that does not satisfy your personal career goals and aspirations. The next chapter looks in more detail at independent working.

Chapter 17
Working independently as a CBT entrepreneur

The previous chapter covered options along the four career development pathways of the ARD model. As discussed, these pathways are flexible as they can be combined, and you can transition in and out of them as needed. The message is that you do not need to feel trapped in one role throughout your career. We now open this up further by considering options for working independently. Setting up your own private practice is often viewed as being a clinical endeavour; however, in this chapter we will explore ideas for making private practice work to your strengths by developing the mindset of a CBT entrepreneur.

There is an abundance of resources available to guide you through the process of setting up a private business that go beyond the scope of this chapter, and other resources and further reading are provided to guide your deeper research on this topic. The main aim of this chapter is to expand your perspective and instil hope that you can create a CBT career that is sustainable and fulfilling based on your strengths, passions and values.

Building your private practice

Most CBT therapists starting up in private practice will want guidance on how to do it. This is natural when approaching a new situation, and advice and stories from those who have been through this process are provided below. However, it is important to start by reflecting on your reasons and motivation for wanting to set up in private practice. This relates to your personal CBT career vision discussed in Chapter 15.

> **Reflection point**
>
> What appeals to you about working independently? Is something missing from your current role that has reduced your job satisfaction and confidence? How long has starting your own business been part of your CBT career vision? How ready do you feel to make this move on a scale of one to ten? What have you done already to facilitate this process?

One of the reflection points asks you to rate how ready you feel to work independently on a scale of one to ten. Regardless of where you scored yourself on the scale, you can move forward. Sometimes we believe we must wait until everything is in place or we feel confident enough to make the transition. It is important not to confuse confidence with certainty. We know that intolerance of uncertainty will increase worry and anxiety, which lead to procrastination and self-doubt. This will also increase the perceived threat associated with making this transition, so we need to break all-or-nothing thinking. Use the threat-opportunity continuum and positive imagery to reinforce the reasons why you want to work independently.

It is important to refer to the building of a CBT therapist model presented in Chapter 2. Remind yourself of the core qualities, skills, knowledge and personal resources you possess and how they have got you to this point. The qualities are compassion, courage, tenacity, curiosity, flexibility, reflection and patience. Coupled with the personal resources of resilience, self-compassion, stress management and support, you will be able to approach this transition as you have every other step in your CBT career journey.

Remember there is always more than one pathway to any CBT career option. This is true for setting up in private practice. When CBT therapists leave an employed position to work independently, some will base their private practice on the role they have left, because this is what is familiar to them. It is important to remember the reasons you chose to change your working practice. Depending on your current situation and your reasons for wanting to work independently, your approach will vary. This means that you can go at your own pace. Most CBT therapists will experiment with private work before setting up their own practice, and others will make a complete transition from employed to self-employed status. Some broad options are presented in Table 17.1.

Getting started

General literature on setting up a business provides broad advice about the fundamentals, but there are specific issues that need attention when working as a private psychotherapy practitioner. The BABCP provides a **private practice toolkit** on its website. Jane Travis (2019) wrote a book called *Grow Your Private Practice*, which documents her experience of setting up and growing her own psychotherapy business.

There are some services and communities specifically focused on helping CBT therapists to set up in private practice. Sarah Rees has developed her role in this area and is recognized as an expert consultant. Sarah now offers her consultancy and support role across a range of services and social media platforms that can be accessed on her website (www.sarahdrees.co.uk). Along with Sophie Wood, Sarah has created a website design and consultancy service called Pocket Site, and an online community called Therapist's Corner. They both provide information and services specifically aimed at therapists setting up and developing their own businesses. Sarah and Sophie have produced a checklist for getting started in private practice on the Therapist's Corner site. This is free to download and can be accessed on the Resources page.

Table 17.1 – Pathways to working independently

Pathway	Description	Tips
Working independently on an ad hoc basis with a private provider while still in a substantive employed position.	Many private healthcare providers who offer psychological therapies have associate positions for CBT therapists to provide therapy on an hourly basis. This is akin to bank or agency work in other core professions such as nursing. These organizations normally cover administration, set up appointments for you and offer supervision. This allows you to try before you commit further.	■ Research the various providers offering associate work. ■ You can do this in social media communities. ■ Clarify any queries by contacting the provider. ■ Register. ■ Trial it, and if you don't like it, try another provider.
Working for one or more private organizations as an independent CBT provider.	It is possible to start private practice by working for private organizations only. You will be self-employed, but referrals, admin and payment will be organized by the provider. This can feel like a safer transition from an employed position as the infrastructure is in place to just do the work and submit invoices. You will need to do a self-assessment for tax at the end of the financial year.	■ As above, you need to research the organizations and their practices. ■ Make sure the fees are acceptable to you. ■ Understand the admin processes expected by each provider as these will vary. ■ Don't feel obligated to stay if it isn't working for you or matching your values.
Building your own private practice slowly alongside an employed position.	You can build your business from scratch without the pressure of having to jump in full time. This allows you to dedicate sufficient time to pay attention to your vision for the business and set up the systems necessary to work independently of private organizations. This includes branding yourself, having a good-quality website, and a clinical records system that meets information governance standards.	■ Read the tips below for setting up in private practice. ■ Use the online resources cited below. ■ Make links with others in social media groups. ■ Use a business development service for professional advice. ■ Find a mentor.
Starting a private practice as your sole source of income.	As above, this requires attention to setting up the infrastructure of your business. You will also need to advertise and market your business. You will need to decide on premises, whether this will be working from your home or having a dedicated rented office space. Having a business mentor familiar with psychotherapy businesses is highly recommended while setting up and growing your business.	As above. It is even more important to have professional support to work through the process and overcome any challenges as they occur. The following section provides useful advice and cites services and resources for setting up your private practice.

Another leader in CBT business development in the UK is Heather Howard-Thompson. She is the director of her own private practice (www.yorkshirepsychotherapy.co.uk) which combines a successful therapy service made up of a team of associate practitioners and her business consultancy services. This includes products to help CBT therapists set up in private practice. She has produced a 'Private Practice Document Toolkit', which comprises all the individual policies and agreements you may need and can be purchased individually on her website.

The steps described below are broad and may occur in a different order, but give attention to each step.

Essentials

Decide on a name and buy the domain.

- This sounds simple but it will become your brand. It needs to be original so that you can purchase the domain name for your website and email address.
- Some therapists will just use their name or combine their name with a therapy descriptor such as 'Sarah Smith Therapy'. Others may use a name that they associate with wellbeing or mental health such as 'Feel Good CBT'.
- It is worth taking time to decide on a business name that you are happy to commit to.

Cover the following legal requirements:

- Professional membership and accreditation.
- Indemnity insurance cover.
- DBS check.
- Information management system that complies with GDPR data protection requirements.
- Register with ICO.
- Set up a **clinical will** – this provides a process for notifying clients in the event of your death or inability to continue working.

Get a supervisor:

- This is a requirement for ongoing practitioner accreditation with the BABCP and maintains accountability for your practice.
- A supervisor with experience of private practice is very useful so they can act as a mentor.

Business logistics

Type of business:

- Sole trader
- Limited company

Clinical record system:

- Use free trials to find one that works for you. WriteUpp is a popular system.
- Alternatively, you can set up your own system. This would need to comply with GDPR requirements.

Premises:

- Working from home – make sure space is secure and does not intrude on personal boundaries.
- Renting premises – how many rooms do you need? Consider access to maximize inclusion. Does a therapy business fit with other services in the building? For example, privacy and noise levels?
- If you will be sharing a space with other therapists, make sure this is allowed within the landlord's agreement.

Business plan:

- Audience.
- Specific services you plan to offer.
- Pricing structure.
- Therapy agreement and other policies.

Business vision

Mission statement:

- This states the vision for your vision and how you want to be identified in the CBT business market.
- Can you describe your business easily to others? If not, then refine your statement.
- This should be embedded into your website and other public platforms.

How many client contacts per week?

- Be realistic, especially if you are combining your business with other paid roles and commitments.
- Plan your diary to allow for peaks and troughs in your business.
- Experiment with different systems.
- Be flexible as your needs and the needs of the market change.

Do you want to specialize?

- Find a niche in the market and associate your identity with that niche.
- Revenue streams – develop your business in line with your passions and skills.

Personal development:

- Stay up to date with any mandatory requirements like DBS checks, safeguarding and information governance training.
- Factor time into your diary for regular CPD that interests you.

Attracting business

Have a clear website with good SEO (search engine optimization). Tag your website in all correspondence and posts.

Know the market and where to advertise:

- Set up social media accounts and have an active presence.
- Network on social media.

Sharing your profile:

- Join therapist directories such as *Psychology Today* where you can share your profile. Often these sites give a free period of six months for you to try before subscribing.
- Become a provider for private insurance companies offering CBT.

Managing your finances

Working independently requires constant attention to your financial security. Talking to others who have set up businesses is helpful, but professional support is available. Most therapists in private practice will recruit an accountant or financial adviser. Business consultancy services are another valuable resource.

Figure 17.1 outlines some of the main financial considerations, but this is not an exhaustive list. The band in the middle contains the essential tasks of registering with HMRC for annual tax assessment and monitoring income and expenses. Keeping on top of your financial transactions is an ongoing process and often requires daily attention. Clinical records systems such as WriteUpp are great for this purpose, as you can record all income and expenses on the system. Alternatively, you can create data spreadsheets to log your financial activities. This information is required for your tax self-assessment. An accountant or consultant can help with this aspect of your business. Other considerations include having a dedicated bank account, payment systems in place, and funds or policies to cover holidays, illness and your pension.

Figure 17.1 – Some financial considerations

Bank account	Payment systems	Quiet periods
Set up a bank account that is dedicated to the business. This does not have to be a business account. As sole trader I set up a second current account for all business transactions. There are pros and cons to both types of account, so seek advice on the best option for your business.	Each session or transaction will need an invoice. This is where you display your payment options. This can be a direct bank transfer or by card (credit or debit), PayPal or similar online system. You can buy a card reader and set up an account to create payment links. Consider fees for the different methods.	Business does not always flow consistently. It is important to have sufficient funds in the bank to cover monthly expenses and personal needs during leaner periods. You can use these times to generate ideas for alternative income streams like putting on a training event.
Monitoring income and expenses		**Tax**
This is a critical part of managing finances and will affect all other areas. If you have a clinical records system, you can manage this on there. Each transaction will be recorded. Alternatively, you can use spreadsheets or an income management app, or hire an accountant or assistant to manage your turnover.		All private work will need to be declared annually on a tax self-assessment form. You must register with HMRC online.
Holidays	**Illness cover**	**Pensions and Retirement**
If you are still working in an employed position, you will have annual leave entitlements. If private practice is your main or sole work, then you need to account for holidays. Most people will base annual income on a 46-week year to allow for six weeks off, but this is flexible.	When employed you receive sick leave benefits. Illness is unpredictable and can have devastating financial consequences. Funds and/or an illness policy are needed to cover time off sick.	You may have pensions from previous employed positions. Some people will stop at a certain age or choose to gradually reduce hours as other financial demands such as childcare responsibilities and mortgage payments lessen. Seek financial advice to plan for your future.

Valuing yourself

Although the information so far provides clear practical advice for setting up in private practice, there can be barriers to this process relating to your beliefs and schemas. These need to be overcome or at least challenged to make the process easier.

One of the most common challenges for a CBT therapist moving from an NHS or other public service position to private practice is related to charging a fee for therapy. This can feel like a conflict of values. In earlier chapters, we identified some common therapist schemas that maintain self-critical thinking and erode self-esteem. The three main ones are **unrelenting standards, self-sacrifice** and **emotional neglect.** Chapter 14 explored how the impact of these schema can be reduced by practicing self-compassion. Stepping out of your comfort zone is likely to trigger negative beliefs. Perceived conflict between values relating to helping others and charging fees is a common source of distress for therapists transitioning into private practice. It is important to remember that the schemas are beliefs, and they can be updated and modified. By undercutting your fee or even providing your service for free, you are strengthening the self-sacrifice and emotional neglect schemas. This will reduce your confidence and self-value, which will potentially risk the quality of your practice.

> **Reflection point**
>
> Identify the values you hold about helping others. Can you apply these values to yourself? Reflect on a situation where you have paid for a service such as getting your clothes dry cleaned. Would you expect the business to provide this service for free? How can we apply this to private therapy practice? How does this feel?

Promoting yourself on your website

Having a good website is a fundamental requirement for your business. There is a popular quote that says "Your website is your shop window", so ensure you make it appealing and that it represents you and your business accurately.

Consider whether you want to build it yourself using website design software or pay a web designer. Beware that doing it yourself may appear cheaper at face value, but factor in all the hours you need to commit to this massive and important task. If you are a perfectionist, you might spend even longer on the task, delaying the promotion of your business. Working in partnership with a web designer means you can still be in control of the vision and ideas but hand over the task to an expert. The web designer can also sort out any other technical details like purchasing a domain with your business name and setting up an email account. They normally host the site for an annual fee. If you are not technically minded, then this option will reduce stress and allow you to focus on other areas of your business. Pocket Site provides web design and consultancy services aimed specifically at therapists.

Here are some tips for building a successful and engaging website:

- Use professional photographs, and lots of them. Don't be shy. It is important that potential clients can identify with you through your images.
- Use video clips – these bring you and the website to life.
- Make your fees easy to access as most potential clients want to know the fee first before even considering your service.
- Make information simple and easy to read. Avoid excessive text and stick to the basic messages.
- Put links to any other social media or events you are advertising.
- Make contact details very clear.
- Make sure you include a privacy and cookie policy to inform website visitors of how the information will be used.

Staying connected

It can be lonely working in private practice if you are a sole trader. It is a vast change from working in a service with other therapists. Although you will have your reasons for making the transition, you may not be prepared for the isolation of working independently. This will not be an issue for some therapists, who value the full sense of independence and autonomy that private practice can afford, and you will have regular supervision to maintain your clinical governance, so this is one contact you can use to start a personal network. You can also include ex-colleagues and therapists you know who are currently working independently.

The Facebook group called 'CBT in Private Practice' was established by Sarah Rees and Heather Howard-Thompson as a space for peer support for any therapist considering or currently in private practice where they share the expertise they gained during their own career development. Although Sarah moved on to build other platforms, at the time of writing Heather still manages the Facebook group which continues to thrive.

As already mentioned, Sarah Rees and Sophie Wood have developed an online community called Therapist's Corner (www.therapistscorner.co.uk) on a platform called Substack. They provide a forum for networking with other therapists in private practice. Their mission statement emphasizes the importance of building a peer community to promote a diverse, accessible, and values-driven practice. There are resources, meetings and webinars on subjects related to developing a successful CBT private practice.

The BABCP have a range of special interest groups (SIGs) you can join. They organize events and have meetings, but these may be infrequent. Another way to connect with fellow therapists is through social media groups. Some may be aimed at therapists in private practice, or you may want to connect with people with the same interests as you. Links to social media groups and BABCP SIGs are provided on the Resources page.

Becoming a CBT entrepreneur

Be proud of having your own business. Making this transition can be difficult for CBT therapists because we focus more on the clinical work and the clients than our changing professional identity. When you work independently, even on a part-time basis, you are free to develop your private practice in line with your strengths and passions. This allows creative thinking and the generation of ideas that will multiply the potential opportunities available to you. In essence, this requires changing your mindset to that of a CBT entrepreneur. Some therapists will already have this mindset before making the transition to independent practice, and it is likely to be the motivation to leave an employed position.

Developing the mindset of an entrepreneur

Brandstätter (1997) explored differences in personality structures of entrepreneurs who set up businesses (founders) compared to those who inherited a business. Using a personality adjective scale, founders were more likely to describe themselves as emotionally stable and independent (self-assertive) than those who did not choose to set up their own business. Segal *et al* (2005) found three factors that significantly increase the motivation to become an entrepreneur: tolerance of risk, perceived feasibility and desirability.

Rigg and O'Dwyer (2012) proposed the notion that becoming an entrepreneur is related to constructs of identity rather than just learning a set of skills. In their study, using a social constructionist approach, they described how an entrepreneurial identity is actively created by talking to, observing, and interacting with family, friends and mentors. This emphasizes the importance of networking and being part of a community that will facilitate this identity formation or transition. The active nature of this perspective goes beyond a set of personality traits to provide an optimistic view that anyone can develop as an entrepreneur.

Lewis *et al* (2016) used a qualitative case study approach to explore the development of an entrepreneurial identity in females. Their findings suggest that overcoming role conflict and actively engaging in entrepreneurial identity transition is associated with increased opportunity-seeking behaviours. This highlights the importance of having a flexible mindset that allows movement from fixed notions of identity and role. We can link this to therapist schemas that can limit confidence and thwart personal development.

We need to adopt a strengths-based approach to our business practice. This will ensure that we stay connected to our values and make the best use of our internal resources. We can draw on our CBT therapist qualities of being tenacious, curious, and brave. This will promote our entrepreneurial identity.

Reflection point

When you hear the word entrepreneur, what image comes to mind? Is there a particular person you think of? List the qualities you have in common with them. Can you identify with the term 'CBT entrepreneur'? If not, reflect on your reasons.

Creative practice

We have emphasized the importance of having a strong business identity, but this does not mean it has to be static or rigid. Flexibility is one of our core strengths. As a CBT entrepreneur, you can be creative with your vision and ideas for developing your business. Being an entrepreneur does not mean taking risks and neglecting security. You can think outside the box while maintaining a functioning business grounded in the practices that have proven successful in the past. Your activities can extend beyond being a clinician.

You can incorporate different roles such as training, clinical supervision and consultancy. One of my passions is CBT career development so this became embedded into my business from the start by offering consultancy, mentoring and free resources, and by creating an online CBT career social media group.

Creative practice also involves thinking on the spot or responding to new information that you see as potentially useful for your business development. For example, attending a training event where an area of your expertise is highlighted as underrepresented in a certain local service. You can respond by contacting that service and discussing your business and how you could help. This might be pitching an idea for training or consultation, or just using this new contact to broaden your local network.

Seizing an opportunity does not have to be spontaneous. Having some information or references to previous projects you have been involved in will keep you prepared for the opportunity when it arises. For example, having an electronic copy of a flyer for your training events or personal CV will allow you to make an immediate impression.

Creative practice allows you time to dream. Make a bucket list for your business, even if many of the items may not come to fruition. By engaging your right brain in this way, you are reducing the rigid, threat-focused thinking that increases anxiety and stress and pushes you into the threat-driven cycle. If you are getting bored in your career, you can make changes.

Iain's story, below, shows how life experiences, personal qualities and creative thinking can be embraced to become an independent CBT entrepreneur.

Iain's story

I left school in 1974 with few qualifications and did not have a career plan. I went into sales and management and worked my way up into senior management, then moved onto the UK board of an international business organization. After the birth of my first child, in 1991, I decided I wanted a career change to work in mental health. I already knew I wanted to work towards becoming a CBT therapist. I started as a healthcare assistant on a mental health ward and then trained as a mental health nurse. After qualifying in 1996, I worked for a year on an adult acute ward while waiting for self-funding to do the eighteen-month CBT training. It was the advanced diploma in CBT known as the ENB (English National Board for Nursing) 650 course. On completion, there were no NHS CBT posts so I set up in private practice in 1998. I was mostly targeting referrals from businesses via occupational health, health and safety and HR.

In 2003, in addition to private practice, I co-founded and was joint managing director of Occupational Mental Health Ltd. This provides clinical CBT, commercial cognitive behavioural coaching, educational workshops and management consultancy. In 2016, I became sole MD following the retirement of my business partner.

In 2018, I commenced two years of research for retirement. In 2020, I moved aboard my narrowboat and continue a bit of private work for previous clients. I am no longer registered with the NMC or accredited with BABCP, but I provide voluntary mental health support to vulnerable boaters and am an advocate of boaters' rights.

Iain's story is inspiring on so many levels. Leaving school without qualifications did not deter him from building a successful career in sales management. This demonstrates his grit and determination from the start. He then had a dream and followed it through. When opportunities were not available, he created them, combining his previous experiences and drive to become a CBT therapist, to develop a successful enterprise targeting a market he was familiar with. Another important feature of his story is how he managed his retirement from his CBT career. Living on a narrow boat allows him to continue helping others in his community in a new and unique way.

Iain's story displays each level of the building a CBT therapist described in Chapter 2. His qualities of being curious, compassionate, brave, tenacious and patient steered his journey. He has used his resources of resilience, self-compassion and stress management to sustain a balanced and fulfilling career into his retirement.

Portfolio working

This is a way of having it all. Many people fall into the trap of all-or-nothing thinking, which forms a dichotomy between employed and private practice. As an independent CBT therapist, you can choose which roles you want to make up your professional identity. When I set up Moya CBT in 2020, I was still working full time in an NHS Talking Therapies service. I condensed my hours to free up Wednesdays and this became my private practice day. Over the next two years, I reduced my hours in the service until I was only working there one day a week and had changed roles from therapist to clinical trainer. This role was created after pitching my idea to develop training materials in response to the COVID pandemic. I produced an online CBT resource for long-COVID and other long-term conditions. During this time, I explored other roles and opportunities rather than just building up my business. I had wanted to do additional training on CBT for children and adolescents for many years, so I sourced a placement in a local mental health support team (MHST) in 2022 and paid for the training from the money generated in my business. At one point in time, my working week looked like the planner in Figure 17.2.

This weekly plan demonstrates how being a CBT entrepreneur does not mean you have to work in private practice only. You can combine jobs and work in services or create roles and source new opportunities in line with your CBT career bucket list and values. For example, this year I have worked purely in private practice and freed up time to focus on writing this book, which has been another item on my bucket list. Portfolio working allows progression into new areas that may not have been an option previously. Using the entrepreneurial skills of creative thinking, opportunity-seeking and pitching ideas, you can genuinely make changes happen. This is independent working at its finest and keeps you in control of your CBT career.

Figure 17.2 – Example of portfolio working

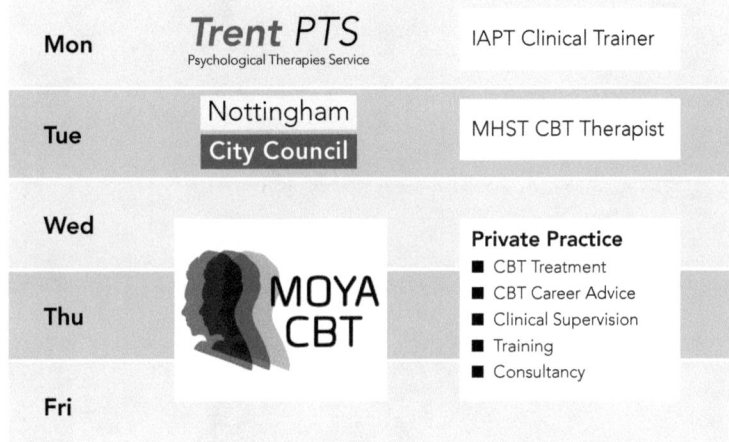

Summary

This chapter has considered independent working beyond a purely clinical CBT practice role. Adopting the mindset of a CBT entrepreneur allows freedom to think creatively and be flexible in the development of your business. Portfolio working provides a model for building your professional identity in line with your strengths, values, and passions so you can achieve more of the items on your CBT career bucket list and maintain a fulfilling career.

Chapter 18
Promoting CBT careers

This book has aimed to guide individuals pursuing and developing careers as CBT therapists. This final chapter addresses how CBT careers can be promoted by service providers and larger educational communities to increase understanding of the role of CBT therapists, the career pathways available and ways to support individuals through this process. The use of the ARD model, CBT career map and building a CBT therapist diagram provide frameworks to bring the content of the guide together so you do not feel alone on this journey.

The section on developing CBT therapists within psychological therapy services is based on an article published in *CBT Today* (Moya, 2022) reproduced with permission of the BABCP. The content of this chapter is intended to be inspirational for all members of organizations, not just managers. Whatever stage you are at in your career journey, it is important to have a clear vision for CBT career development within the UK's primary psychological therapy services. Some of this material is presented in earlier chapters, but here it has a more specific focus on service development to facilitate CBT career development for the individual therapist.

The promotion of CBT careers within the wider community includes information in schools for children at GCSE and A-level stages before selecting a university course. Chapter 5 provided a map of the different pathways to becoming a CBT therapist. Now, we consider how this information can be integrated into education settings at all stages to provide informed choices and accurate information on the requirements for a CBT career.

The chapter finishes with some of the main messages echoed throughout the book.

Developing CBT therapists within psychological therapy services

Currently, there is an ongoing expansion of the original IAPT enterprise. Development of NHS Talking Therapies will continue beyond 2024, when the Five-Year Forward View for Mental Health is reviewed (Mental Health Taskforce, 2016; NHS, 2019b). This expansion to increase access will likely continue way beyond this time. To keep up with demand and changing targets, a robust and flexible training provision is essential. Often overlooked as a significant stakeholder in psychological therapy services, the education system is key to providing a workforce that is fit for purpose. The following extract is taken from the recent NHS long-term plan (published by NHS England in 2019a, section 4.3, p78):

> **"To make this Long Term Plan a reality, the NHS will need more staff, working in rewarding jobs and a more supportive culture.** By better supporting and developing staff, NHS employers can make an immediate difference to retaining the skills, expertise and care their patients need. They can, and will, also do more to improve equality and opportunities for people from all backgrounds to work in the NHS."

There is a bottleneck of potential trainees seeking a career as a CBT therapist. Most of these will be graduates with a psychology degree with varying levels of clinical experience. It takes, on average, eight years of high-level study and clinical commitment to become a CBT therapist. Currently, the average salary of an NHS CBT therapist is around £40,000 a year. High-intensity training, designed to prepare the workforce to meet the requirements of the BABCP minimum training standards (MTS) for accreditation, is at risk of becoming a stepping-stone for other career options such as private practice. It is essential that psychological therapy services not only attract potential therapists and train them, but also focus on retention and career development. Without a robust model in place, there is a risk that more therapists will leave to set up by themselves to earn more money, or to gain a better balance in the use of their skill sets.

Challenges for psychological therapy services

- Staff recruitment
- Staff retention
- Rapidly expanding services to supply therapy to more people
- Staff development to supply the changing demands
- Maintaining standard mandatory and accreditation training requirements
- Co-ordinating such a large operation

One of the difficulties of delivering training and developing the workforce in the NHS is the allocation of duties. Often, internal training is delivered as part of another role within the organization (such as clinical lead), which means the trainer may not be skilled or interested in delivering training. The option of buying in external expertise is costly and may not fit the specific needs of the individual service and staff.

An extended version of the ARD model includes support during training (Figure 18.1). This version of the model is divided into four levels or stages:

1. Before training – aimed at potential CBT trainees.
2. During training – to monitor CBT Trainee progress through training.
3. Ongoing in-house mandatory and accreditation-specific training and skill development (basic level CPD), but the proposal suggests including the attending of conferences by full-time staff.
4. Career development level – with four pathways to follow.

Figure 18.1 – Four stage ARD model for psychological therapy organizations

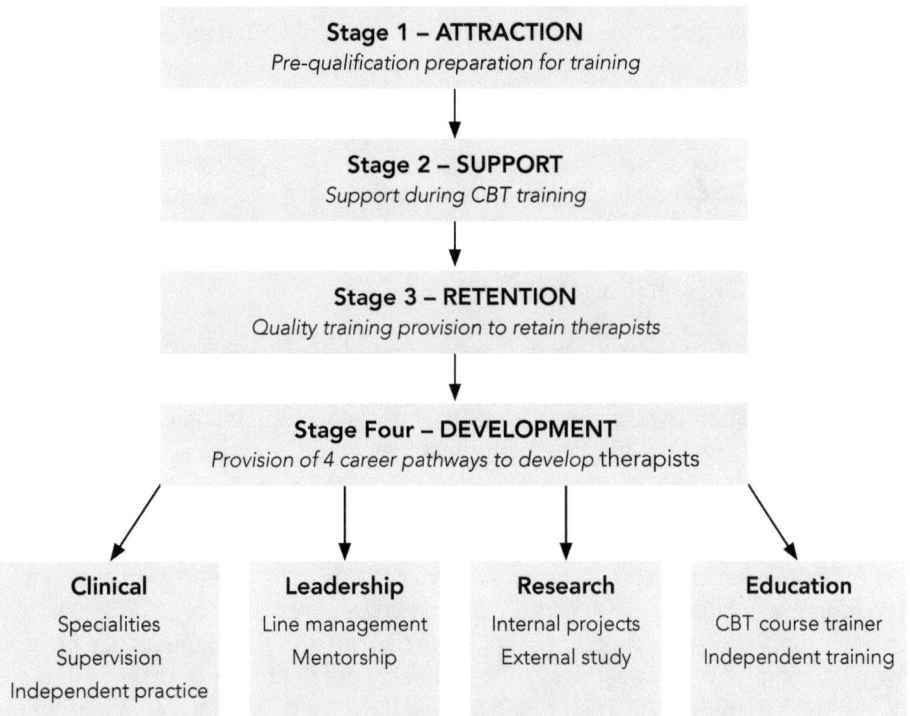

A key part of the model is the proposal to employ a **dedicated training manager** (or lead) in each service. This post would be paid at the same level as a clinical lead (currently 8a, but salary gradings are subject to change). To provide a comprehensive and cohesive training provision, there must be a designated person responsible for the operations at every level. It is suggested that this model would crown organizations with training expertise and a clear investment in staff development.

Case example: Trent Psychological Therapy Service (PTS) clinical development manager post

Trent PTS have contracts with local CCGs across Derbyshire to offer NHS Talking Therapies services in local communities. With a clinical workforce of over 150, they have suffered the same problem of attrition, particularly with CBT therapists. To address this, they have developed a new post of clinical development manager to develop training pathways from PWP to high-intensity CBT therapist. This is a Band 8b position dedicated to developing the workforce. It is an example of how training can be placed at the heart of the service.

Staff recruitment

Most NHS organizations only recruit and employ accredited CBT therapists (or those who meet the requirements and can work towards accreditation). From my personal experience of being involved in recruitment for the CBT trainee posts (as an educationalist), it was clear that most applicants are *not prepared* for these positions.

If a potential candidate does not have a core profession, then they need to prepare a KSA portfolio before interviewing for a CBT training programme. This is notoriously problematic, and many potentially suitable candidates are rejected because they do not have an adequate KSA, or it is incomplete.

Part of this proposal is to create an initial stage of training provision, which is aimed at preparing potential candidates (both internal and external), by preparing either an online KSA tool or a workshop (which they would pay for), generating income. This could be run several times a year, and marketed at psychology graduates with sufficient clinical experience as well as PWPs in other services.

Another pathway would be to develop PWPs in-house for CBT training. Attracting a steady flow of PWPs to enter the service, either as trainee PWPs or as qualified practitioners who want to progress to high-intensity CBT, is another strategy. This is not to diminish the career opportunities or the role of the PWP – they are vital in the maintenance of good-quality psychological therapy services. It is just being open-minded to the idea that some PWPs will want to pursue this career pathway, so having a good succession plan in place to allow for this flow is prudent.

Coordination of trainee development

One of the difficulties with having trainee CBT therapists in different locations across a large organization is the lack of consistency, the potential for overlooking coursework deadlines, staff leaving in the middle of a supervision period, and the general demands on supervisors' time. The training manager (TM) or dedicated training lead can be the link between the organization and the universities, to make sure the course requirements are being adhered to and the right information and support are available for the trainee and their supervisors.

Not all trainees will be funded through Health Education England (HEE). A growing number of people independently fund their training. This requires a suitable placement or place of work to gain clinical practice and apply skills taught on the course. Many NHS Talking Therapies or related services offer placements, but this is currently on an ad hoc basis. It is necessary to plan and ensure the infrastructure is in place to support trainees.

> ### Case example – supporting independent trainees
> The requirements for supporting independent trainees were outlined in a recent round-table discussion among non-IAPT managers of psychological therapies services. It is hoped that a directory of suitably prepared placements will be created and shared to marry up potential CBT trainees to appropriate services that will meet their needs.

Staff retention

The provision of ongoing continued professional development (CPD) and mandatory training is a requirement of every organization. In most cases, this will be the only stage of the ARD model that is currently in operation. While basic training to maintain minimum accreditation requirements and wider national directives regarding patient safety is available, it can become a 'tick-box' exercise that, in some cases, is reduced to a set of online resources or face-to-face sessions that lack creativity. This risks staff disengaging and developing a negative attitude towards training.

Recognizing the costs attached to training, in terms of both time and money, I still believe (from my experience as an educationalist) that, with the right skills, experience and attitude, training can be designed to engage staff by making it more interactive and providing even a small amount of choice over specific options to develop their individual interests. This can be achieved with minimal tweaking of existing resources with a dedicated training manager (TM) with a positive attitude to training and development. The payoff would be increased motivation to learn and develop within the workforce, and an enhanced feeling that the organization is supporting and investing in them.

Within this version of the model, I propose a rolling programme of support for each full-time therapist to attend one conference run by their accrediting body every three years. The rationale for this is to develop and maintain their identity as a therapist in the wider community, to learn, and to represent and promote their service nationally. The esteem developed from this will enhance job satisfaction and will appeal to potential employees when posts are advertised. Despite conference fees often being high, some provide group offer discounts – or the organization could agree to fund part of the conference.

Developing careers within NHS Talking Therapy services

Currently, there is very little choice in terms of career development within NHS Talking Therapy services. Unless you want to become a clinical lead or team leader, there are no other pathways. This means there is an extremely well-qualified and talented workforce with a substantial percentage working beneath their potential. The Band 7 salary (at the time of writing), while attractive to the younger members of the workforce at the start or middle points in their career, is not satisfactory for those with substantially more experience and qualifications and career aspirations to move up from a purely clinical role.

There is an amazing wealth of talent in psychological therapy organizations, but people are hitting a career ceiling. The ARD model provides a framework for career development based on other healthcare professions. Figures 18.2 and 18.3 provide a comparative SWOT (strengths, weaknesses, opportunities, and threats) analysis for the current provision versus the proposed ARD model for career development within NHS Talking Therapies services.

Figure 18.2 – SWOT analysis for career development in NHS Talking Therapies services

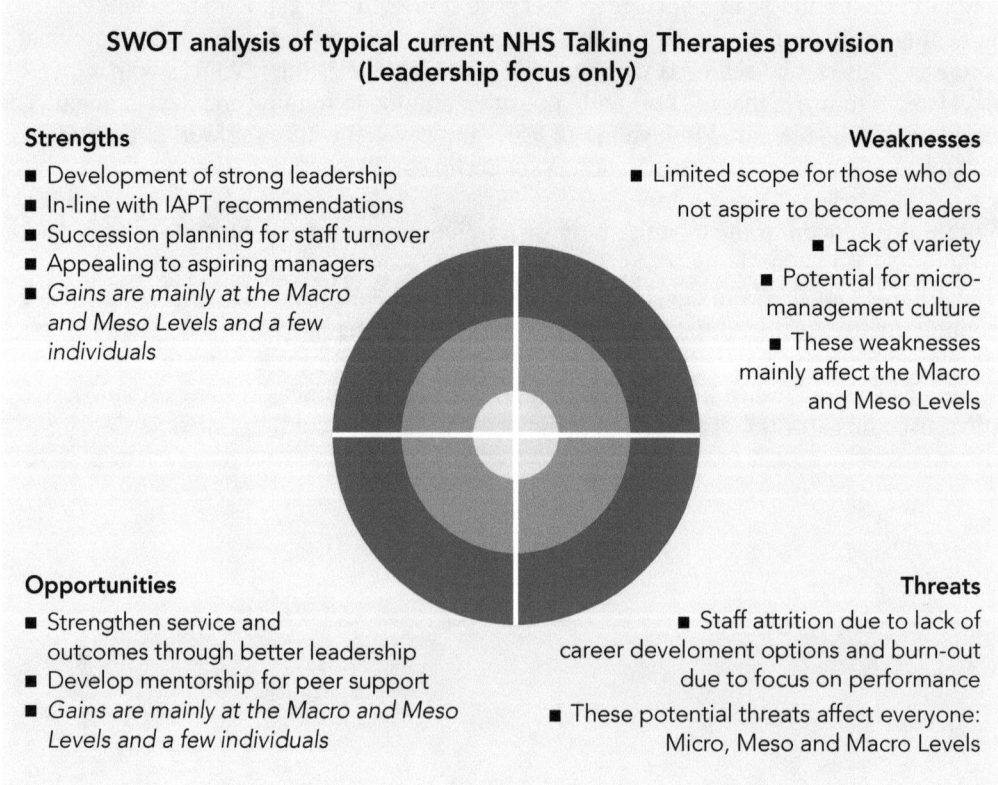

Figure 18.3 – SWOT analysis for the ARD model

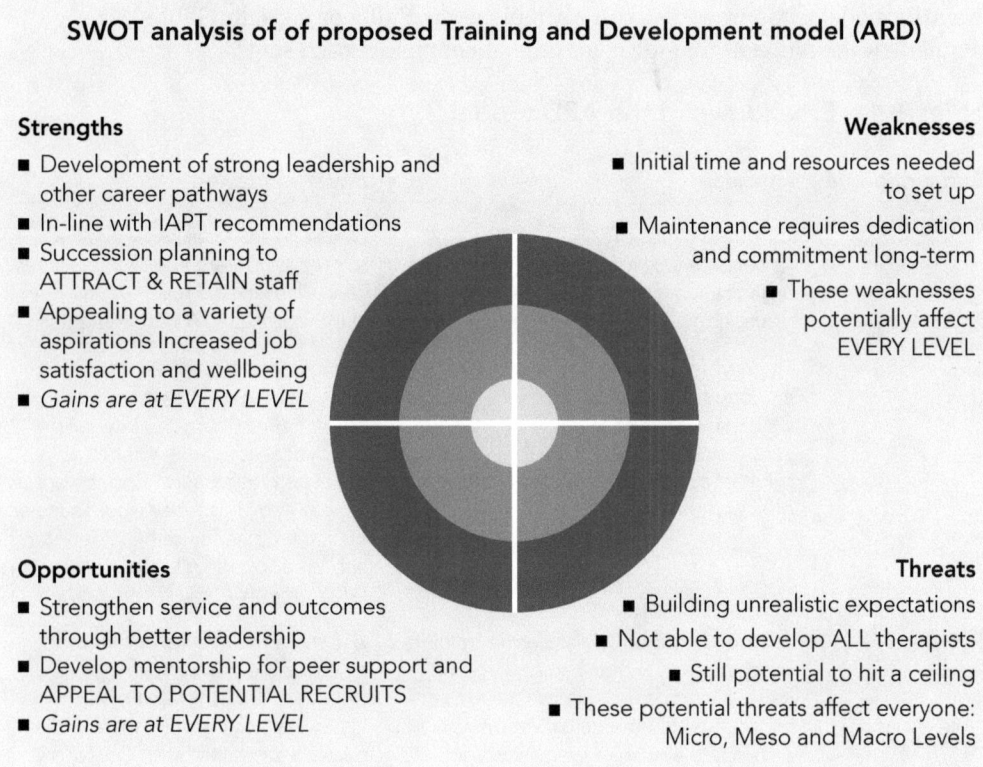

This comparison highlights the pros and cons of the proposed model. By using the helicopter view, we can see that the ARD model provides the most benefit across each level.

Implementing the ARD model in organizations

The ARD model is robust and so can be implemented fully or partially. Table 18.1 summarizes the rationale and ideas for implementation at each stage.

Table 18.1 – Breakdown of the ARD model

Stage of model	Rationale	Implementation
Attract	To attract the *appropriate* candidates to become CBT trainees in your organization if they do not have a core profession.	Develop resources and workshops to prepare potential KSA candidates. This will cover the minimum training standards and KSA requirements.
Supporting training	To provide a coordinated, consistent and structured training experience for CBT trainees. Consistency of provision across sites, support for supervisors and point of contact for trainees other than their supervisor.	Designate a dedicated person (training manager) as the coordinator of the trainee journey. They will be the clinical education contact within the organization and liaison between service and HEIs. They would support both the trainee and the supervisor and be a sounding board to clarify the requirements of the training course.
Retention	To provide ongoing mandatory training in accordance with organizational, national and professional requirements by those within the organization who are passionate about training. This will build an internal training structure based on existing talent, maximizing the internal skill mix of the existing workforce. To build the reputation of the organization for investing in staff training and development.	Use the annual review process to discover the passions and goals of individual CBT therapists within the organization. Identify those with a passion for training. In addition to standard ongoing training, each therapist will be encouraged and supported to attend a conference run by their accrediting body every three years. This will build a professional identity and encourage networking outside the organization.
Development	To provide clear career pathways within NHS Talking Therapies and related services. To increase career opportunities beyond management to retain staff through active career development. This will increase job satisfaction and motivation of the workforce. To create an innovative service that will become self-sustaining through the use of the existing staff talent pool, and be attractive to potential employees.	Offer four career pathways – clinical, leadership, education and research – that all have the potential to progress to Band 8a. Encourage a culture of sharing ideas to maximize the existing talent within the organization.

Benefits to the organization of the proposed model

- Centralized training provision with a dedicated role to oversee and coordinate operations across the service.
- A training provision that is fit for purpose – ensuring staff access the right training for their personal needs and preferences.
- Gain a reputation for investing in staff development. This will make the organization more attractive to potential employees.
- Four level model ensures that we are planning for the future in terms of staff recruitment (by supporting KSA portfolio development before interview), consistent support for CBT trainees, and staff development (by offering career pathways to enhance job satisfaction and support promotion to more senior roles within the organization) to encourage staff retention over time.

Although the focus of the discussion has addressed issues within NHS Talking Therapies services, the model applies equally to other providers of psychological therapies where CBT is offered. The current situation presents a challenge for all services, so making career development central to their ethos will attract potential CBT therapists to those services.

The take-home message for service providers

This discussion has provided a conceptual model to address how we can grow the CBT workforce in psychological therapy services. The lack of current career development options for CBT therapists threatens to exacerbate the problem of high attrition rates from NHS Talking Therapies and related services. A robust training provision that offers options and variety for therapists and grows their talent will help services attract, retain, and develop their workforce.

> **Reflection point**
>
> Does the ARD model resonate with your service goals? How can you integrate it? Which stage could be addressed first? What further resources might you require?

Promoting CBT careers in the education community

It is essential that we address the issue of growing the NHS Talking Therapies workforce before Stage 1 of the ARD model (see Appendix 1). We need to prepare potential CBT therapists to grow into the position where they can access training. This requires clear career advice that provides information on potential pathways to access CBT training based on the individual's current qualifications and clinical experience. This includes sound career advice in colleges before students select degree options. Psychology degrees are attractive, but they do not guarantee access to a clinical career. A core profession in mental health provides psychology theory in an applied manner, giving the student more options in their career, with CBT being just one of many.

Let's look again at the CBT career roadmap diagram (first introduced in Chapter 5).

Figure 18.4 – the CBT career roadmap

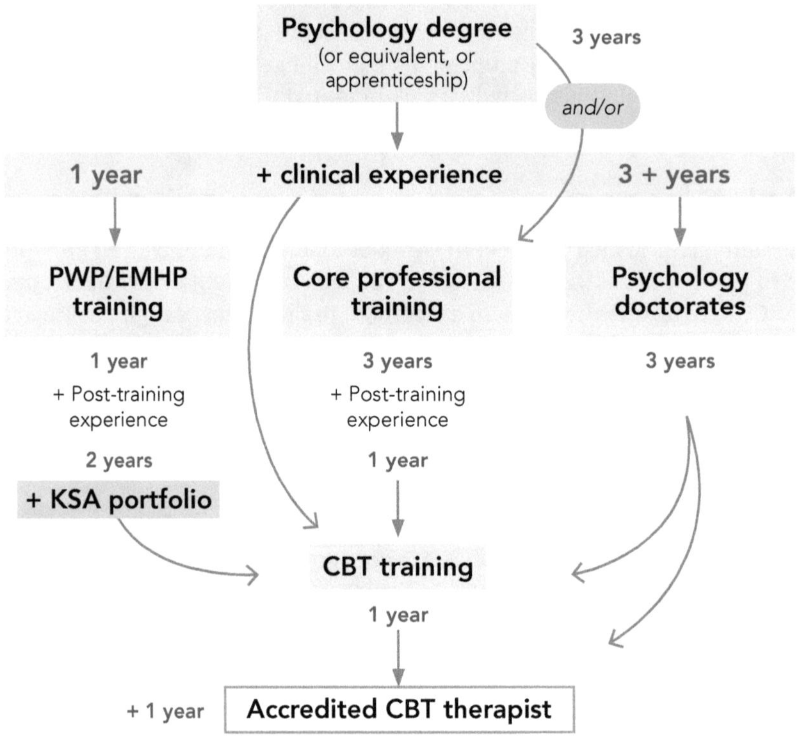

The roadmap goes beyond a CBT career. It identifies the different pathways to a clinical career in mental health. This bigger-picture perspective is essential for educationalists and career advisers at all stages of education to be aware of. Current advice tends to be narrow, focusing on psychology degrees as an initial higher education option for a mental health career. It has been suggested that more knowledge and understanding of mental health core professions is provided to broaden students' choice. These degree programmes provide high psychology content, which is applied through clinical skills, leading to a professional role immediately upon completion of the undergraduate degree. This also includes a clear and well-paid career. Psychology graduates form the largest group of graduates wanting a mental health career, making it the most competitive pathway to move forward.

For students who want to do a pure psychology degree, information on gaining relevant clinical experience, in addition to the degree, is necessary to prepare them for postgraduate clinical options. Due to the competitive nature of postgraduate clinical courses, relevant work experience is essential. Chapter 6 provides suggestions for this and the guide on the Resources page is also relevant for organizations and educationists to extend their knowledge to support students.

Teachers in schools and colleges need to understand the different roles identified on the CBT roadmap. Many psychology teachers and lecturers focus on the doctoral pathways which limit options for psychology students and graduates. We have considered the mental health core profession option, but there is also the low-intensity CBT route into a clinical career in mental health. These are funded courses and have a clear and varied career development trajectory, often overlooked by school and college career advisers.

Reflection point

If you have a role as a career adviser, are you aware of all the career options leading to a CBT career? If not, what can you do to learn more? How can your organization change its approach to promoting psychological therapy careers?

Concluding comments

This book has provided a guide to a career as a cognitive behavioural therapist from initial contemplation, through the stages of becoming a CBT therapist and developing your career. With the ARD model providing a clear framework for this process, the guide has been divided to reflect the journey at each level. The CBT career map is another central feature of the guide to give a clear representation of the pathways available. Although a long and intense road, with many challenges, the storied accounts of people from different backgrounds and stages of their journey offer hope. The online resources that accompany this book mean that it can be used flexibly. Whatever stage you are at, I hope that this guide will become a useful part of your CBT career journey.

Appendix 1: The ARD model of CBT career development

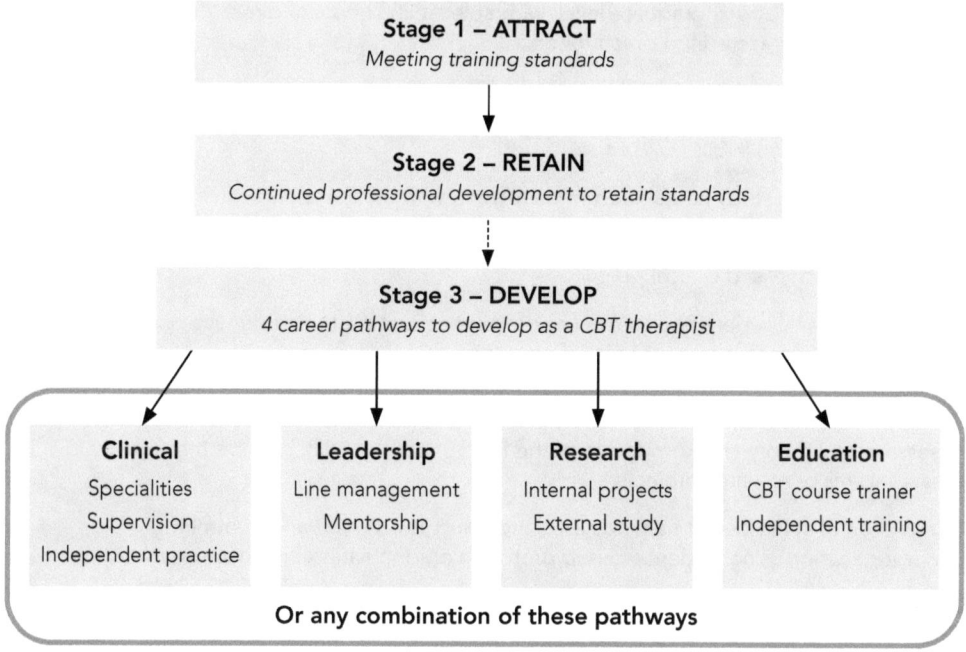

Appendix 2:
The BABCP minimum training standards and core curriculum

BABCP minimum training standards (MTS) and core curriculum requirements for CBT training checklist

450 hours of study at postgraduate level, with at least 200 hours of direct structured training by BABCP-accredited practitioners.	
Of the 200 hours structured teaching, at least 100 hours needs to have been completed by graduation of a postgraduate course and validated by the Higher Education Institution (HEI).	
The remaining 250 study hours need to be logged with evidence and can include self-directed study.	
200 hours of supervised clinical practice.	
40 hours of clinical supervision as this needs to be at a ratio of one hour supervision for every five hours of clinical practice during training.	
There must be a 50:50 split between theory and clinical skills teaching.	
Assessment of theory and knowledge of the fundamentals of CBT can be through essays, exams or research projects.	
Completion of at least eight training cases, including assessment and treatment under supervision using evidence-based protocols or formulation-driven approaches.	
Across the eight cases there must be at least two anxiety disorders, or one anxiety disorder and a trauma or stressor-related disorder as well as a mood disorder presentation.	
At least four of the eight training cases need to be presented as case studies, covering at least three different presentations, and need to be formally assessed.	
Three cases need to be closely supervised with live material formally assessed either in vivo or through marking of recorded sessions.	
Of these three cases, at least two anxiety disorders or one anxiety disorder and a trauma or stressor-related disorder as well as a mood disorder presentation.	
A closely supervised case needs to be taken to supervision at least five times with at least two examples of live practice shared during the supervision of these cases.	

N.B. Always refer to the most up-to-date versions of the minimum training standards and core curriculum on the BABCP website.

Appendix 3: The CBT career roadmap

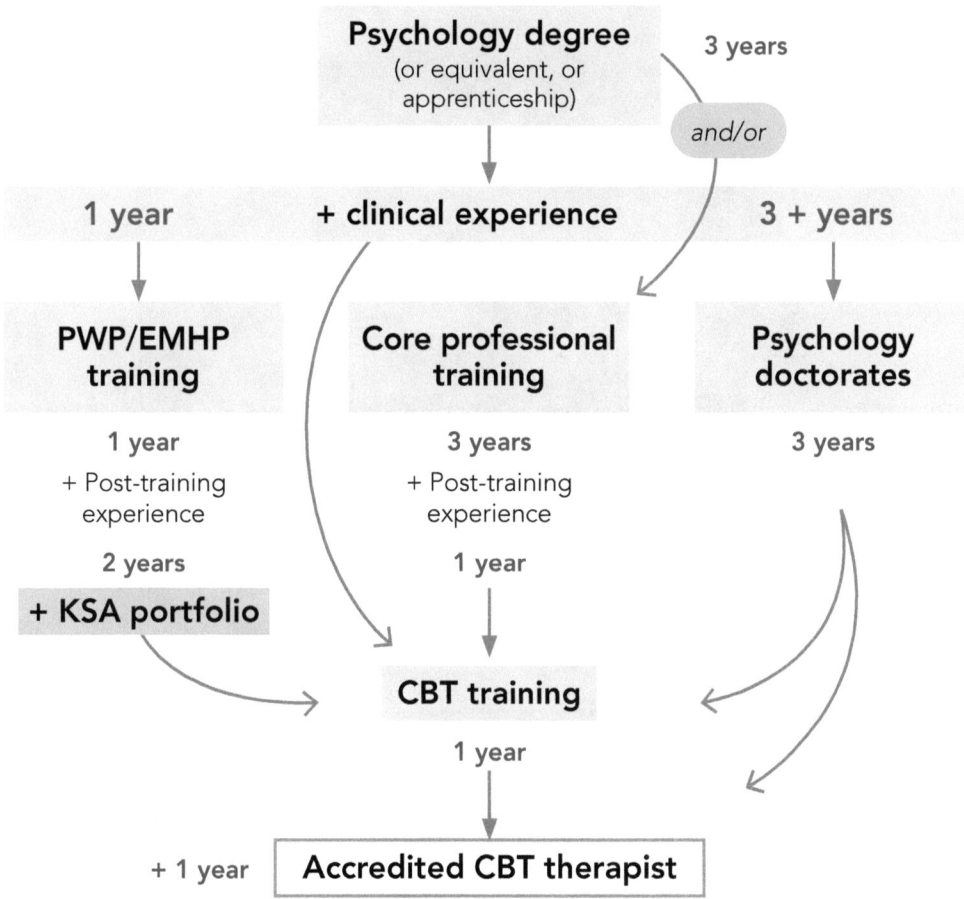

Appendix 4: CBT therapy process model

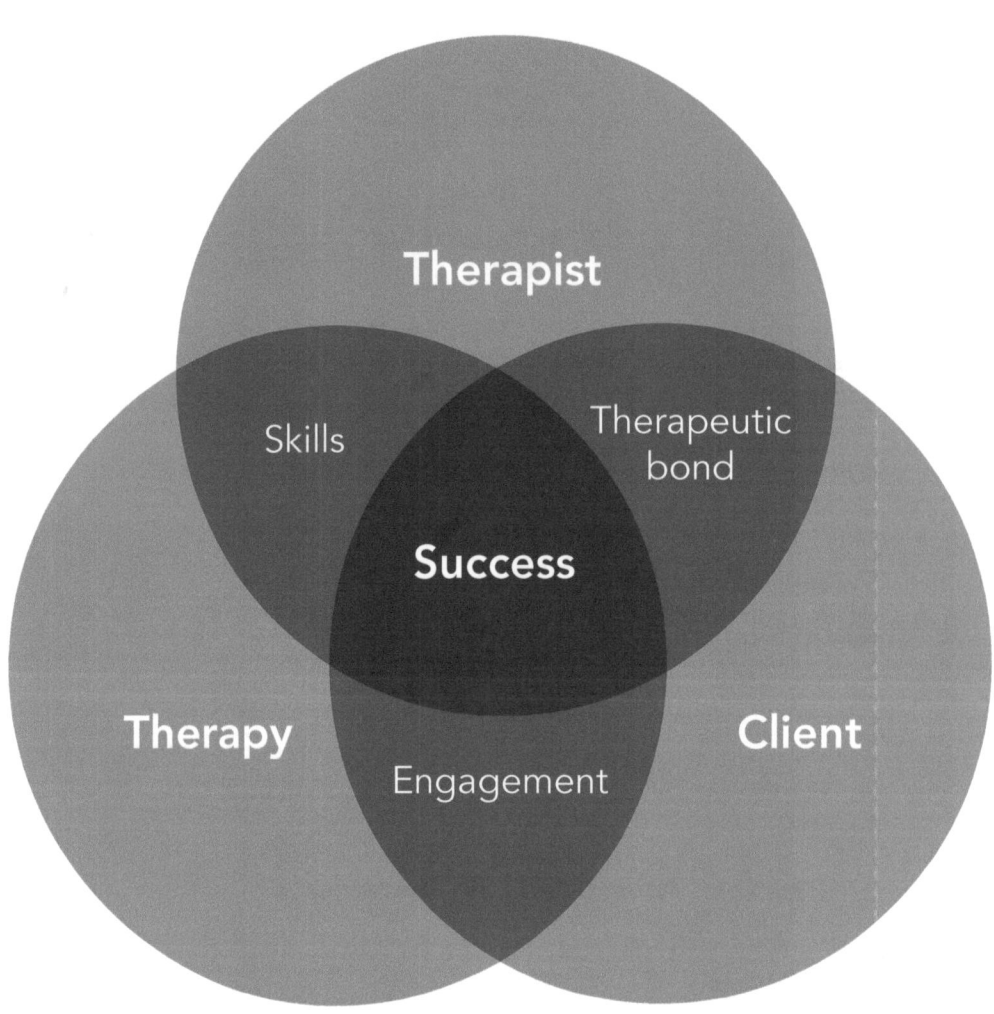

Appendix 5: Using the CBT process model in clinical supervision

Skills
Are you working within skill set? What skills need to be practiced? For example, imagery rescripting for depression. Practice in supervision and read up on it.

Therapeutic bond
Have expectations of therapy been clearly stated? Is therapist taking too much responsibility? Address boundaries and therapist schemas (see Leahy, 2001)

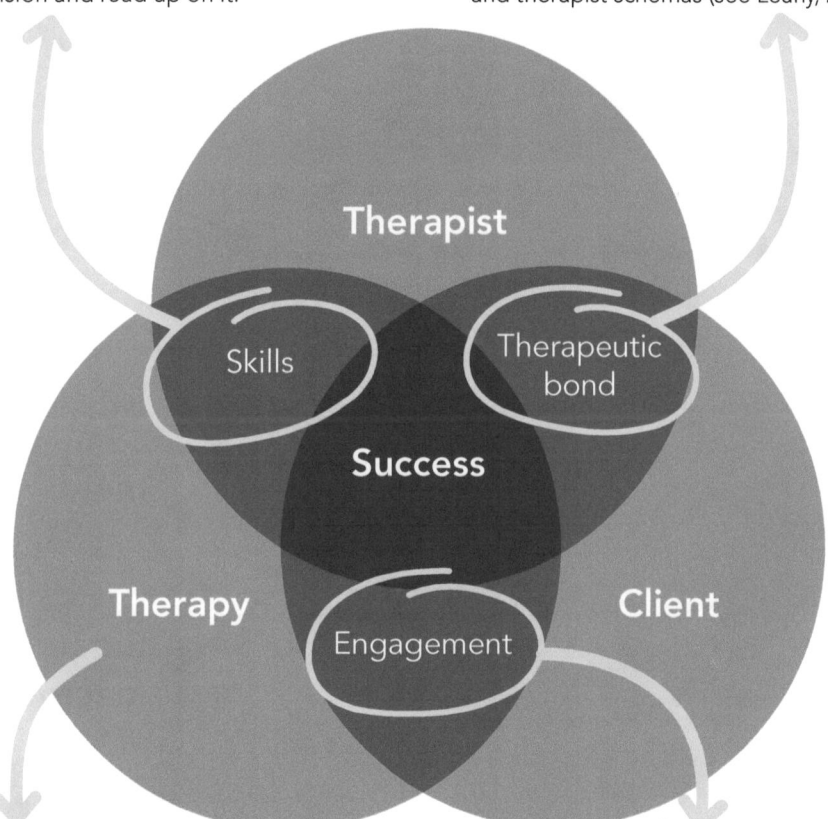

Systemic issues
Are there any issues with family or relationships that need attention? Has the bigger picture been considered such as work and school? Include in the formulation

Engagement
Is client engaging? Are they doing homework? Are they avoidant in sessions? Do role plays in supervision and consider creative methods. Is CBT the right approach for them? Is now the right time?

Appendix 6: Helicopter view model of critical reflection

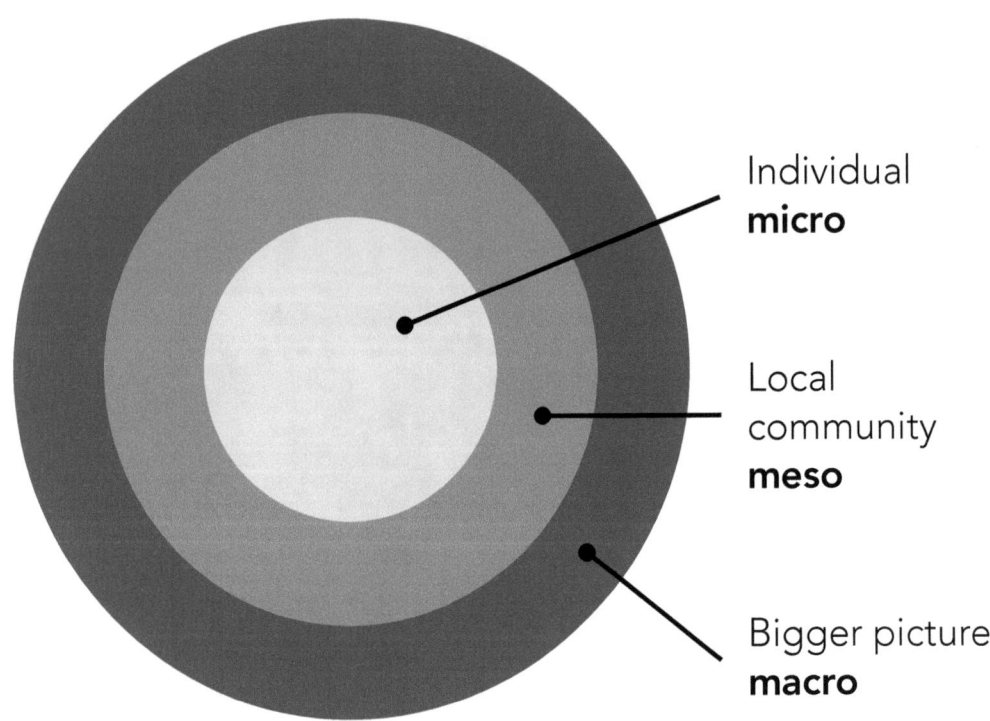

Appendix 7: The four stage ARD model of CBT career development for organizations

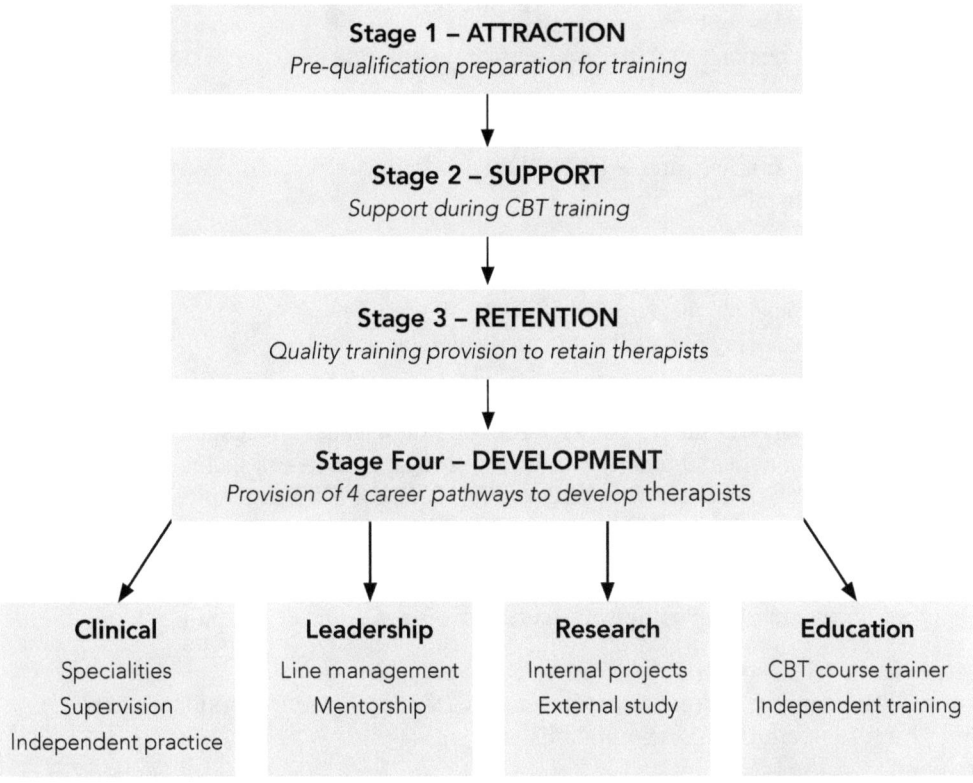

Appendix 8: Websites and other resources

Websites

BACP Private practice toolkit:
www.bacp.co.uk/media/12921/bacp-pp-toolkit-private-practice-checklist.pdf

NHS England Education website: www.hee.nhs.uk

Information on healthcare careers on NHS England Education website: www.healthcareers.nhs.uk

NHS Leadership Academy website: www.leadershipacademy.nhs.uk

NHS Leadership Academy description of the Healthcare Leadership Model: www.leadershipacademy.nhs.uk/healthcare-leadership-model/

Compassionate and inclusive leadership described on the NHS Senior Leadership and Onboarding Support website: https://senioronboarding.leadershipacademy.nhs.uk/creating-compassionate-and-inclusive-cultures/compassionate-and-inclusive-leadership-resource/#:~:text=Compassionate%20leaders%20take%20a%20genuine,do%20something%20to%20alleviate%20distress

Skills for Care (provides information on the Care Certificate): www.skillsforcare.org.uk/resources/documents/Developing-your-workforce/Care-Certificate/Introduction.pdf

Details of the 15 standards of care can be accessed at: www.skillsforcare.org.uk/resources/documents/Developing-your-workforce/Care-Certificate/The-Care-Certificate-Standards.pdf

If you require information about how the **Care Certificate** is assessed and certified see:

- Health Education England (www.hee.nhs.uk)
- Skills for Care (www.skillsforcare.org.uk or)
- Skills for Health (www.skillsforhealth.org.uk)

Key documents

Mental Health Taskforce (2016) The five-year forward view for mental health.

NHS England (2019) NHS long-term plan.

NHS England (2019) NHS mental health implementation plan 2019/20 – 23/24.

NHS Equality and Diversity Council (2015) Improving Lesbian Gay Bisexual and Trans (LGBT) Equality Across the NHS: a Paper for the Equality and Diversity Council. Available at: www.england.nhs.uk/wp-content/uploads/2015/11/edc1-lgbt-equal-pap-20-10-15.pdf (accessed January 2024).

Roth and Pilling CBT competency framework

The CBT competency framework can be accessed on the UCL website. It comprises of a series of documents. Main page with all the links:

www.ucl.ac.uk/pals/research/clinical-educational-and-health-psychology/research-groups/competence-frameworks-0 (accessed January 2024).

The self-assessment tool:
www.ucl.ac.uk/pals/sites/pals/files/migrated-files/self_assessment_tool_manual.pdf (accessed January 2024).

Resources and guides

Cumbria, Northumberland, Tyne and Wear NHS foundation provide CBT self-help leaflets covering a number of issues. There are audio and translated versions available on the website: https://web.ntw.nhs.uk/selfhelp/ (accessed January 2024).

Royal College of Psychiatrists have translated information:
www.rcpsych.ac.uk/mental-health/translations (accessed January 2024).

Therapist Aid Problem-solving worksheet:
www.therapistaid.com/worksheets/problem-solving.pdf (accessed January 2024).

Therapist Aid progressive muscle relaxation script: https://www.therapistaid.com/worksheets/progressive-muscle-relaxation-script (accessed January 2024)

Listen to a video version:
https://www.youtube.com/watch?v = 86HUcX8ZtAk&t = 184s&themeRefresh = 1 (accessed January 2024)

MIND wellness action plan for hybrid working: www.mind.org.uk/media/12143/mind-wellness-action-plan-hybrid-work.pdf (accessed January 2024)

MIND wellness action plan for workplace: www.mind.org.uk/media-a/5760/mind-guide-for-employees-wellness-action-plans_final.pdf (accessed January 2024)

Mindshift app link: www.anxietycanada.com/resources/mindshift-cbt/ (accessed January 2024)

CBT Bristol (Andrew Grimmer) website: www.bristolcbt.co.uk/publications/psychosexual-articles/clinical-issues-for-cbt-therapists-when-working-with-gender-sexuality-and-relationship-diversity/ (accessed January 2024)

Health & Safety Executive website page on work-related stress: www.hse.gov.uk/stress/ (accessed January 2024)

Health & Safety Executive (HSE) 'working together to reduce stress' guide for employees: www.hse.gov.uk/pubns/indg424.pdf (accessed January 2024)

ACAS guide to managing stress in the workplace: www.acas.org.uk/managing-work-related-stress (accessed January 2024)

Dr Kristian Neff's website provides self-compassion focused guided practices and exercises: https://self-compassion.org/category/exercises/#exercises (accessed January 2024)

Advancing mental health equality toolkit produced by the Royal College of Psychiatrists: www.rcpsych.ac.uk/improving-care/nccmh/service-design-and-development/advancing-mental-health-equality (accessed January 2024)

Police Care UK for information on CBT careers in the police force: www.policecare.org.uk

House of Healing CBT. Jodie's private CBT practice offering Islamic cognitive behavioural therapy for Muslims: www.houseofhealingcbt.com

BABCP Let's talk equality video: www.youtube.com/watch?v = fjRlABAmwus (accessed January 2024)

References

Adler, J.M. & McAdams, D.P. (2007) Telling stories about therapy: Ego development, well-being, and the therapeutic relationship in Josselson, R., McAdams, D.P., & Lieblich, A. (Eds.). *The Meaning of Others: Narrative Studies of Relationships* (pp. 213-236). American Psychological Association.

Adler, J.M., Skalina, L.M., & McAdams, D.P. (2008) The narrative reconstruction of psychotherapy and psychological health. *Psychotherapy Research* **18** (6) 719-734.

Alfonsson, S., Parling, T., Spännargård, A., Andersson, G. & Lundgren, T. (2018) The effects of clinical supervision on supervisees and patients in cognitive behavioral therapy: a systematic review, *Cognitive Behaviour Therapy* **47** (3) 206-228, DOI: 10.1080/16506073.2017.1369559

Balsam, K. F., & Mohr, J. J. (2007) Adaptation to sexual orientation stigma: a comparison of bisexual and lesbian/gay adults. *Journal of Counselling Psychology* **54** 306-319.

Bamber, M.R. (2011) *Overcoming your work-based stress A CBT-based self-help guide*. Routledge.

Beauchamp, T.L., & Childress, J.F. (1979) *Principles of Bioethics*. Oxford University Press: Oxford.

Beauchamp T.L., & Childress J.F. (2013) *Principles of Bioethics* (7th ed). Oxford University Press.

Beck, A. (2016) *Transcultural Cognitive Behaviour Therapy for Anxiety & Depression: A practical guide*. Routledge.

Beck, A. (2019) Understanding Black and Minority Ethnic service user's experience of racism as part of the assessment, formulation, and treatment of mental health problems in cognitive behaviour therapy. *The Cognitive Behaviour Therapist* **12** E8. doi:10.1017/S1754470X18000223

Beck, A. T., Rush, A. J., Shaw, B. F., & Emery, G. (1979) *Cognitive Therapy of Depression*. New York: The Guilford Press.

Beck, A., Naz, S., Brooks, M., & Jankowska, M. (2019) *IAPT Black Asian and Minority Ethnic Service User Positive Practice Guide*. BABCP.

Bennett-Levy, J., Thwaites, R., Haarhoff, B., & Perry, H. (2014) *Experiencing CBT From the Inside Out: A self-practice/self-reflection workbook for therapists*. The Guilford Press.

Bernal, G., Bonilla, J., & Bellido, C. (1995) Ecological validity and cultural sensitivity for outcome research: issues for the cultural adaptation and development of psychosocial treatments with Hispanics. *Journal of Abnormal Child Psychology*, **23**(1), 67-82.

Beshai, S., Clark, C. M., & Dobson, K. S. (2013) Conceptual and pragmatic considerations in the use of cognitive-behavioral therapy with Muslim clients. *Cognitive Therapy and Research* **37** (1) 197-206.

Blackburn, I.-M., James, I. A., Milne, D. L., Baker, C., Standart, S., Garland, A., & Reichelt, F. K. (2001). *Revised Cognitive Therapy Scale* (CTS-R, CTS) [Database record]. APA PsycTests.

Bostwick, W., & Hequembourg, A. (2014) 'Just a little hint': bisexual-specific microaggressions and their connection to epistemic injustices. *Culture, Health, and Sexuality* **16** 488-503.

Bouman W.P., Claes L., Brewin N., Crawford J.R., Millet N., Fernandez-Aranda F., & Arcelus J. (2017a) Gender Dysphoria and Anxiety: A comparative study between transgender people and the general population. *International Journal of Transgenderism* **18** (1) 16-26.

Bouman W.P., Suess Schwend A., Motmans J., Smiley A., Safer J.D., Deutch M.B., Adams N.J., & Winter, S. (2017b) Language and Transgender Health. *International Journal of Transgenderism* **18** (1) 1-6.

BPS (2019) *Guidelines for Psychologists Working with Gender, Sexuality and Relationship Diversity: For adults and young people (aged 18 and over)*. British Psychological Society: Leicester.

Brandstätter, H. (1997) Becoming an entrepreneur — A question of personality structure? *Journal of Economic Psychology* **18** (2-3) 157-177.

British Association for Behavioural and Cognitive Psychotherapies (BABCP) (2021). Standards of Conduct, Performance and Ethics. Available at: www.babcp.com/Portals/0/Files/About/BABCP-Standards-of-Conduct-Performance- and-Ethics%20Feb%202021.pdf?ver = 2021-02-24-142904-080

Bruner, J. (1978). The role of dialogue in language acquisition. In A. Sinclair, R. Jarvella and W. J. M. Levelt (Eds.), *The Child 's Conception of Language* (pp. 241-256).

Burgess, A., van Diggele, C., Roberts, C. *et al*. (2020) Planning peer assisted learning (PAL) activities in clinical schools. *BMC Medical Education,* **20** (Supplement 2) 453 (2020).

Campling P. (2015) Reforming the culture of healthcare: the case for intelligent kindness. *BJPsych Bull* **39** (1) 1–5.

Care Quality Commission (2018) *Are we listening? Review of children's and young people's mental health services*. First published 8 March 2018.

Carvalho, S., Castilho, P., Seabra, D., Salvador, C., Rijo, D., & Carona, C. (2022). Critical issues in cognitive behavioural therapy (CBT) with gender and sexual minorities (GSMs). *The Cognitive Behaviour Therapist* **15** E3.

Castonguay, L.G., & Hill, C.E. (Eds.) (2017) How and why are some therapists better than others? American Psychological Association.

Chaskalson, M. (2011) *The mindful workplace: Developing resilient individuals and resonant organizations with MBSR*. John Wiley & Sons Ltd.

Clegg, S., Heywood-Everett, S., & Siddiqi, N. (2016) A review of cultural competence training in UK mental health settings. *British Journal of Mental Health Nursing* **5** 176–183.

Cook, C.H., Powell, A., & Sims, A. (2009) Spirituality and Psychiatry. London: Gaskell.

Corrie, S., & Lane, D. A. (2015) *CBT supervision*. Sage.

Cresswell, C., Parkinson, M., Thirlwall, K., & Willetts, L. (2019) *Parent-led CBT for child anxiety: Helping parents help their kids*. Guilford Press.

Department of Health (2011) No Health without mental health. A cross-government mental health outcomes strategy for people of all ages. London.

Department of Health (2012) Compassion in practice: Nursing, midwifery and care staff our vision and strategy. Published by NHS Commissioning Board Chief Nursing Officer and DH Chief Nursing Adviser, December 2012: www.england.nhs.uk/wp-content/uploads/2012/12/compassion-in-practice.pdf

Dugas, M. J., & Robichaud, M. (2007). *Cognitive-behavioral treatment for generalized anxiety disorder: From science to practice*. Routledge/Taylor & Francis Group.

Dummett, N. (2010) Cognitive -behavioural therapy with children, young people and families: From individual to systemic therapy. *Advances in Psychiatric Treatment* **16** (1) 23–36.

Dyar, C., & London, B. (2018) Longitudinal examination of a bisexual-specific minority stress process among bisexual cisgender women. *Psychology of Women Quarterly* **42** 342–360.

EAHC (2013) *European Profile of Prevention and Promotion of Mental Health*. Executive Agency for Health and Consumers, Brussels.

Edwards, D. & Potter, J. (1992) *Discursive Psychology*. Sage.

Egan, G. (1975) *The Skilled Helper: A systematic approach to effective helping*. Pacific Grove, CA: Brooks/Cole.

Elliott, M. N., Kanouse, D. E., Burkhart, Q., Abel, G. A., Lyratzopolous, G., Beckett, M. K., Schuster, M. A., & Roland, M. (2015) Sexual minorities in England have poorer health and worse health care experiences: a national survey. *Journal of General Internal Medicine* **30** 9–16. doi: 10.1007/s11606-014-2905-y

Engel G.L. (1977) The need for a new medical model: a challenge for biomedicine. *Science* **196** 129–136.

Etherington, K. (2016) Personal experience and critical reflexivity in counselling and psychotherapy research. *Counselling & Psychotherapy Research* **17** (2) 1–10.

Faheem, A. (2023) 'It's been quite a poor show' – exploring whether practitioners working for Improving Access to Psychological Therapies (IAPT) services are culturally competent to deal with the needs of Black, Asian, and Minority Ethnic (BAME) communities. *The Cognitive Behaviour Therapist* **16** E6.

Farooq, R., Oladokun, O., Al-Mujaini, R., & Addy, C. (2023) Unsettling the 'master's house': A critical account and reflections on developing a clinical psychology anti-racism strategy. *Psychotherapy & Politics International,* **21**(1&2), 1-17.

Farooq, R., Abuan, B., Griffiths, C., Usman-Dio, F., Kamal, O.J., Toor, P., Hajaji, Y., & Yeebo, M. (2022) "I didn't feel as though I fitted in": critical accounts from aspiring clinical psychologists from racially minoritized backgrounds. *Journal of Critical Psychology, Counselling & Psychotherapy* **22** (3) 6–17.

Fernando, S. (2017) *Institutionalised Racism in Psychiatry and Clinical Psychology: Race matters in mental health.* Palgrave Macmillan e-book.

Foy, A., Morris, D., Fernandes, V., & Rimes, K. (2019) LGBQ adults' experiences of Improving Access to Psychological Therapies and primary care counselling services: Informing clinical practice and service delivery. *The Cognitive Behaviour Therapist* **12** E42. doi:10.1017/S1754470X19000291.

Gazula, S., McKenna, L., Cooper, S., & Paliedelis, P. (2017) A systematic review of reciprocal peer tutoring within tertiary health profession education programs. *Health Professions Education* **3** (2) 64–78.

Gibbs, G. (1988) *Learning by Doing: A guide to teaching and learning methods.* London: Further Education Unit.

Gilbert, P., & Leahy, R. (Eds.) (2007) *The Therapeutic Relationship in the Cognitive Behavioural Psychotherapies.* Routledge: Hove.

Gilbert, P. (2010) *The Compassionate Mind.* London: Constable & Robinson.

Gillon, R. (1994) Medical ethics: four principles plus attention to scope. *BMJ.* **309** (6948) 1848.

Goffman, E. (1963) *Stigma: Notes on the management of spoiled identities.* Penguin.

Graham, A.R., Soronsen, S., Hayes-Skelton, S.A. (2013) Enhancing the cultural sensitivity of cognitive behavioural interventions for anxiety in diverse populations. *Behaviour Therapy* **36** (5) 101–108.

Grey, N., Deale, A., Byrne, S., & Liness, S. (2014) Making CBT supervision more effective. In A. Whittingham & N. Grey (Eds.), *How to become a more effective CBT therapist: Mastering metacompetence in clinical practice* (pp. 269–283). Wiley & Sons.

Grimmer, A., (2021) *Clinical issues for CBT therapists when working with gender, sexuality and relationship diversity.* Bristol CBT. Available at: www.bristolcbt.co.uk/publications/psychosexual-articles/clinical-issues-for-cbt-therapists-when-working-with-gender-sexuality-and-relationship-diversity/ (accessed January 2024).

Haarhoff, B. (2006) The importance of identifying and understanding therapist schema in cognitive therapy training and supervision. *New Zealand Journal of Psychology*, **35**(3), 126-131.

Hathaway, W. (2013) Pathways toward graduate training in the clinical psychology of religion and spirituality: A spiritual competencies model. In: K. I. Pargament, A. Mahoney, & E. P. Shafranske (Eds.), APA Handbook of Psychology, Religion, and Spirituality: Volume II (pp. 635–649). Washington, DC: APA.

Hays, P. (2008) *Addressing cultural complexities in practice: Assessment, diagnosis, and therapy.* 2. Washington, DC: American Psychological Association; 2008.

Hays, P. A. (2006). Developing culturally responsive cognitive-behavioral therapies. In P. A. Hays, & G. Y. Iwamasa (Eds.), *Culturally-responsive cognitive-behavioral therapy: Assessment, practice, and supervision* (pp. 3–19).

Heath, G. & Startup, H. (Eds.) (2020) *Creative Methods in Schema Therapy: Advances & innovation in clinical practice.* Routledge: Oxon

Hogarth, R.A. (2019) The myth of innate racial differences between white and black people's bodies: lessons from the 1793 yellow fever epidemic in Philadelphia, Pennsylvania. *American Journal of Public Health* **109** 1339–1341.

Huey, S.J. Jr, Park, A.L., Galán, C.A., Wang, C.X. (2023) Culturally Responsive Cognitive Behavioral Therapy for Ethnically Diverse Populations. *Annual Review of Clinical Psychology* **9** (19) 51–78.

Johns, C. (1994) Nuances of reflection. Journal of Clinical Nursing 3 71–75.

Kelly, M.R., Robbins, R., Martin, & J.L. (2019) Delivering Cognitive Behavioral Therapy for Insomnia in Military Personnel and Veterans. *Sleep Med Clin* **14** (2) 199–208.

Kendall, P.C. & Hedtke, K. (2006a) *Cognitive-behavioral Therapy for Anxious Children: Therapist manual.* Ardmore, PA: Workbook Publishing; 2006a.

Kendall, P.C. & Hedtke, K. (2006b) *The Coping Cat Workbook.* Ardmore, PA: Workbook Publishing; 2006b.

Kennerley, H., Kirk, J. & Westbrook, D. (2016) *An Introduction to Cognitive Behaviour Therapy: Skills & applications* (3rd edition). Sage.

Kinsella, P. & Moya, H. (2021) *CBT for Long-Term Conditions and Medically Unexplained Symptoms: A guide for practitioners.* Routledge: London.

Kolb, D. A. (1983) *Problem management: Learning from experience. The Executive Mind*. San Francisco: Jossey-Bass.

Lago, C. (ed) (2011) *The Handbook of Transcultural Counselling and Psychotherapy*. McGraw-Hill Education, UK.

Laungani, P. (2004) *Asian Perspectives in Counselling and Psychotherapy*. London: Psychology Press.

Lawton, L., McRae, M., & Gordon, L. (2021) Frontline yet at the back of the queue: improving access and adaptations to CBT for black African and Caribbean communities. *The Cognitive Behaviour Therapist* **14** e30, 1-19.

Leahy, R. (2008) The therapeutic relationship in cognitive behavioural therapy. *Behavioural and Cognitive Psychotherapy* **36** (6) 769-777.

Leahy, R. (2002) A model of emotional schemas. *Cognitive & Behavioral Practice* **9** 177-190.

Leahy, R. (2001) *Overcoming Resistance in Cognitive Therapy*. Guilford Press.

Lewis, K.V., Ho, M., Harris, C. & Morrison, R. (2016) Becoming an entrepreneur: opportunities and identity transitions. *International Journal of Gender and Entrepreneurship* **8** (2) 98-116. https://doi.org/10.1108/IJGE-02-2015-0006

Liu, J.J., Ein, N., Forchuk, C. *et al*. (2023) A meta-analysis of internet-based cognitive behavioral therapy for military and veteran populations. *BMC Psychiatry* **23** 223.

Lopez, S. R., Grover, K. P., Holland, D., Johnson, M. J., Kain, C. D., Kanel, K., & Rhyne, M. C. (1989) Development of culturally sensitive psychotherapists. *Professional Psychology: Research and Practice* **20** 369.

McAdams, D.P. (2001) The psychology of life stories. *Review of General Psychology* **5** 100-122.

McNally Keehn, R.H., Lincoln, A.J., Brown, M.Z., & Chavira, D.A. (2013) The Coping Cat program for children with anxiety and autism spectrum disorder: a pilot randomized controlled trial. *J Autism Dev Disord* **43** (1) 57-67. doi: 10.1007/s10803-012-1541-9.

Meyer, I.H. (2003) Prejudice, social stress, and mental health in lesbian, gay, and bisexual populations: conceptual issues and research evidence. *Psychological bulletin* **129** (5) 674.

Meyer, I.H., & Frost, D.M. (2013) "Minority stress and the health of sexual minorities". In: C.J. Patterson & A.R. D'Augelli (Eds.) *Handbook of Psychology and Sexual Orientation* (pp252-266). Oxford University Press.

Meichenbaum, D. (1993) Changing conceptions of cognitive behavior modification: retrospect and prospect. *Journal of Consulting and Clinical Psychology* **61** (2) 202-204.

Milne D. (2008) CBT supervision: From reflexivity to specialization. *Behavioural and Cognitive Psychotherapy* **36** (6) 779-786.

Milne, D., & Dunkerley, C. (2010). Towards evidence-based clinical supervision: The development and evaluation of four CBT guidelines. *The Cognitive Behaviour Therapist* **3** (2) 43-57.

Milne, D. L., & Reiser, R. P. (2014). SAGE: A scale for rating competence in CBT supervision. In C. E. Watkins, Jr. & D. L. Milne (Eds.), *The Wiley international handbook of clinical supervision* (pp. 402–415). Wiley Blackwell.

Milne, D.L. (2017). *Evidence-based CBT Supervision: Principles and practice*. John Wiley and Sons.

Moya, H. (2022) CBT career development: introducing a conceptual model. *CBT Today*, 28-30.

Murray, T. & Arroyo I. (2002). *Toward Measuring and Maintaining the Zone of Proximal Development in Adaptive Instructional Systems*. Submission to the 2002 International Conference on Intelligent Tutoring Systems.

Muse K, Kennerley H, McManus F. The why, what, when, who and how of assessing CBT competence to support lifelong learning. *The Cognitive Behaviour Therapist*. 2022;15:e57.

Muse, K., McManus, F., Rakovshik, S., & Thwaites, R. (2017). *Assessment of Core CBT Skills (ACCS)* [Database record]. APA PsycTests.

Nazroo, J.Y., Bhui, K.S., & Rhodes, J. (2020). Where next for understanding race/ethnic inequalities in severe mental illness? Structural, interpersonal, and institutional racism. *Sociology of Health & Illness* **42** 262-276.

Naheem, F., Sajid, S., Naz, S., & Phiri, P. (2023) Culturally adapted CBT: the evolution of psychotherapy adaptation frameworks and evidence. *The Cognitive Behaviour Therapist* **16** e10, 1-21.

Naeem, F., Ayub, M., Gobbi, M., & Kingdon, D. (2009) Development of Southampton Adaptation Framework for CBT (SAF-CBT): a framework for adaptation of CBT in non-western culture. *Journal of Pakistan Psychiatric Society* **6** 79-84.

Naz, S., Gregory, R., & Bahu, M. (2019) Addressing issues of race, ethnicity, and culture in CBT to support therapists and service managers to deliver culturally competent therapy and reduce inequalities in mental health provision for BAME service users. *The Cognitive Behaviour Therapist* **12** E22. doi:10.1017/S1754470X19000060

NHS Equality and Diversity Council (2015) *Improving Lesbian Gay Bisexual and Trans (LGBT) Equality Across the NHS: a Paper for the Equality and Diversity Council* [online]. Available at: www.england.nhs.uk/wp-content/uploads/2015/11/edc1-lgbt-equal-pap-20-10-15.pdf (accessed January 2024).

NHS England (2019a) NHS long-term plan.

NHS England (2019b) NHS mental health implementation plan 2019/20 – 23/24

NHS (2017) Transforming children's and young people's mental health provision.

NHS (2016) The Five Year Forward View for Mental Health. The Independent Mental Health Taskforce to the NHS in England.

NHS England (2015) *Future in Mind: Promoting, protecting and improving our children's and young people's mental health and wellbeing.* NHS England Publication gateway ref. No 02939

NHS (2012) Compassion in practice. NHS Commissioning Board and Department of Health: London.

NICE (2011) *Common mental health problems: Identification and pathways to care* (CG123).

NICE (2019) *Depression in children and young people: identification and management* (NG134).

O'Lynn C & Krautscheid L (2011) How Should I Touch You? A Qualitative Study of Attitudes on Intimate Touch in Nursing Care. *American Journal of Nursing* **111** (3) 24–31

Okamoto A, Kazantzis N. (2021) Alliance ruptures in cognitive-behavioral therapy: A cognitive conceptualization. *Journal of Clinical Psychology* **77** (2) 384-397. doi: 10.1002/jclp.23116. Epub 2021 Jan 29. PMID: 33513280.

Pachankis, J. E. (2007). The psychological implications of concealing a stigma: A cognitive-affective-behavioral model. *Psychological Bulletin*, **133**(2), 328–345. https://doi.org/10.1037/0033-2909.133.2.328

Pachankis, J.E., & Goldfried, M.R. (2004) Clinical issues in working with lesbian, gay, and bisexual clients. *Psychotherapy: Theory, research, practice, training* **41** (3) 227.

Pachankis, J.E., Soulliard, Z.A., Seager van Dyk, I., Layland, E.K., Clark, K.A., Levine, D.S., & Jackson, S. D. (2022) Training in LGBTQ-affirmative cognitive behavioral therapy: A randomized controlled trial across LGBTQ community centers. *Journal of Consulting and Clinical Psychology* **90** (7) 582–599. https://doi.org/10.1037/ccp0000745

Pachankis, J.E. Harkness, A.R., Jackson, S.D., & Safren, S.A. (eds) (2022) 'Introduction to LGBTQ-Affirmative Cognitive-Behavioral Therapy', in *Transdiagnostic LGBTQ-Affirmative Cognitive-Behavioral Therapy: Therapist Guide* (New York, online edn, Oxford Academic, 1 Aug. 2022).

Padesky, C.A. & Mooney, K.A. (2012), Strengths-Based Cognitive–Behavioural Therapy: A Four-Step Model to Build Resilience. *Clinical Psychology & Psychotherapy* **19** 283–290.

Pass, L., & Reynolds, S. (2020) *Brief Behavioural Activation for Adolescent Depression: A clinician's manual and session by session guide.* Jessica Kingsley Publications.

Plöderl, M., & Tremblay, P. (2015). Mental health of sexual minorities. A systematic review. *International Review of Psychiatry* **27** 367–385.

Potter, J. & Wetherell, M. (1987) *Discourse and Social Psychology: Beyond attitudes and behaviours.* Sage.

Qalehsari, M.Q., Khaghanizadeh, M., & Ebadi, A. (2017) Lifelong learning in nursing: A systematic review. *Electronic Physician* **9** (10) 5541–5550.

Quiddington, J. (2009) Breaking Significant News. In: Glasper, A., McEwing, G. & Richardson, J. (eds) Foundation Skills for Caring: Using Student-centred Learning. Palgrave Macmillan, Hampshire.

RCP (2018) Supporting transgender and gender-diverse people. A position statement by the Royal College of Psychiatrists. PS02/18.

Reiser, R.P., Cliffe, T., & Milne, D.L. (2018). An improved competence rating scale for CBT supervision: Short-SAGE. *The Cognitive Behaviour Therapist* **11** E7.

Repper, J., & Perkins, D. (2003) *Social Inclusion and recovery: A model for mental health.* Balliere Tindall.

Richards, C., Bouman, W.P., Seal, L., Barker, M.J., Nieder, T.O., & T'Sjoen, G. (2016) Non-binary or genderqueer genders. *International Review of Psychiatry* **28** (1) 95–102.

Rigg, C. & O'Dwyer, B. (2012) Becoming and entrepreneur: researching the roles of mentors in identity construction. *Education and Training* **54** (4) 319–329.

Rimes, K.A., Broadbent, M., Holden, R., Rahman, Q., Hambrook, D., Hatch, S., & Wingrove, J. (2018) Comparison of treatment outcomes between lesbian, gay, bisexual, and heterosexual individuals receiving a primary care psychological intervention. *Behavioural and Cognitive Psychotherapy* **46** 332–349. doi: 10.1017/S1352465817000583

Robichaud, M., Koerner, N., & Dugas, M. J. (2019). *Cognitive behavioral treatment for generalized anxiety disorder: From science to practice* (2nd ed.). Routledge/Taylor & Francis Group.

Rogers, C. (1951) *Client-Centered Therapy: Its current practice, implications and theory*. London: Constable.

Roscoe, J. (2021a) Maximizing trainee cognitive behavioral therapists use of clinical supervision: Can a bespoke workshop help to broaden their horizons? *Journal of Applied Psychology and Social Science* **6** (1) 58–89.

Roscoe, J. (2021b) Conceptualising and managing supervisory drift. *The Cognitive Behaviour Therapist* **14** E37.

Roscoe, J., Taylor, J., Harrington, R., & Wilbraham, S. (2022) CBT supervision behind closed doors: Supervisor and supervisee reflections on their expectations and use of clinical supervision. *Counselling and Psychotherapy Research* **22** 1056–1067.

Roth, A., & Pilling, S. (2007) *The Competences Required to Deliver Effective Cognitive and Behavioural Therapy for People with Depression and with anxiety disorders*. Department of Health: London.

Sabki, A., Zuraida, Sa'ari, Zarrina, C., Muhsin, S., Basirah, S., Kheng, Lei, G., Sulaiman, H., Ahmad, G Koenig, & Harold. (2019) Islamic Integrated Cognitive Behavior Therapy: A Shari'ah-Compliant Intervention for Muslims with Depression. *Malaysian Journal of Psychiatry* **28** (1) 29–38.

Saddichha, S., Kumar, A., Pradhan, N. (2012) Cognitive schemas among mental health professionals: Adaptive or maladaptive? *J Res Med Sci.* **17** (6) 523–6.

Saewyc, E.M. Respecting variations in embodiment as well as gender: Beyond the presumed 'binary' of sex. Nursing Inquiry. 2017 Jan 1;24(1).

Safren, S.A., Sprich, S.E., Perlman, C.A., & Otto, M.W. (2018) *Mastering Your Adult ADHD: A cognitive behavioural treatment program*. Oxford University Press.

Segal, G., Borgia, D., & Schoenfeld, J. (2005) The motivation to become an entrepreneur. *International Journal of Entrepreneurial Behaviour & Research* **11** (1) 42–57.

Semlyen, J., King, M., Varney, J., & Hagger-Johnson, G. (2016) Sexual orientation and symptoms of common mental disorder or low wellbeing: combined meta-analysis of 12 UK population health surveys. *BioMed Central Psychiatry* **16**.

Shabani, K., Khatib, M., & Ebadi, S. (2010) Vygotsky's zone of proximal development: Instructional implications and teacher's professional development. *English Language Teaching* **3** (4) 237–248.

Sharples N (2013) Relationship, Helping and Communication Skills. In: Brooker C, Waugh A (eds) *Nursing Practice: Fundamentals of holistic care*. Mosby Elsevier, London.

Singer, J. A. (2005) *Personality and Psychotherapy: Treating the whole person*. New York: The Guilford Press.

Simmons, J., & Griffiths, R. (2017) *CBT for Beginners* (3rd edition). Sage.

Skerven, K., Whicker, D., & LeMaire, K. (2019). Applying dialectical behaviour therapy to structural and internalized stigma with LGBTQ clients. *The Cognitive Behaviour Therapist* **12** E9.

Social Work England (2023) *Guidance of practice placements* [online]. Available at: www.socialworkengland.org.uk/standards/practice-placements-guidance/ (accessed January 2024).

Sprich, S.E., Knouse, L.E., Cooper-Vince, C., Burbridge, J., Safren, S.A. (2012) Description and Demonstration of CBT for ADHD in Adults. *Cogn Behav Pract* **17** (1) 10.1016/j.cbpra.

Stallard, P. (2020) *A Clinician's Guide to CBT for Children to Young Adults: A companion to think good, feel good and thinking good & feeling better* (2nd edition). Wiley.

Stanley, M.A., Bush, A.L., Camp, M.E., Jameson, J.P., Phillips, L.L., Barber, C.R., Cully, J.A. (2011) Older adults' preferences for religion/ spirituality in treatment for anxiety and depression. *Aging & Mental Health* **15** 334–343. http://dx.doi.org/10.1080/13607863.2010.519326

Stickley T. (2011) From SOLER to SURETY for effective non-verbal communication. *Nurse Educ Pract.* **11** (6) 395–8. doi: 10.1016/j.nepr.2011.03.021. Epub 2011 Apr 13. PMID: 21489877.

Stonehouse, D. (2017) The use of touch in developing a therapeutic relationship. *Journal of Healthcare Assistants* **11** (1) 15–17.

Sue, D.W., Capodilupo, C.M., Torino, G.C., Bucceri, J.M., Holder, A., Nadal, K.L., & Esquilin, M. (2007) Racial microaggressions in everyday life: implications for clinical practice. *American Psychologist* **62** 271.

Testa, R.J., Michaels, M.S., Bliss, W., Rogers, M.L., Balsam, K.F., & Joiner, T. (2017) Suicidal ideation in transgender people: gender minority stress and interpersonal theory factors. *Journal of Abnormal Psychology* **126** 125–136. https://doi. org/10.1037/abn0000234

Teunissen, P.W., & Dornan, T. (2008) The competent novice: lifelong learning at work. *BMJ Practice* **336** 667–9.

Thwaites, R., Bennett-Levy, J., Davis, M., & Chaddock, A. (2014) Using self-practice and self-reflection (SP/SR) to enhance CBT competence and metacompetence. In: Adrian Whittington and Nick Grey (Eds.) *How to Become a More Effective CBT Therapist: Mastering Metacompetence in Clinical Practice*, First Edition. John Wiley & Sons.

Townend, M., Iannetta, L. and Freeston, M.H. (2002) Clinical supervision in practice: a survey of UK cognitive-behavioural psychotherapists accredited by the BABCP. *Behavioural and Cognitive Psychotherapy* **30** 485–500.

Townend, M., Iannetta, L., Freeston, M. & Hayes, J. (2007) *Supervision Practices of UK Cognitive- Behavioural Psychotherapists, 2001 and 2006*. Paper presented at the 5th World Congress of Behavioural and Cognitive Therapies, Barcelona, 11–14 July.

Topping, K.J. (1996) The effectiveness of peer tutoring in future and higher education: a typology and review of the literature. *Higher Education* **32** (3) 321–45.

Travis, J. (2019) Grow your private practice. Independently published.

Triste, A. (2023) *CBT for young people: The complete CBT workbook for kids, children, teens, and adolescents*. Independently published.

Tucker, L., & Webber, M. (2021) 'Maybe a Maverick, Maybe a Parent, but Definitely Not an Honorary Nurse': Social Worker Perspectives on the Role and Nature of Social Work in Mental Health Care, *The British Journal of Social Work*, Volume 51, Issue 2, March 2021, Pages 545–563, https://doi.org/10.1093/bjsw/bcaa202

Vallianitou, C. & Mirovic, T. (2020) Therapist schema activation and self-care. In: G. Health & H. Startup (Eds.) *Creative Methods in Schema Therapy: Advances & innovation in clinical practice*. Routledge.

Varkey, B. (2021) Principles of clinical ethics and their application to practice. *Medical Principles & Practice* **30** 17–28.

Verenikina, I. (2008) Scaffolding and learning: Its role in nurturing new learners. In: P. Kell, W. Vialle, D. Konza, & G. Vogl (Eds.) *Learning and the learner: Exploring learning for new times* (pp161–180). Wollongong: University of Wollongong, Australia.

Vygotsky, L.S. (1978) *Mind in Society: The development of higher psychological processes*. Cambridge, MA: Harvard University Press.

Waller, R., Trepka, C., Collerton, D., & Hawkins, J. (2010) Addressing spirituality in CBT. *The Cognitive Behaviour Therapist* **3** 95–106.

White, M. & Epston, D. (1990) *Narrative Means to Therapeutic Ends*. W.W. Norton & Company: New York.

Whittingdon, A., & Grey, N. (Eds.) (2014) How to Be a More Effective CBT Therapist: Mastering meta-competencies in clinical practice. Wiley Blackwell.